GAMES AND SETS

Selling sport
(Reproduced by kind permission of Peter Brookes and *The Times*)

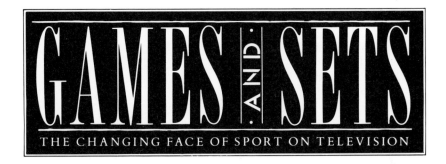

GAMES AND SETS

THE CHANGING FACE OF SPORT ON TELEVISION

· STEVEN BARNETT ·

bfi

BFI PUBLISHING

First published in 1990 by the
British Film Institute
21 Stephen Street
London W1P 1PL

British Library Cataloguing in Publication Data
Barnett, Steven
    Games and sets: the changing face of sport on television.
    1. Television programmes: Sports programmes
    I. Title
    070.449796

    ISBN 0-85170-267-8
    ISBN 0-85170-268-6 pbk

Cover design: Geoff Wiggins

Typeset in Plantin by
Fakenham Photosetting Limited
Fakenham, Norfolk

Printed in Great Britain by
St Edmundsbury Press Ltd
Bury St Edmunds, Suffolk

For Alexandra and the future
For Hilary and the past

CONTENTS

ACKNOWLEDGMENTS

In compiling the background and factual information for this book, I was dependent on the co-operation of a number of people who were generous with their time and advice. For Chapter 1, thanks are due in particular to John Cain at the BBC History Unit for his invaluable assistance and knowledge; and to Asa Briggs for his comments and advice. For Chapters 1 and 2, to Jackie Kavanagh and Jeff Walden for steering me round the labyrinth of the BBC Archive Centre in Caversham. For Chapter 3, to Jonathon Martin, John Bromley and Adrian Metcalfe, then respectively in charge of sport at the BBC, ITV and Channel 4 (the latter two now moved on), for their reflections; and similarly to Peter Dimmock, responsible for BBC sport throughout most of the 1940s and 1950s. For Chapter 4, to Philip Mitchell of British Market Research Bureau for providing access to and permission to publish confidential research data; and to Andrew Hemming of the BBC's broadcasting research department for assistance with audience data. For Chapters 5 and 6, to the various representatives of sports governing bodies who responded punctually and expansively to letters and phone calls. For Chapter 8, to Derek Etherington of the Sports Council, Peter Lawson of the Institute for Sports Sponsorship and Ken Parker of Research Services Ltd for their valuable advice; and to Mike Reynolds of Courage, Blackett Ditchburn of Prudential, Stuart Errington of Mercantile Credit and John de Bank of the National Westminster Bank for agreeing to be interviewed. And for Chapter 9, to Bob Hunter at British Satellite Broadcasting and Paul McDowell, then at Superchannel, for their thoughts.

The photographic illustrations were prepared by the National Film Archive, and are courtesy of the Hulton-Deutsch Collection, the BBC, London Weekend Television, Channel 4 and Eurosport, Sky Television. The cartoons are reproduced by kind permission of Peter Brookes and *The Times* (frontispiece), the *Listener* (pp. 63, 117), and Kevin Macey and the *Independent* (p. 136). The chart on p. 139 is reproduced from *Broadcast* magazine.

On a general level, thanks are due to BFI Publishing for taking on the original proposal; and in particular to David Wilson for his support, advice and efficiency in steering the project through to completion. Thanks also to colleagues past and present at the Broadcasting Research Unit for moral and material support; to those sportswriters and academics whose deliberations (with due acknowledgment) have been liberally quoted; to members of the Archery Tavern Cricket Club for their constructive suggestions (mostly unrelated to the book and unprintable); to David Docherty, Matthew Engel, Jon Epstein, Jill Greatorex, Barry Horton, Kenny King, Michael Warren, and all those I have approached at some time in the last eighteen months for information, clarification or speculation. And finally to Sasha for her enthusiasm and encouragement throughout.

I have tried to eliminate any errors of fact or interpretation, but no doubt some will remain; for these, I take full responsibility and offer apologies in advance.

STEVEN BARNETT
London, April 1990

INTRODUCTION

Around the same time that spectators in classical Rome were indulging their passion for chariot racing and bloody gladiatorial contests, the ancient Mayans of Central America invented a more civilised pastime. In a game reminiscent of today's basketball, competing teams attempted to kick or head a ball through a metal hoop. Although the game itself was relatively civilised, post-contest rituals were less so: losing teams were ceremonially sacrificed to the appropriate deity while the victors were rewarded with the goods and chattels of their vanquished opponents. The terminal consequences of a poor result would, one assumes, lend a tension to the contest which even a Cup Final or a Superbowl might find hard to match. The difference, of course, is that Mayan contests – as for every sporting contest in the world until the 1930s – remained the private experience of those spectators who chose to attend the event.

Two millennia later, the consequences of defeat have diminished while the rewards of victory are steadily enhanced – without recourse to predatory raids on opponents' possessions. Meanwhile, the varieties of sport have increased exponentially as the ancient athletic skills of the original Olympics (Olympia, Greece, 776 B.C.) have been extended by ingenuity, technology and banality to chess, motor racing and synchronised swimming (Los Angeles, USA, 1984 A.D.).

In the thousands of years in which sport has played an integral part in many very different societies, the last fifty years have been unique in one important respect: the major sporting contests have been available not just to spectators who choose to witness the event in person, but to many millions more who can view the spectacle in the comfort of their own homes. Television has become the medium through which the vast majority of people now have access to their favourite sports.

Two completely unrelated activities – the screening of television programmes and the spectating of sporting events – have become inextri-

1

cably intertwined. Some sports owe their popularity and participation rates almost entirely to television exposure. A few professional sportsmen and women owe their sometimes considerable personal wealth to television. Meanwhile television, constantly trying to balance greater scheduling time with apparently diminishing budgets, will frequently turn to sport as a means of filling airtime without laying out the huge sums required for the creation of original programming.

It is a mutually beneficial relationship, from which millions of television viewers can derive enormous pleasure. Like all close relationships, however, there are times when this mutual advantage can be unproductive, even destructive. A sudden surge of interest in a sport, or a sudden influx of television cash, can have surprisingly unhappy consequences both for professional athletes and for amateur governing bodies. And, once television has purchased its valuable screen commodity, it will frequently expect concessions which may have little to do with the sport's best interests.

This book examines that relationship at a critical point in its evolution. For television in the UK, and throughout Europe, is about to undergo a period of enormous change which will have a direct impact not just on televised sport but on sport itself. Since sport was first featured on the small screen in the late 1930s, with experimental and barely decipherable pictures, technological progress has brought immense improvements in sharpness, breadth of coverage, colour and commentary. Despite the speed of this progress, changes in the number of channels, their funding and organisation, have been gradual. Compared to the last fifty years, the next decade is destined to move at breathtaking speed.

Throughout Europe, two major agents of change have already started to alter the face of television. First, new satellite technology is being introduced, potentially capable of providing dozens more channels. Many of these will be specialist channels, including 24-hour sports channels. Second, spurred on both by new technology and by the fashion for laissez-faire economic policies, there is increasing pressure from governments towards greater competition and less regulation throughout broadcasting. While the nature and scope of such changes are the subject of controversial debate in all European countries, two consequences are inescapable. First, the amount of available airtime will triple or quadruple. Second, the increasing emphasis on competition within even established channels will provoke soaring prices for all television product which does not require expensive investment in creation and production processes. Prices for imported series, particularly American, have already doubled. Sport is even more attractive because it is generally home-produced and is therefore not included within the import quota. For television channels increasingly desperate to fill airtime, sport is starting to become one of the most sought after commodities.

In the UK, a new Broadcasting Bill about to become law is destined to reshape the structure of British broadcasting. Channel 4 will be required to sell its own airtime; a new commercial fifth channel will start in 1993; and ITV companies, forced to make a lump sum payment in return for their franchise, will face increasing financial pressures. In addition, the BBC's financial position is increasingly constrained, with a licence fee pegged to the Retail Price Index and a government injunction to move towards subscription as a means of replacing licence funding. Consequently, the BBC's ability to compete in the market-place will become increasingly eroded.

In a period of such rapid change, there is almost limitless scope for approaches to the theme of television and sport. Astonishingly, there has been little systematic attempt to examine this relationship in the UK, although it has been a popular theme in the United States. Given the recurring theme throughout this book – the impact on sport of increasing competition within the television industry – events in the US are examined in each chapter as illustration and counterpoint to the British context. This comparative analysis, with a competitive television environment established for many years, provides an insight into the potential dangers of television's intimate involvement with sport. Even now, that impact is starting to make itself felt within the UK; the lesson from America is that for British sport the repercussions may not be good news.

This book was not written to demonstrate a particular theory or propound a particular view. Its emphasis is descriptive and analytical, involving interviews with heads of television sport, representatives of sponsoring companies, and executives from a variety of sports governing bodies. Unless otherwise indicated, all quotations come from these first-hand interviews (except for the well-known television heads of department, identities have been kept anonymous). A considerable body of written evidence was also consulted, and a full bibliography appears at the end of the book.

Each chapter is designed to pursue a particular theme of the television/sport relationship. Chapter 1 examines some of the early history, as this new medium gained in confidence and pervasiveness, making comparisons with the evolutionary process in America. Chapter 2 looks at the costs of sport relative to other programming areas, and in particular the

3

effect of competitive television on the cost of exclusive rights. Chapter 3 examines how the structure and philosophy of television channels in Britain and the United States directly influences decisions about the nature, extent and type of sports programming. Chapter 4 looks at the audience, and provides a portrait of audience trends in televised sport over the last twenty years. Chapters 5 and 6 are complementary, looking first at the benefits which sports can derive from television: and then at some of the pitfalls and problems which American experience in particular suggests should not be underestimated. Chapter 7 looks at some of the difficulties involved in the very process of turning a live event into a television programme, and how this process is itself transformed by fierce competition between channels. Chapter 8 reviews the increasingly fraught area of sponsorship and television's vital role in unlocking additional revenue for sport. Finally, Chapter 9 looks forward to the advent of satellite and cable channels in the UK, and to what difference their appearance is likely to make to televised sport.

Inevitably, given the number of complex interrelationships, there is some overlap between chapters: sign-posting is provided where appropriate. Equally inevitably, some areas have not been explored in the detail which they might ideally deserve, since each of these chapters could represent a book in itself. Other areas have barely been touched: televised sport in the rest of Europe, for example, is itself a fascinating theme which highlights important cultural differences between countries. Similarly, the history of technological changes in televised sport and its impact over the years is only featured in the context of other issues. This, too, requires more detailed research and examination.

This book is not designed to be a comprehensive review of the field, but a contribution to a debate of mounting significance for both sport and television. British and European broadcasting is at a crossroads, and its direction over the next decade could have long-term consequences for sports which have traditionally comprised an influential element of television schedules. There will, certainly, be more opportunities for watching sport on television. But as commercial pressure on television channels increases, sport will inevitably find itself on the receiving end of unforeseen and unfamiliar forces. In seeking to exploit both the financial and publicity rewards which television can offer, sports might find themselves recast as useful but disposable television commodities. American experience serves as a potent reminder of the consequences.

1
IN THE BEGINNING

Ladies and Gentlemen. Everyone knows that the Lawn Tennis Championship meeting is taking place at Wimbledon over the next two weeks, starting today. By the courtesy of the All England Lawn Tennis Club we've been able to make arrangements to televise matches in the Centre Court throughout the fortnight. For the first time, anywhere in the world, then, Television will bring into viewers' homes pictures of outstanding international events at the exact moment they are taking place *without* the aid of an intermediate link of special cable. . . . . It's a great experiment.

So ran the script for a BBC Television announcer on Monday 21 June 1937, setting the scene for the first day of Wimbledon. The opening match, a three sets to one defeat of G. L. Rogers by the British champion Bunny Austin, may not have been a very memorable game of tennis, but at 3 o'clock in the afternoon it became a match of historic significance. Blurred though they were, pictures could clearly be seen by the 2,000 or so Londoners sufficiently monied and innovative to have acquired one of those new-fangled television sets.

The relationship innocently launched by a relatively insignificant tennis match has in the last fifty years had almost immeasurable consequences for sports athletes, events, spectators and administrators. Throughout the developed world, at almost every level beyond recreational parks and back gardens, television considerations have influenced, often dictated, the progress of sports. Prize money has escalated beyond the wildest dreams of early participants. Rules have been changed. Events have been tailored, rescheduled or abandoned. Amateurism has almost vanished in all but name. And in the meantime, huge numbers of the previously disenfranchised, those prohibited by financial or physical disadvantage or simply disinclined to attend a live event, have been able to share in the successes and failures of national teams and national athletes.

Even at the very beginning, before the world's first live sporting picture was ever transmitted, there was a hint of things to come. During tests, interference with signals from the mobile transmitter at Wimbledon had been traced to Hornsey Central Hospital, jeopardising the experimental transmission. The Secretary of the hospital was contacted and agreed to suspend all 'diathermy activities' during transmission periods. If any patient at Hornsey hospital wondered why their internal organs were not heated by electric current on that day, it is unlikely they were told the truth. It would presumably have been of little comfort to know that theirs was the first experience of an increasingly common occurrence: the ability of televised sports to influence extraneous decisions.

The presence of cameras at Wimbledon that day can be directly attributed to some assiduous courting of the Secretary of the All England Lawn Tennis Club by the BBC's first Director of Television, Gerald Cock. After the success of this experiment, he began to explore the possibilities of live coverage of other events. Saturday 9 October saw the world's first televised motor race, the Imperial Trophy Road Race from Crystal Palace. And on 10 December, Cock wrote to Stanley Rous at the Football Association suggesting that both the international England v Scotland soccer match and the FA Cup Final would be suitable for live telecasting the following year. While Rous himself was amenable to the idea, the FA Council was less enthusiastic. The following month he outlined to Cock the Council's fears, which foreshadowed arguments to be propounded by governing bodies of almost every major sport over the next twenty years. What would be the effect of the live transmission of a blue riband event on all the smaller matches being played in the London area at the same time? Newsreels, which had traditionally provided highlights of big games for the football-hungry who were not among the Wembley crowd, were never a threat. Their films were transmitted days, if not weeks, later. This was a new, unpredictable and potentially ruinous development. Administrators were wary.

Gerald Cock was persistent but apparently unsuccessful. By 22 February he had heard nothing; he wrote promising that permission would 'not be regarded as a precedent but as a trial'. He was confident that attendances at other matches would not be affected, and anyway only 2,000 sets had been installed in homes at that time. In the final paragraph, with just a hint of hyperbole, Cock tried to convey to Rous his own appreciation

Early days: televising the 1939 Boat Race (© BBC)

of the significance of the moment. 'Television is on trial. Here is the beginning of a great new industry, the progress of which depends to a great extent on the co-operation of institutions such as the Football Association.' This plea seemed to fall on deaf ears, but Cock refused to give up. On 17 March, with the international just 23 days away, he wrote asking for a decision. The next day, Rous telephoned: the Council had consented to the televising of both the England-Scotland international and the FA Cup Final. Arthur Elvin, Managing Director of Wembley Stadium, promised every co-operation with Wembley events, and on 9 April 1938 England *v* Scotland provided the world's first live television pictures of a soccer match for the benefit of a tiny number of set owners.

Even more excitement was generated by the first televised Cup Final on 30 April. The match, between Huddersfield Town and Preston North End, was to be a royal occasion. Elvin was most concerned that the Royal Party should be introduced to this new scientific wizardry, and wrote to the BBC asking for a television receiver to be made available in the Royal Retiring Room: 'I think that Their Majesties are likely to be most interested to see the Machine in the Room when they arrive.' In terms of capital letters, at least, the Machine commanded as much gravity as the Royal Family itself.

7

Coverage was not faultless. According to Cock's own post-mortem, 'the preliminaries were a disaster' mainly because the radio commentary (which television was carrying) failed for the first half-hour. Viewers, however, were clearly delighted. Responding to one uncharitable (and not very prescient) complaint that 2¾ hours of continuous viewing would prove too taxing on people's eyesight, Cock wrote:

a) Every letter, telegram and telephone message we have had (and there have been many) has particularly appreciated the whole match being televised to the very end, and not one has mentioned any strain at all. Speaking from memory, it has brought in about the largest correspondence we have had.
b) It has resulted in probably the best Press that any television has had since the Coronation . . .

With the first televised Boat Race on 2 April (also broadcast simultaneously with John Snagge's radio commentary), the stage had been set for a series of live events to be televised the following year. The 1939 Boat Race and Cup Final had their own television commentary, and the medium was beginning to come of age. As a result, the potential threat to live audiences, and therefore to revenue, began to concentrate the minds of sports administrators. Even before war had been declared, and television had begun its seven-year banishment, the era of sympathetic experimentation was giving way to more hard-nosed assessments of potential damage. In the immediate aftermath of the war, sporting bodies became extremely concerned.

Post-war
Even before BBC television restarted in June 1946, there were the first stirrings of concern. At this stage, it was not the potential effects on gates or ticket sales that caused alarm but the suggestion that cinemas might 're-diffuse' the television pictures and charge for admission. Led by the Greyhound Racing Association, those sports bodies particularly apprehensive formed themselves into the Association for the Protection of Copyright in Sports (APCS). Some were more committed to the Association than others, but all sought reassurances from the BBC that no pirated re-diffusion would be permitted. On 13 March Maurice Gorham, Head of Television Service, wrote to the Director General that nothing could be done about broadcasting the Derby until 'we have come to a satisfactory arrangement with the Association for the Protection of Copyright in Sports'. The following day Ian Orr-Ewing, Manager of

Outside Broadcasts, wrote that Lord's would need reassurances about cinema pirating before agreeing to the televising of Test Matches. Three months later the Amateur Athletics Association, which had agreed to the televising of its Championships on 19 and 20 July, withdrew after joining the APCS. With promoters' fears increasing, there was concern about whether any sporting events would be available for the coming year.

In fact, the resumption of television in 1946 saw a great deal of sport in the schedule. Wightman Cup tennis in mid-June was followed by two days of the first Test Match against India at Lord's, and the Wimbledon tennis championships. There was speedway from West Ham and Wimbledon stadiums, racing from Ascot, and the Varsity Rugby Union match from Twickenham. The first post-war soccer match was an amateur Athenian League match between Barnet and Wealdstone – whose transmission, according to Asa Briggs, had to be interrupted fifteen minutes from the end because of bad light.

Towards the end of 1946, Maurice Gorham could confidently report that 'we are now getting full co-operation from the majority of sports promoters', and he listed only two refusals. The first, an ice show from Wembley Pool, was resisted by Arthur Elvin for reasons unconnected with fears of either pirating or falling attendances. According to Gorham, he apparently 'objected to our additional lighting, not only because it tended to melt the ice surface but because he was afraid his patrons would expect similar lighting on evenings when we were not there to provide it.' The second was more serious and more indicative of the tensions which the new medium was about to create. On 28 October, a middleweight boxing championship between Roderick and Hawkins was scheduled for transmission. Although pirating was unlikely, the BBC could not offer an absolute guarantee that cinemas would not re-diffuse. The British Boxing Board of Control took fright and banned the transmission. Even this event was almost rescued at the last minute. The fight's promoter, Jack Solomons, was aware of the financial possibilities of television rights, and refused to accept any Board control over his financial arrangements with the BBC. While he reluctantly accepted the ban on Roderick/Hawkins, he was prepared to consider offering television rights for the Baksi fight on 5 November. The BBBC, worried that money from boxing might find its way into promoters' pockets rather than boxers', insisted that Solomons should disclose both the rights fee and its apportionment. Solomons declined and the fight went untelevised.

Some forty years later, it might seem strange that money did not feature as a major issue. Boxing, predictably, was shortly to force the pace, but for the moment permission to televise did not stand or fall on

9

whether the financial carrot was sufficiently large. As Gorham noted at the end of 1946, 'The question of permitting television will continue to be judged solely on its promotional value until much larger fees are paid.' This was partly due to the still limited availability of television sets, which even by the end of 1947 had not exceeded 20,000. It was also in no small measure due to the non-commercial and overtly public service nature of the BBC. A corporation accountable to its licence payers, and with one channel on which to cater for all television tastes and preferences, was obliged to marshal its resources carefully. It could not make outrageous payments for single events.

More importantly, promoters and administrators were quite aware of the BBC's financial limitations and its difficulty in acceding to any but the most modest demands. Public service obligations, and the absence of any commercial competition, naturally inhibited any tendency towards spiralling costs. Furthermore, any attempt to introduce discreet commercialism through the back door was firmly rejected. In March 1947 Solomons, inevitably, offered the Woodcock-Baksi fight to the BBC in return for an opening announcement along the lines of 'by courtesy of Jack Solomons and Vernons Pools'. The response from Gorham was unequivocal: 'I am afraid I must turn down the suggestion of acknowledgement . . . without further reference, though I shall inform the Director-General of it. . . . Vernons Pools are not the organisers of the fight, and to acknowledge them as well as Solomons would be sponsorship without alloy.' If money was not the dominant issue, the effect on attendances certainly became so. As of 1 May 1947 unauthorised cinema rediffusion became impossible without a special licence from the Postmaster-General, who would issue them only once promoters or the BBC had been consulted. Although the possibility of pirating still haunted many promoters – who either did not understand or were unaware of the new provision – it was attendances that increasingly began to concentrate promoters' minds.

Opinions were divided. There were those who were convinced that television was valuable free publicity which would encourage viewers to venture out for the live event and increase gates; and those equally certain that television would encourage would-be paying spectators to watch at home. This difference of opinion was understandable. Not only were some parties, notably Wimbledon, Rugby, Cricket and the Football Association, positive towards television anyway, but it was quite plausible that television would have a differential effect on individual sports. Thus at the beginning of 1949 Orr-Ewing reported on a visit to Colonel Prentice at Twickenham. For the first time, tickets for the

10

England/France international had been over-subscribed; many applicants for the England/Scotland match had also been disappointed. Prentice was 'thoroughly pro-television', and not just because it seemed to boost live attendance: 'He says television is a "Godsend" to him since it keeps all the old gentlemen at home and they write long letters afterwards commenting on the play and don't bother him on the day.' Similarly, an all-time attendance record for steeplechasing at Sandown Park was 'further proof of the fact that television does nothing but good' since it had long been known that the three main races were to be televised. Attendances for ice hockey matches at Earls Court were 'up by 30%' since they had encouraged telecasting. And at the first Saturday of the previous year's Wimbledon, when most matches on Centre and No. 1 courts had been televised, 'all records were broken when 33,000 people paid for admission'.

Pressure was mounting, however, within the opposition lobby. At the end of 1947, the Chairman of the British Boxing Board of Control had written that 'Stewards ... remain unconvinced that Television ... cannot be but detrimental to Professional Boxing.' In other sports, there was particular anxiety about the impact of a major televised event on less important matches taking place simultaneously. In April 1949 Peter Dimmock, then assistant to Orr-Ewing, reported that Arthur Elvin was complaining of the adverse effect of a televised ice hockey match on a simultaneous Wembley event. Dimmock was dubious (the Wembley match had been a minor one), but the fear was contagious. Fuelled by evidence from the United States, and a steady increase in television households which was approaching a quarter of a million by the end of 1949, the hawks began to dominate the argument. A complete ban on live telecasting of sports was proposed, to take effect from 1 January 1950.

Although at this stage the ban was only implemented on a limited scale – there were too many disparate interests represented for total unanimity to prevail – the Association for the Protection of Copyright in Sports was sufficiently influential to have a marked effect on sports output. Its motives were not financial. An APCS document in February 1950 stated explicitly that 'it is not the object to get more money for the promoters by selling the rights but to protect the whole sporting spectacle system'. They acknowledged that television could 'awaken interest' in sports, and that major event attendances might not be affected. Anxiety was focused almost entirely on simultaneous and less significant events elsewhere.

Right on cue, the televised 1950 Cup Final – at a time when there was still a full football programme elsewhere on the same day – caused controversy. In a classic match, Arsenal beat Liverpool 2–0. Attend-

11

ances elsewhere dropped. Although the weather was foul, an excerpt from a Midlands newspaper was circulated within the BBC to show how easy it would be to blame television:

> In Birmingham there were crowds round the demonstration sets in city stores. One Midland viewer is reported to have been watching at home when he was interrupted by two callers . . . who asked if they could come in and join him. They explained that they belonged to a larger group which had split up and gone in search of television aerials in the neighbourhood.

Two days later, Controller of Television Norman Collins anticipated the repercussions and advised:

> Please bear in mind when . . . Rous blames television for the poor attendances at the gates of other football matches on the Cup Final Day, that the weather was so shocking that there would anyhow have been a big drop without any television at all. This is precisely the kind of point that is likely to be overlooked when the conversation turns on what television did to football in the 1950 Cup Final.

By this stage the reduction in televised sport and the influence of the APCS had become sufficiently serious to provoke Parliamentary questions. Despite the limited availability of sets, MPs – whether prompted by personal exposure to the medium's sporting potential or by the expressed concern of their constituents – were greatly exercised. On 17 May 1950, Ernest Marples MP asked Postmaster-General Ness Edwards: 'Will the right honourable Gentleman bear in mind that undoubtedly sporting events are at the moment the most effective spectacle on television?'

Recognising the rising level of anxiety on this issue, the Postmaster-General established a Sports Television Advisory Committee (STAC). Sports associations agreed to allow the BBC to show 'sports events of the order of 100 events per annum' for an experimental period to allow the Committee to assess the direct and indirect effects of television. The Committee was to report 'from time to time as it may see fit'. It delivered its first (and only) report in May 1951. Its focus was statistical, con-centrating on attendance returns, information received from clubs re-sponding to questionnaires, and representative surveys of the television audience. Although the restricted geographic availability of television facilitated some unique – and unrepeatable – controlled experiments, the Committee's findings were predictably inconclusive. Football attendance figures on Cup Final day tended to confirm the views of those opposing televised sport: estimated gates in first-class matches down 42% and 39% respectively in the transmission areas of London and Birmingham, compared to 34% down in the rest of Britain. More significantly, the estimated shortfall for second-class matches was 56% in Birmingham compared to 37% elsewhere (only one game was played in London: attendance down 59%).

Weather interfered with any realistic conclusions about the effects on county cricket of televised Test Matches. Ice hockey, an indoor sport, seemed impervious. And speedway seemed to suffer marginal but not conclusive reductions. Responses from football clubs established that 'the Cup Final is the one match which worries both Associations and Clubs'. On the other hand, analysis of audience data gave credence to the supporters of televised sport: 'There were large audiences for many different kinds of event, even though some of them attract comparatively small attendances, and it is reasonable to conclude that television is helping to develop interest in sporting activities.'

Broadcasters and sporting interests alike had been nervously looking across the Atlantic where, as we shall see, the debate was both more advanced and a good deal more heated. Dimmock had returned from the United States at the beginning of the year, brandishing a copy of a report compiled on behalf of the Thoroughbred Racing Associations of America. In a hopeful letter to the Racecourse Owners' Association ('Please do not think I am trying to lobby you'), he described how one racecourse had been persuaded by the publicity value to provide television facilities at no charge: 'It is significant that with the help of television, American racecourse attendances rose by fifteen per cent during 1950, whereas every other major sport showed a decline in attendances.'

Systematic studies had also been commissioned, with conflicting conclusions. The STAC report quoted a study by the National Opinion Research Centre at the University of Chicago which came to the same tentative conclusions about the possible damage to minority sports. Also in internal circulation at the BBC, and known to the Director General, was a counter-study commissioned by the National Association of Broadcasters which claimed to demonstrate that those who had television sets in fact attended *more* sporting events. Those who read it were almost certainly unaware that the author of this thesis, Jerry Jordan at the University of Pennsylvania, was the son of an executive vice-president at

13

Ayer and Son – an advertising agency which handled several large sports accounts.

The debate continued to generate more heat than light on both sides of the Atlantic. The 11–page STAC report conclusions were succinctly summarised by G. R. Barnes, Director of Television:

1. Some time must elapse before it is possible accurately to estimate the effect of Television on gates.
2. It is the televising of important events like the Cup Final and Professional boxing which have a marked effect on attendance.
3. This effect is greatest on the smallest clubs.

The result of these deliberations was that little was resolved and some bans remained in place. Predictably, and not for the last time, it was televised soccer which bore the brunt of the controversy. In contrast to the Football Association, whose concern was for the welfare of the game at every level, the Football League had set its face against television at an early stage. Fred Howarth, the League's Secretary, was convinced of the damage which would be inflicted on attendances. But even the friendly FA decided in August 1951 that the 1952 Cup Final could be televised in full only if it were postponed one week. There was no postponement, and for the first time since 1936 an FA Cup Final went untelevised.

This particular debate continued into 1953. It was only in the face of intense resistance that the FA agreed to the televising of the classic 1953 final when Stanley Matthews electrified the nation and Blackpool beat Bolton Wanderers 4–3. De Lotbiniere complained to Barnes that 'The Football League have been doing everything they can to embarrass the Football Association over their original decision to let us televise the Cup Final in full.' As we shall see, the Football League were not quite so reticent when it came to large financial inducements just two years later.

In the meantime, there were clear signs of a relaxation of attitudes as both promoters and broadcasters geared themselves to the imminent arrival of competitive television. The prospect of a commercial competitor, desperately opposed by many influential people within and outside the BBC, had repercussions for all areas of programming but particularly for sport. For the first time, the BBC would not be able to offer a price on a take it or leave it basis. They would face both the possibility of escalating costs for television rights and – far more seriously – the real risk of losing the right to cover major sporting occasions. As early as May 1950 the BBC had announced a list of 'events from which the BBC would not wish to be excluded'. This comprised boxing (world professional title fights); foot-

14

ball (Cup Final plus internationals); cricket (Test Matches); horse-racing (Derby, Grand National, St. Leger, Royal Ascot); tennis (Wimbledon plus Wightman and Davis Cups); Rugby Union internationals; and the Boat Race.

Once the decision on a commercial broadcaster had been taken, the problem of exclusivity had to be discussed. While accepting that its automatic monopoly was to evaporate, the BBC was concerned that it should not be ousted from major events by a cash-rich commercial sector with limited geographic availability. Its position was described by Barnes following a meeting with the Postmaster-General on 22 October 1953: 'This must be thought of as not so much giving an exclusive right to somebody as preventing somebody else from exercising an exclusive right.' Thus any negotiation with the BBC would not preclude an agreement with other television stations. Similarly no one should be able to exclude the BBC by virtue of agreements with other stations.

The most revealing and important meeting at this stage of the relationship was that called by Director General Sir Ian Jacob at Broadcasting House on 21 April 1954 with representatives of the APCS. Its purpose was to discuss Section 5 of the proposed Television Bill, which applied special conditions to 'important sporting events'. Nowhere is the early relationship between sports promoters and broadcasters more clearly documented.

Jacob made it clear that the BBC was not interested in exclusive rights but in obtaining facilities for broadcasting 'all events of interest to the public'. The BBC was conscious of the dangers of too much television sport; it was also conscious of television's ability to raise the popularity of sports. It therefore wanted to co-operate with promoters to ensure that sport could reap the benefits of television without undue damage: 'The question of the money payment involved was less important, in the Corporation's view, than that of preserving all forms of sport in a healthy condition.' Jacob warned of the inclination of competitive television to strive for exclusivity and to 'exploit sports to the utmost'; evidence from abroad showed that sport was the eventual loser. Nevertheless, the proposed Section 5 would be virtually unworkable and the BBC would prefer 'sensible and businesslike negotiations' to settle each case. In the event, as Chapter 2 explains, Parliament was prepared to concede to the BBC a complicated clause which effectively prevented exclusive coverage of any event of national interest.

In subsequent discussion, sports representatives exhibited loyalty to the BBC even while reserving the right to take financial advantage of the new competition. Rous for football, Prentice for rugby, Aird for cricket,

15

and Reay for tennis all agreed that the BBC 'had proved generally beneficial'. While Mrs Topham representing Aintree and Arthur Elvin for Wembley Stadium acknowledged that the size of the fee would be influential, Asa Briggs describes them as having 'recognised the length and import of the history of their dealings with the BBC'.

The first non-BBC transmission was broadcast to the London area by Associated Rediffusion Television on 22 September 1955. Although it was to be almost another year before reception of commercial television covered more than half the country, the fledgling service needed a major attraction to announce its arrival and seduce viewers from their entrenched non-commercial viewing habits. The country's most popular sport was a prime candidate; and in a move precisely emulated by their first commercial competitor nearly thirty-five years later, ITV went for live coverage of League football.

Fred Howarth, however, had not altered his opposition to live soccer on Saturday afternoons. In August 1955 he assured Peter Dimmock that if the League Management Committee decided to the contrary the BBC would be given equal opportunity. Even now, Howarth was disinclined to exploit the new competition. His words, quoted by Dimmock, were indicative of the wary attitudes of sports promoters: 'The BBC have always been very straightforward with us and we don't even know who are behind these commercial people.' The following year, however, the Midlands ITV franchise had upped the stakes considerably. With £40,000 on the table in return for live coverage of matches postponed until 6.15 p.m., the BBC had to decide whether to compete head to head. According to Dimmock's (almost certainly accurate) intelligence, the Football League Management Committee were finding it hard to refuse such a high offer for transmission over a limited area. From the BBC's standpoint, however, he advised against a bidding free-for-all for reasons which had as much to do with sport as with a concern about escalating costs: 'It might very well transpire that to televise League football every Saturday is not in the best interests either of the sport or the televising authority.' Meanwhile he would continue to press for film rights, so that 'telerecording' – recorded highlights – could be transmitted at a later time. He would argue that the BBC should not be deprived of all facilities, 'particularly in view of our long-standing good relations with the League'. When three weeks later ATV added £10,000 to their offer, Dimmock recognised the permanent effect that commercial television was to have on sport, and that these negotiations probably represented 'the first of many similar situations that will arise as ITV gathers strength and increases its coverage'.

16

One month later, the issue became academic. The Football League rejected all proposals and deferred indefinitely the whole question of live coverage of League matches. It was not until 1964 that the BBC initiated what was to become the hallmark of British football coverage and the centrepiece of Saturday night programming – recorded highlights on *Match of the Day*. Almost eleven years previously de Lotbiniere had wondered whether 'we now make up our mind that certain sport is always going to be beyond the reach of live television' and should therefore be 'canned'. His concern was the potential danger of losing live events and therefore depriving the viewer, once promoters had seen all the advantages of recorded action which would not interfere with live attendances. It was a prophetic suggestion, but he could not have anticipated the enormous popularity of this new recipe for packaging sport outside the stadium.

Meanwhile Dimmock's assumption (widely shared by many outside the BBC) that an ITV of gathering strength would challenge and possibly steal the BBC's sporting crown appeared increasingly unfounded. As Bernard Sendall wrote in his history of independent television, 'ITV handled sport rather gingerly' with coverage which was 'sparse, random and sometimes amateurish'. Commercial television's weakness originated in several factors. First, the fledgling ITV network was barely functional. Given its constitutional structure as a series of regional franchises, each with different starting dates, the first transmission in the London area reached a minority of television households. It was seven years before the last franchise – in Wales – was in operation and a truly national competitive network in place. The emphasis on regionalism, and the difficulty of efficient and centralised network planning when different regions themselves had different sporting priorities, militated against a determined and co-ordinated stand against the BBC.

Secondly, the infusion of a commercial element into television was an unknown quantity which caused some nervousness among established sporting bodies. At one level, of course, the possibility of additional cash was a welcome development – not just for the professionals whose livelihood depended on participation income, but for all sporting bodies desperately keen to raise the profile of their sport and earn some much-needed revenue for its development. At another level, commercial imperatives did not quite fit with a tradition of public service broadcasting in which the public interest rather than financial gain dictated decisions. As Dimmock wrote at the time, 'I think . . . we can safely assume that the ITA will be frowned upon by most of the amateur associations . . .'

17

Finally, there was the powerful but unquantifiable presence of the BBC as the traditional purveyor of great British events. For nearly twenty years, with interruptions only for war and the occasional copyright problem, the BBC had brought to increasing numbers of British citizens the cream of Britain's sporting achievements. This 20-year advantage had allowed the BBC to develop what Asa Briggs calls 'a remarkable team of commentators'.

It is even more remarkable, when looking at the commentary names from over thirty years ago, that some of them still represent the BBC's voice of sport. Their familiarity and authority evoke some sympathy with those administrators who may have been reluctant to surrender their respective sports to the obscurity of anonymous commentators. Dan Maskell, from 1950, and Freddie Grisewood were the familiar voices of Wimbledon. The inimitable Kenneth Wolstenholme, who was to engrave himself on every soccer fan's memory in the closing seconds of the 1966 World Cup, and Alan Weeks were quickly established as the resident soccer representatives. Boxing had Raymond Glendenning and, from early on, Harry Carpenter. Harold Abrahams provided the voice of athletics with a young unknown called David Coleman. And cricket bubbled with knowledgeable, entertaining and occasionally poetic contributions from the likes of John Arlott, E. W. Swanton, Rex Alston, Peter West and the indestructible Brian Johnston. They were pioneering days for the Outside Broadcast department, which by the end of the 1950s had developed a formidable reputation as the only serious communicator of British sports to television viewers.

This reputation was consolidated by the beginning of a sports magazine programme which quickly established a loyal following. *Sportsview*, with Paul Fox as editor, was first broadcast on 8 April 1954, and switched to its regular Wednesday evening slot just over a year later. It was a fast-moving, current and authoritative look at sporting events and issues which assured the BBC of its place as the prime sports channel. As Briggs has written, 'It was with *Sportsview* as a main weapon in its armoury that the BBC faced competition in sport from commercial television.'

ITV's disadvantage survived well into the 60s. Even once *World of Sport* had started its Saturday afternoon challenge to *Grandstand* in Autumn 1964, it was only two years before calls came for its abandonment in favour of a sports/entertainment mix (a drastic admission of competitive failure which was, in fact, ultimately implemented in 1986). Perhaps Sendall is right that 'in organisational and institutional terms the dice were always loaded in favour of the BBC'. Certainly, by the end of the 50s, it had developed an enviable reputation for its sports coverage, based on a

20-year advantage over the commercial network and on a series of carefully nurtured and mostly happy relationships. It is, however, an analysis rendered easier by hindsight. At the time, the advent of competition was an innovation whose impact the sports department could not accurately gauge but which created genuine anxiety. It was therefore little wonder, as broadcasters assessed the prospect of a competing channel with substantial financial resources, that they looked with increasing nervousness at recent developments in the United States.

Over the Atlantic

Two years after that first Wimbledon broadcast, an experimental television station in New York transmitted some rather hazy pictures of a college baseball game at Columbia University's Baker Field. According to Benjamin Rader, the following Sunday's *New York Times* announced, without a great deal of foresight, that 'the televiewer lacks freedom; seeing baseball on television is too confining, for the novelty would not hold up for more than an hour if it were not for the commentator'.

This 'novelty' became a money-spinner which, less than twenty years later, had transported at least one baseball team from East to West Coast in search of higher television fees. The Brooklyn Dodgers had represented a focal point for the residents of Brooklyn who lived within the greater New York City area but fostered a proud sense of separate community spirit. The team was profitable and maintained a large and loyal following, but played within a television reception area which included two other major baseball teams. The franchise owner 'dreamed of locating the Dodgers in an uncontested media market', and Los Angeles was a prime location. Leaving behind a Brooklyn community bereft of one of its key focal points, the franchise went in search of television megabucks.

Ten years earlier, in the late 40s, questions had started to arise about the effects of television on attendances in boxing and baseball (American Football was then a minority sport with a small following). In 1948–9, 10–12,000 spectators turned up to watch the Madison Square Garden fights. By 1957, after fourteen years of weekly televised fights and some years of almost nightly coverage, attendances were averaging 1,200. The effect on minor league baseball was even more dramatic. Live transmission of major league games in New York, without a blanket ban in the match area, destroyed baseball in nearby Jersey City and Newark, New Jersey. Just as the STAC study in Britain had found the greatest impact of live soccer to be on second-class clubs, so minor league baseball suffered from simultaneous coverage of major league games. Why should a sports

19

fan watch an inferior game unless out of some sense of loyalty? The decline was precipitate: from 42 million spectators in 1949 to 15 million in 1957 and 10 million in 1969.

The fortunes of one team epitomised the potentially ruinous effects of television. In 1948, in winning the National League pennant, the Boston Braves drew 1.5 million fans to their home games. After the TV rights had been sold, attendances dropped to under 300,000 by 1952. In 1953, to avert financial disaster, the team was moved to Milwaukee where it achieved tremendous success. Despite the highest National League attendances for six consecutive years, new owners in 1966 transferred the franchise to Atlanta where the television rights were worth almost three times as much. Just like the Brooklyn Dodgers, supporters' loyalty was rewarded by wholesale defection to a new city simply because higher broadcast revenues were on offer.

To some extent the decline in attendances was due as much to social and economic factors as to the influence of television. Private wealth and the amount of leisure time were both on the increase, as were the options for spending them. The 50s saw a general slump in sports attendances, with even major league baseball losing a third of its paying spectators between 1948 and 1956. It was precisely these extraneous factors, in both the United States and Britain, that made any precise computation of the effect of live television almost impossible. Nevertheless, that did not prevent the National Opinion Research Centre, on the basis of its study of college football, from concluding that attendances would have been 40% higher had games not been televised. In 1951 a moratorium was imposed on wholesale telecasts, and the NORC continued its monitoring by introducing new variables. Their long-term analysis confirmed the original hypothesis that television was responsible for the slump in attendances at college football games.

From the beginning, American Football began to use television skilfully to elevate itself from a relatively insignificant status to the most popular American sport. Television helped would-be sports fans to understand a difficult and fast-moving game, to the point where the televised version became preferable to the live spectacle. Compared to televised games, according to one critic quoted by Rader, 'live games now seem peculiarly inept, lethargic and pedestrian'. During the 50s, the game's fascination grew inexorably. Just as the Olympic Games show-jumping triumph launched a major British television sport in 1948, it was one event which triggered the widespread popularity in American Football in the United States. With seven seconds to go in a 1958 championship game, the Baltimore Colts tied their game with the New York

20

Giants. A sudden death play-off (American sport has never permitted the sacrilege of a draw) was won by the Colts, and the drama witnessed by millions on TV. The stage was set for a television-led invasion of American Football not just by new players and spectators, but by a whole new league.

In 1959 the American Football League was founded, and struggled on for two unprofitable years. Its prognosis was not healthy until, in 1962, the CBS network bought exclusive rights to National Football League games. By this time football was a big enough television draw to constitute a major plank in network programming, and NBC wanted some. Immediately after losing the NFL rights battle to CBS, it agreed a television deal with the new AFL worth 8 million dollars a year which bought it sudden and profitable respectability. With the financial clout to offer lucrative contracts to the best players, it took only four years for the AFL to establish itself as a serious rival to the long-standing NFL. Soaring fees for players forced the NFL to come to the negotiating table in 1966 and accept a compromise which contained two vital provisions. Since the NFL still maintained a 2–1 advantage in the TV markets, three teams were to be transferred to the AFL to restore some financial equilibrium. And a championship game or 'Superbowl' to decide the top national team would have its debut in 1967. America's biggest event of the modern sporting calendar, now watched on TV by over half the population every year, is directly attributable to the economic power of television.

A fair comparison?

Major social and geographic differences between the two countries make precise comparisons difficult. Franchises are not for sale in the UK: even the most ambitious entrepreneur could no more uproot Manchester United from Manchester than make an offer for Buckingham Palace. Local television markets do not have the same buying power, and are centred on regions rather than cities. The traditions of sports themselves, even at the senior professional levels, owe more to their role within the community than to hard-headed commercialism. Nevertheless, a critical and decisive factor in the development of the sport/television relationship in the UK was a national, non-commercial and monopolistic broadcaster with an implicit responsibility for looking after the best interests of sport as well as the interests of viewers. The absence of purely financial criteria allowed broadcasters to take decisions which were, in their view, not detrimental to the sports they televised.

For the promoters, certainly, this meant less money on the table. Arguably, this factor alone deprived British viewers in the 1930s, 40s and early 50s of major boxing events and some horse-racing. Given the amateur traditions within much of British sport at the time, this was of less importance than two other considerations: allowing millions who had never had access to live events a chance to savour some of the excitement; and allowing minority sports, which might never have any opportunity for exposure in a purely commercial environment, a chance to exploit the new medium of communication. An extract from Board of Management minutes in November 1950 captured the flavour of the BBC approach: 'The Corporation's obligation was recognised therefore to televise a proportion of the smaller events as well as the major ones, and it was hoped that by so doing a reasonable basis of payment would be reached for both classes of sporting events.' It was an approach which, with the help of sympathetic and knowledgeable commentators, was to stimulate interest in a variety of different sports throughout the 50s and 60s without requiring any overt forms of packaging. While in the United States teams were being uprooted and sports like hockey and basketball were deprived of airtime because they were unable to attract substantial audiences, in Britain sports were being aired with as little interference as possible.

Traditions had been established which would endure for the next thirty years and in some cases transform both sporting interest and participation. On the one hand, new channels would double the available airtime and hopefully encourage constructive rivalry in the presentation of sporting events. On the other hand, a bidding war and escalating prices were real possibilities. It was hardly surprising that Peter Dimmock, in the 1958/9 Football Association Year Book, looked with some trepidation at events in America. There, he said, television interests had taken over; there was a danger that the same could happen in Britain: 'The more sensible answer both for sport and television in Great Britain must . . . surely be mutual co-operation with sporting bodies that already exist. I am optimistic enough to believe that it can and will be achieved.'

2
COUNTING THE COST

Programme cost comparisons

Compared to the cost of producing plays, current affairs programmes or even quiz shows, sports coverage apparently comes cheap. Analysis of BBC expenditure figures by programme category shows the current costs of sport to average around £30,000 per hour, the lowest for all domestically produced programmes. Cost is a crucial consideration, given the strict traditions within British broadcasting of scheduling home-produced programmes rather than imports. The BBC is committed by custom to ensure that 86% of its output is originated in the UK. The IBA's guidelines insist on the same proportion for ITV companies. The alternative, as was recognised when the guidelines were discussed and laid down, would be increasing proportions of material from abroad (predominantly from the US), simply because it is substantially cheaper to import than to create.

The attraction of sport, at least in theory, is that it can help to fulfil the mandatory quota of domestic programmes while at the same time not imposing undue pressure on programme budgets. Compared to other programme categories, the relative value for money which sports provide is entirely logical. Crews rarely have to be transported to expensive foreign countries; and there is no need for groups of editors, producers and assorted assistants to wait for days in anticipation of a news story or in preparation of a half-hour documentary. Major sporting events are predictable in that their times of transmission and the details of the competition are generally known well in advance. They almost always start and finish on time, they can be trailed in advance, and free publicity will be generated through the sports pages of the print media. On the day, the unpredictability of the event itself may be a commentator's nightmare; in advance, the programme is a cost controller's dream.

Precise figures on costs are difficult to calculate. The difficulty comes not so much from a reluctance by the BBC and independent companies to provide detailed breakdowns as in judging how certain fixed costs should be apportioned within a large and disparate organisation (this is not a problem peculiar to broadcasting, although it is more acute). An exception, because of its structure, is Channel 4. Because Channel 4 commissions programmes, including sport, from independent producers it is able to generate more precise figures on its overall cost and its relative standing to other programme categories.

Channel 4 have produced their own documentation which provides valuable information on the relative costs of programme types in the financial year 1986/7. The table opposite is an interesting graphical representation of how the cost of sport on Channel 4 compares to other television output.

Sport is cheaper on Channel 4 than all other programme types except feature films and cartoons – most of which would be acquired rather than originated material. There are, however, two critical qualifying factors which makes this a confusing and ultimately invalid conclusion.

Factors affecting cost
The first is the form which the programme takes. Channel 4 have themselves calculated the differential costs of three types of sports programme to illustrate how costs can vary.

The first was a one-hour sports documentary which was not untypical of the time, effort and costs which go into regular television documentaries. A four-week production period was preceded by two weeks of research and advance planning and followed by seven weeks of 'post-production' (editing, dubbing, special effects, title sequences etc.). The total cost, excluding profit margins for the independent company and a contingency fee, was just over £80,000. Salaries, for technical and production staff, accounted for just over half of this total.

The second was a series of four 75-minute programmes covering an international volleyball tournament at Alexandra Palace. This comprised three weeks of pre-production, four days of production at the venue, and five weeks of post-production (mostly video editing). The total cost of £117,500 for the whole series represented a notional budget of £23,500 per hour. Salaries represented around 20% of this total, while studio and tape costs comprised over half. This total does not include the cost of exclusive television rights, bought from the English Volleyball Association, which in this case is unlikely to have been significant.

The third was the 1987/8 season of American Football which has come

24

Table 1

Cost per hour of programme by category

COST PER HOUR

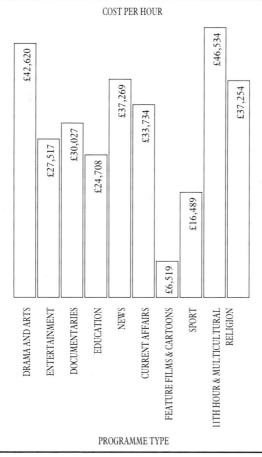

Programme type	Cost per hour
DRAMA AND ARTS	£42,620
ENTERTAINMENT	£27,517
DOCUMENTARIES	£30,027
EDUCATION	£24,708
NEWS	£37,269
CURRENT AFFAIRS	£33,734
FEATURE FILMS & CARTOONS	£6,519
SPORT	£16,489
11TH HOUR & MULTICULTURAL	£46,534
RELIGION	£37,254

PROGRAMME TYPE

Source: Channel 4.

to symbolise Channel 4's sports coverage. Although a great deal of editing, packaging, interviews and previews are incorporated, the core of these programmes is the pictures and commentaries produced by the American networks. The bulk of the cost, therefore – about two-thirds – is devoted to editing in both the US and the UK. The weekly cost for two 75-minute programmes is £30,000, representing a notional hourly budget of £12,000.

The form a sports programme takes can therefore have a major impact on the cost of production. Even more important is the second qualification to the overall cost of sports, the nature of the sport itself. Any discussion of the nature or cost of sports programming must tackle the central fallacy of the question itself: that there is something tangible and generic which can be defined as 'sports'. There are a very small number of people indeed who would claim to enjoy playing or watching every conceivable sport. Most of us will find one or two sports exhilarating, a few boring, and the majority more or less interesting. In comparing sports, there are more differences than similarities.

This will be a common theme, but it is particularly true when assessing the cost of translating sport on to television. There are essentially three determining factors whose relative influence will fluctuate dramatically with each sport: location, duration, and time of day. Location is self-explanatory. When action is taking place within a concentrated space, such as snooker or bowls, the number of cameras and the complexity of the operation will be limited. Once the action moves to a large playing area or a fast-moving event, like football or motor racing, the scale and expense of the operation increases. The increase in cost will clearly bear no relation whatsoever to the numbers of people interested in or concerned to watch that particular sport: considerably fewer people will watch the British Grand Prix than the much more accessible and easily covered World Snooker Championships.

The problem is exacerbated once the location moves overseas to a venue from which local pictures or local coverage cannot be shared by British broadcasters. When the England cricket team toured the West Indies in 1986, fresh from its Ashes defeat of Australia and amid much optimistic speculation about the revival of England cricket fortunes, the BBC alienated many cricket followers by failing to provide coverage. Feelings were strong, as the *Listener* wrote at the time: 'The chorus of criticism this has provoked now shows all the signs of developing into a controversy about the BBC's public service role. Cricket, after all . . . is the national summer sport.' True, agrees the BBC's Head of Sport Jonathon Martin, but even public service must at some point be constrained by cost considerations. Given the disparate nature of the West Indies, and the limited character of their own television facilities, proper coverage would require flying out special film units: 'Then you ship it back to London and you put it on for half an hour, and you get maybe a million people if you're lucky.' In other words, public service considerations must be tempered by financial responsibility, especially given the universal nature of the licence fee.

Strictly speaking, these considerations should also be applicable to

26

ITV, which has been subject to public service requirements in some ways just as stringent as those observed by the BBC. Sports programming within ITV, however, has not generally assumed any of those public service functions adopted by other areas of programming. Traditionally, as Chapter 3 explains, any decision to invest large sums of money in a sporting event – whether because the venue was in some inaccessible part of the world or required a particularly complex operation – has only been justified by the size and quality of the resulting audience.

Duration is the second fact which materially affects the cost of sports. When all the set-up costs, staff payments, transmission fees etc. are devoted to the televising of a single 20-minute boat race, say, or a single horse race, the hourly cost is expensive. When *Match of the Day* featured as the linchpin of BBC Saturday night programming, deploying two Outside Broadcast units at weekends, the total programme budget was up to £80,000 an hour (including payment for rights). Test cricket, however, requires only one OB unit to provide over six hours of daytime programming for twenty-five or thirty days a year. Similarly Wimbledon fortnight, although a more substantial operation, provides 130 hours of daytime television in two weeks. And snooker, of course, combines the best of both worlds: a simple operation, concentrated on a small area, providing hours of uninterrupted television.

The third consideration is time of day, significant only in terms of relative costs of other programming. The most expensive programmes are, for self-evident reasons, generally scheduled at times when most people are free to watch television. There would be little point in spending half a million pounds on an extravagant drama if it was scheduled at a time when the majority of the population were asleep or at work. Viewers' ability to watch television is crucial to considerations of programme timing. Generally speaking, the rule for both commercial and BBC television is that considerably less money is spent on daytime, very late night and breakfast programming than on peak-time evening viewing.

Most outdoor sports, if they are to be covered as live events, will constitute daytime programming. Given that the budget for daytime programmes averages out at little more than £5–6,000 an hour, almost any sport will be relatively expensive – even for one Outside Broadcast unit at Lord's for six hours. Evening sports television, however, whether live coverage or recorded highlights, will be relatively cheap – even for the transmission of a live soccer match from another European country.

All these considerations therefore render the average cost per hour of sport a meaningless concept. Unfortunately, the publication of such stark programme expenditure statistics has provoked forthright criticism from some administrators who are convinced that their own sports are being exploited. From their standpoint, exploitation can only be alleviated through one mechanism: adequate payment in return for the exclusive rights to televise the event. As we shall see, these payments have transformed (and transfixed) American sports. In the UK, from the beginning of BBC sports coverage, the emphasis has been on minimising the rights fees charged to broadcasters.

The cost of exclusive rights

For that very first Wimbledon broadcast in 1937, the All England Tennis Club were prepared to accept that their reward would be a contribution to science and the general interest. Charges were waived, but with a note of prescient caution: 'You will appreciate that if the experiment proves to be successful, the factor of commercial values must of course enter into . . . future calculations.' At this stage, any payment which the Corporation was prepared to make was strictly in the form of a charge for broadcasting facilities or rent, not for the 'right' to televise. During the period of difficult negotiations with the Football Association preceding the first televised Cup Final, Stanley Rous drew attention to the fees paid by newsreel companies, which after all did not even represent a threat to minor match attendances. The BBC's non-commercial constitution was at this stage clearly influential in guiding such negotiations. Gerald Cock recorded his own response, that 'we were a public service, and did not rely on sales for income, but I said that I thought a moderate payment for facilities or rent would be possible.' It was implicitly acknowledged, however, that 'facilities' were a convenient euphemism for disguising the truth: the BBC were paying for the right to televise.

Predictably, perhaps, it was boxing that made the running in the immediate post-war era. Here was a sport ideally suited to the new medium: indoor venues were not subject to unpredictable weather; a small playing area did not overstretch a technology still in its infancy; and title fights were expensive to watch live and frequently sold out. Financially, however, promoters had no need to concern themselves with the promotion of the sport in general as opposed to their own match. Professional boxing existed to make money, which it did by charging spectators to watch. Television was a means of reaching more people who would be prepared to pay, and the rights would have to reflect the number of viewers. Furthermore, since 1944 boxing had been televised in America to the very lucrative advantage of participants. British promoters wanted a similar deal for their own fights.

28

A demand of £2,000 for the Woodcock-Mills fight in 1946, subsequently reduced to £500, was refused but provoked debate at the highest levels of the BBC about what would constitute acceptable practice. The dilemma was acknowledged in a note by the Director General to the Board of Governors on 20 June 1946: 'In principle we claim free access and facilities wherever they are given to the Press. In practice, after periods of offering to pay for the actual extra cost of our facilities . . . we have usually arrived at a compromise on a fairly nominal fee.' The exception even at that stage was the two big horse races, the Grand National (standard payment £350) and the Derby (£300). Test Matches were charged at £100 for the full five days, Wimbledon at £75 for the full fortnight, and for all professional football (including the Cup Final) a scarcely extortionate five guineas! It was proposed to raise the level of fees for boxing matches from the pre-war £100 a fight to £300 'for the very top-line fights'. The tone throughout this note was that a hike in fees for one sport would inevitably have an inflationary effect on all others, and that 'we would be faced with a landslide, and merely end with the same necessity to call a halt at a more expensive point.' In fact, given the potential benefit which television could bring to sport, perhaps even the existing fees were out of proportion to the facilities offered. Without the competitive pressure of a rival broadcaster, the BBC was in a position to set the negotiating pace. It was for sporting bodies to decide at what point the potential benefit to the sport should be sacrificed by refusing to accept inadequate payment.

Some three years later, little had changed. Five events were the exception to the facility fee rule, and were deemed sufficiently important to warrant a price tag of 'something nearer what the individual event is worth to us'. The Boat Race had been added to the two horse races, boxing and Test Matches. Jack Solomons had again been threatening to review the fees available for professional fights, in view of a forthcoming World Heavyweight Championship fight in London. In reviewing the options, de Lotbiniere again expressed anxiety about the potential inflationary effect of changing existing policy to a calculation for every event of its worth to the BBC. He favoured the status quo 'even at the expense of losing some big boxing broadcasts' – although he indicated a willingness to relent on the five guineas Cup Final payment. A year later, although dramatic increases had been resisted, there were clear signs of sporting bodies starting to flex some muscles: Wimbledon was up to £40 a day, Test Matches to £100 a day, and the Football Association had finally extracted a more realistic £250 for the Cup Final.

In 1950 boxing again provoked a revision of the payment structure, leading this time to a provision for 'maximum fees' – a means of ensuring that inflationary pressure was restrained while allowing some discretion in the negotiating process. This set the maximum fees at £750 for the Cup Final, £1,000 for World Championship professional fights, £200 a day for Test Matches, £1,000 each for the Grand National and the Derby, £100 a day for Wimbledon, and £200 for rugby internationals. For the first time, in recognition of the greater availability of audiences during weekends and evenings, a differential fee was applied for 'miscellaneous championship events': £200 for evenings and Saturday afternoons, and £100 for weekday afternoons.

Two years later, as television became increasingly widespread, it was clear that flexibility would be required in negotiations with sporting bodies. De Lotbiniere recommended a new scale of maximum fees, with an acceptance of the principle that the relative importance of different events could not be legislated for in advance: 'They will vary according to the day of the week and to the ballyhoo of the moment, and in consequence some latitude is desirable . . . I should like to state maxima for a few outstanding events and then to be allowed to negotiate other events along proportionate lines.' The proposed ceilings for the major events were substantially increased. The Cup Final was up 33% to £1,000, while the fee for Scotland-England soccer internationals doubled to the same amount; World Championship boxing was up 50% to £1,500, as were the Derby and the Grand National; Wimbledon went up 75% to £175 per day; and rugby internationals up 25% to £250. Only Test Matches stayed where they were.

Towards the end of 1953, the Chairman of the Football League was suggesting a television fee of £10,000 for the Cup Final. While this was generally dismissed as 'ridiculous' by other football representatives, the FA did eventually demand another 50% increase to £1,500. Once again, it was the repercussions on other major events which most concerned de Lotbiniere, who assumed that the same proportionate increase would be applied across the board. Somewhat reluctantly, he recommended acceptance of the FA terms and the inflationary consequences.

Over the next eighteen months, it was not competition among the different events which dictated negotiations but competition from an entirely different source. With rivalry from the new commercial network due to begin at the end of 1955, the BBC were acutely aware of the potential impact on negotiations for prestigious live events. Surely the advent of competitive pressure for the first time would provoke an expensive battle for exclusive television rights? In practice, however, the BBC were less concerned with exclusivity than continued access. Several factors governed its position. First, it was entirely consistent with a now long-standing and realistic approach designed to avoid 'astronomical' rises in fees which could only prove detrimental to both broadcasters. Second, it was politically sensible. As Peter Dimmock, now Head of Outside Broadcasts, said at the beginning of 1955 after outlining the non-exclusive contracts he had negotiated so far: 'This seems to me to offer a safeguard for BBC viewers without precipitating the political storm that might arise if we bought exclusive rights. It would also enable us to protest strongly if the ITA obtained exclusivity at a major event.' Finally, it was an approach formulated in the certain knowledge that the new competitor was not in a position to bid realistically for exclusivity.

Inevitably, given the highly controversial decision to start a commercial service at all, Parliament was drawn into the debate. When it came to that section of the new Television Act which dealt with exclusivity and events of national interest, Parliament found itself in a quandary. While welcoming the advent of a new service, many Conservative MPs were aware of the electoral consequences of major sporting events being transmitted on a channel available to barely half the population. As Bernard Sendall has recorded, there were 'apprehensions that wealthy commercial interests might outbid the BBC and . . . deprive BBC viewers of events they expected to see on the "national" service'.

There was, however, simultaneous concern that the legitimate interests of sporting promoters should not be inhibited, and that sporting bodies should be allowed to reap the proper rewards for their most prized events. It was an insoluble dilemma for the Government, captured in the words of one Government spokesman during the Bill's Committee stage in the House of Lords. According to Sendall, Lord De La Warr 'virtually threw himself on the mercy of the House' in attempting to reconcile conflicting demands: 'I am not giving any secrets away when I say that the Government draftsman produced something like ten drafts on this subject; it has been the most difficult problem in the Bill.' The Gordian knot was severed by a truly British compromise which gave the Post-master-General the power to draw up a statutory instrument 'with a view to preventing the making of exclusive arrangements for broadcasting of sporting or other events of national interest'. In the event, this power was never invoked because the broadcasters co-operated. Although the Act itself did not specify which events were covered (and would not be expected to do so), a list of ten was mutually agreed by ITV and BBC. These were: the English and Scottish FA Cup Finals; the Grand National and the Derby; Test Cricket involving England; the Boat Race; Wimbledon tennis; soccer's World Cup finals; the Olympics; and the Commonwealth

31

Traditionally a BBC preserve: Wimbledon, a Ladies Doubles Match in 1957 (© BBC)

Games when held in Britain. While adopted as a response to unique developments in 1955, the philosophy engendered by this clause subsequently became an accepted part of the broadcasting landscape. It was carried forward in its entirety into Section 30 of the 1981 Broadcasting Act, which initiated Channel 4.

History repeated itself when cable was launched in 1982–3 amid a fanfare of optimistic forecasts. Authoritative sources were projecting considerable economic power for cable companies, eventually enough to challenge the BBC/ITV duopoly. It was, however, never likely to become universally available and therefore attracted the same concern about viewers' right of access to major events. Once again, Government and Parliament were generally agreed about the need for protection, but were greatly exercised about its precise form. Different regimes of protection were suggested, first by the Government-appointed Hunt Committee on the future of cable, then by the Government's own White Paper, and finally by the published Bill. After further amendments during its passage through Parliament, what finally emerged in Section 14 of the 1984 Cable and Broadcasting Act was a new two-tier system of protection.

Under the first tier, safeguards imposed on the original listed events were retained and extended to cable operators. Rather than leave anything to chance, the list was for the first time published by the Secretary of State in a written Parliamentary answer on 12 July 1985. Additionally, Section 14 defined a second tier of 'protected' events which – while permitted for exclusive purchase as part of a subscription package – could not be shown on pay-per-view terms. This group consisted of any events which had regularly been part of broadcasters' schedules, thereby extending the net to virtually every sporting occasion of any moment. The logic of this extension was clear: given the small audiences which cable would attract initially, operators would only be able to raise sufficient cash to outbid terrestrial broadcasters by charging a premium fee for a single event. Such potential viewer deprivation was not to be tolerated. For thirty-five years, a consistent underlying philosophy has therefore prevailed: that while rights holders should reap the just rewards of selling their product to television, viewers should not be deprived of access to events of national importance. It was a natural and logical extension of the public service philosophy applied to sports broadcasting. In the delicate balance of power between viewer and rights holder, the viewer was to remain sovereign.

Nearly thirty-five years later Peter Dimmock, the original architect of a listed events mechanism, confessed to some amazement that these restrictions on competitive bidding have survived. Certainly, it is a barrier to maximising revenue through unrestrained competition which seems out of step with the prevailing emphasis on an unfettered free market. Right on cue, the Government's 1989 Broadcasting Bill proposes to abolish the listed events provision. Any channel, regardless of its availability, will be able to buy exclusive rights to major events, thereby breaching the long-standing principle of universality. Only the restriction on exclusive acquisition for pay-per-view purposes is to remain.

As satellite channels proliferate, competing both with each other and with established terrestrial broadcasters, increasingly vigorous competition will ensure a considerably enhanced price for these sporting showpieces. Chapter 9 explores the potential repercussions of this policy shift, but it is unlikely to be long before at least one event of national interest is snapped up by a satellite channel as a means of encouraging reluctant viewers to invest in new channels. For viewers, it may mean an unwelcome transition from 'free' television to restricted and expensive access. For sporting bodies, this relaxation comes as a welcome outcome given that full-blooded competition between the networks never fully materialised after 1955.

During the 60s and 70s, the BBC reaped the benefit of their flying start and ITV's federal structure. In soccer, there were cosy agreements which preserved the BBC's Saturday night highlights while allowing ITV a Sunday afternoon presence. Most non-listed events stayed with the BBC, although for fees which arguably better represented their true worth to the broadcaster in relation to other programming. Of major sports, the only real battles to develop were in athletics and football, both detailed in the following chapter. While professional sport may not have reaped the financial rewards of outright competition between two equally matched rivals, intense network battles in the United States took American sport to the other extreme: spiralling rights fees and a rampant commercialism which many believe has had fatal consequences for the health of American sports.

Exclusive rights in the US
While the 1951 Test Matches were available in their entirety to the BBC for £200 per day, the 1951 baseball World Series earned rather more for the team owners and participants. The deal struck in 1951 gave the American national game $1 million a year over six years for its blue riband event, a minimum of nearly $150,000 (or £50,000) a day (assuming each of the best of seven games was played, and each on a separate day). Eight years later, the BBC was proposing a fourfold increase to the Test and County Cricket Board, allowing £800 a day for a forthcoming Test series against India. The differential had narrowed: by this time, baseball had renegotiated a mere threefold increase, which gave them $2.5 million a year, or a minimum of $350,000 a game. In 1983, aggressive competition for rights fees resulted in a staggering $1.2 billion contract over six years, worth $4 million to each club annually.

The driving force behind American sports rights for the last forty years has been a ferocious battle between the three major networks, ABC, CBS and NBC. Chapter 3 details the crucial importance which each network attached to sport in their schedule; and few sports were sufficiently popular and adaptable to commercial television to be worth pursuing. The two key sports which satisfied both criteria were the classically all-American games of baseball and American Football. With some help from Congress, the network dogfights to secure exclusive rights to football produced some quite astonishing settlements.

By the early 60s, football, a relative newcomer to the American sporting landscape, had become established as the biggest crowd-puller of all American sports. More importantly, while baseball consolidated its reputation as the traditional national game, many thought it did not

34

translate well on to television. Baseball fans were happy to watch, but the more casual viewer was not captivated by the long pauses and slow build-up. Football, on the contrary, was a gift to television. Here was a game which, to the uninitiated, appeared violent and virtually incomprehensible. The complex tactical manoeuvres which preceded plays were lost in the ensuing melee, whose only objective seemed to be to render the maximum number of opponents unconscious in the minimum possible time. Those who went to the stadium understood and enjoyed the intricacies. Those who did not dismissed it as a game for lunatics.

Television transformed American Football because it was the perfect medium for explanation. In much the same way that Channel 4 has gradually initiated millions of British viewers, so American television performed the same function in the early 1950s. Even casual viewers and former sceptics began to understand the rules, appreciate the subtleties and enjoy the ebbs and flows of the match. In an astonishingly short time, television converted a fringe pastime into a national obsession. And networks were prepared to pay to keep the newly converted spectators locked into their channel. Spiralling television rights fees for American Football reflected its transformation into a hot telegenic property. In 1951, ignored by CBS and NBC, the entire National Football League made only $50,000 from television. League championship rights for 1951–3 were sold to the ill-fated Dumont network for $95,000 a year. CBS bought the entire 1955 season's schedule for $1 million. At this stage of football's relationship with television, broadcast rights fees constituted a mere 15% of NFL revenue.

Until 1960 individual teams struck their own television deals which depended on their own success and the size of their local television market. In 1960, the scene changed dramatically with the formation of a rival American Football League (AFL). Spurred on by the AFL's revolutionary decision to divide broadcast revenues equally between teams, the NFL persuaded CBS to sign a unified, national contract through which each NFL team was guaranteed twice the revenue of their AFL counterparts. As well as ensuring a minimum income for those teams in less lucrative markets, pooled television contracts would strengthen bargaining power with the three television markets. At this point, just as the British Parliament had intervened in the television/sport relationship five years previously, Congress became equally involved, though from a very different perspective.

In a country which almost worshipped competition and regarded monopolies as anathema both to economic growth and to the national psyche, antitrust laws were rigorously applied to every sector of econ-

35

omic life. The NFL decision to pool contracts was ruled out of order: packaged media contracts, it was argued, constituted restraint of trade and therefore violated federal antitrust law. The NFL fought back against the very backbone of American competition law. It lobbied hard, arguing that pooled contracts were fundamental to the survival of modern sports leagues. By the end of 1961 Congress had passed the Sports Broadcasting Act, which permitted professional sports franchises to negotiate the sale of broadcasting rights as a single economic unit. These antitrust exemptions applied to professional baseball, hockey and basketball as well as football. All Congress asked in return was a promise (willingly given) not to schedule games against Friday night high school matches or Saturday afternoon college games. In Britain, Parliament had deliberately restrained the bargaining power of sports bodies to ensure universal access to important events. Congress, however, went out of its way to guarantee to sports bodies the economic power they craved. It was a decision which paved the way to gold.

The effects were immediate and startling, but entirely predictable given American television's hunger for football. In 1962, CBS won the battle for exclusive rights with a package worth $4.6 million a year. Two years later, assisted by a 50% increase in ratings and therefore even fiercer bidding by all three networks, CBS agreed to a 300% increase and a package of $14 million for each of the next two years – a contract which incidentally ensured the survival of the Green Bay Packers, who proceeded to dominate the league for years afterwards. In 1967, the last year before the NFL/AFL merger, a modest 33% increase gave the NFL $18.5 million a year. No sooner was the ink dry on the merger than Congress passed a rider to an unrelated Bill which extended the antitrust exemption to the new Football League.

The increases continued inexorably. In 1977, television rights went for over $160 million a year, contributing $5.5 million to each team's annual income and exceeding gate revenue for the first time. And the five-year agreement concluded in 1982, following 1981's best ever football ratings, resulted in a $2 billion package which contributed $14 million to each of the twenty-eight teams. In return, teams had to concede one additional minute of advertising during televised matches. After 1981, however, America's love affair with televised football began to pall, and declining ratings meant a halt to spiralling rights fees. An agreement reached in 1987, which involved all three networks and the cable sports channel ESPN, totalled $1.4 billion over three years – a $12 million drop from 1986 levels. As a direct result, for the first time since agreeing to pooled contracts each team had to accept a half-million dollar reduction in network revenues. With broadcast revenue constituting 65% of the total, such reductions became critical; there was considerable speculation as to whether the principle of pooled contracts – an ideal arrangement for the years of plenty – could survive a period of famine. In fact, most recent negotiations demonstrate the enduring attraction of televised football: deals with all three networks plus TBS and ESPN on cable are likely to exceed $3 billion over four years from 1990.

One means of escape from this unfamiliar and uncomfortable financial straitjacket – moving into the fast-expanding European market – could have enormous implications for sport on European television. With American television revenues saturated, sale of European television rights could provide the new source urgently required to maintain those vital TV revenues. Although generating a paltry $2 million for the National Football League in 1988, the new generation of satellite and cable channels throughout Europe looks tempting: sufficiently so for the NFL to announce their commitment to a satellite league based in Europe and scheduled to start in 1990 or 1991. With similar initiatives well advanced in baseball, hockey and basketball, Europe's satellite revolution will find willing customers for their airtime from traditional American sports. Traditional European sports may well find themselves in uncomfortable competition with a new influx of American sports being packaged and heavily promoted on new specialist sports channels.

In one major international sporting arena the power of American influence and the financial consequences of their network battles for exclusive rights have already been graphically illustrated. Most of the world has felt the full force of aggressive bargaining techniques through the fight to secure coverage of the Olympic Games. Table 2 (overleaf) gives the stark inflationary figures for every Olympic Games since satellite technology allowed foreign cameras to send pictures back home. Behind those figures are some extraordinary stories of chicanery and hard determination to achieve exclusive access.

For American television, both the 1960 and the 1964 Winter and Summer Games were little more than news material. Primitive technology meant time delays in getting footage back home, and anyway the Games had at this stage achieved nothing like their magneticism for American television of later years. By 1968, as Chapter 3 describes, ABC was attempting to establish itself in the national psyche as *the* sports channel. The first major American Olympic production in Grenoble saw $3 million (half a million dollars more than the rights themselves) poured into facilities and production costs. Twenty-seven hours of programming was transmitted from France to the USA via forty cameras and the

Early Bird satellite, including some spectacular ice-skating by gold medallist Peggy Fleming. Even this did not whet viewers' appetite for Olympic coverage enough for networks to launch a major offensive. The 1972 rights fees were decided after only moderate competition which reflected moderate audiences. It was the horrific drama of terrorist kidnapping and the subsequent massacre of both terrorists and Israeli hostages at the Summer Games in Munich which sent ratings skywards and announced the permanent arrival of the Olympic Games as a price-less television commodity. While the drama was unfolding on American screens, ABC sport's architect and shrewd negotiator Roone Arledge realised the Games had come to stay and immediately made the Canadians a 24-hour-only offer for the 1976 games: $25 million with 10% payable immediately. Cash was in short supply, and it was a fantastic sum at the time; the Canadians accepted.

Table 2

American rights fees for Olympic Games 1960–1992

Year	Summer/ Winter	Venue	Winner	Price
1960	Winter	Squaw Valley	CBS	$50,000
	Summer	Rome	CBS	$394,000
1964	Winter	Innsbruck	ABC	$597,000
	Summer	Tokyo	NBC	$1.5m
1968	Winter	Grenoble	ABC	$2.5m
	Summer	Mexico	ABC	$4.5m
1972	Winter	Sapporo	NBC	$6.4m
	Summer	Munich	ABC	$7.5m
1976	Winter	Innsbruck	ABC	$8.0m
	Summer	Montreal	ABC	$25m
1980	Winter	Lake Placid	ABC	$15m
	Summer	Moscow	NBC	$85m
1984	Winter	Sarajevo	ABC	$91m
	Summer	Los Angeles	ABC	$225m
1988	Winter	Calgary	ABC	$309m
	Summer	Seoul	NBC	$300m
1992	Winter	Albertville	CBS	$243m
	Summer	Barcelona	NBC	$401m

After such a successful coup, and unparalleled success in coverage of the 1976 Montreal Games, it was open warfare for the 1980 Moscow Games. Despite difficult time zones, fewer facilities for sophisticated coverage and political differences, each network was prepared to pull out any campaigning trick to further their cause. While negotiations proceeded, the Russians made it clear that favourable political coverage would not harm the competitors' chances. Each obliged: ABC provided a week of glamorising images of life in Russia; CBS produced a special prime-time feature on the Bolshoi ballet; and NBC covered a Russian festival of music and dance. However entrenched the American antagonism to all things Communist, ideological purity was temporarily waived. In his colourful book *Supertube*, Ron Powers described the only possible silver lining: 'If the three major networks could find one scrap of satisfaction in the way they performed in contending for the rights in Moscow, it was this: they managed to make the Communist bureaucracy of Mother Russia itself behave like a bunch of grovelling capitalists.' In the end, NBC's victorious offer of $85 million looked a little generous when Jimmy Carter pulled the US out of the Games in response to Russia's invasion of Afghanistan.

By 1984, the stakes had nearly trebled. $225 million from ABC bought the showpiece Los Angeles Games, a Russian boycott, and a great deal of nationalistic coverage. And four years later, Canada's convenient time zones attracted a phenomenal $309 million for the Calgary Winter Games, which exceeded the sum eventually paid for the Seoul Summer Games. At this stage, the United States can reasonably be said to underwrite the Olympic Games themselves: payment for exclusive rights from American television networks now constitutes two-thirds of the host city's total revenue. Such financial dependency does not come without repercussions, and some of the consequences for this pinnacle of international sporting competition are discussed in Chapter 6.

Drawing conclusions

Who wins and who loses from these very different traditions of paying for televised sport depends on perspective. Critics of the British tradition, looking across the Atlantic, can point to the money which sport might have derived from a more competitive broadcasting system. It is not an unusual complaint from some of the major sporting bodies that television gets its sporting events 'on the cheap'. Critics of the American tradition might envy British sport its integrity and British broadcasting its willingness to schedule more than just the high-rating events or most popular sports. Later chapters are devoted to a more searching examination of the

39

price which television has exacted in the United States in return for its dollars. For the moment, it is more constructive to outline two reasons why comparisons between the bargaining practices of the two countries can be invidious.

First is the sheer economic power of the United States. Its television household population is four times the size of the United Kingdom's and its economic capacity six times as great. In economic terms, broadcasting is a 'public good' – that is, it costs the same amount to produce regardless of the number of customers ultimately attracted to the product. Thus once a television programme has been made, the economic power of the total audience dictates its worth; the greater the number of available viewers, the greater the fee such a programme can command.

In the British context, such considerations are as material for the non-commercial BBC as they are for commercial television, and they explain some of the huge differential between the two countries in payments for exclusive rights. A television household size comparable to that of the United States would quadruple the BBC licence income. And ITV, with access to audiences with equivalent spending power to pass on to advertisers, would also be well placed to make more generous offers. More important, perhaps, is the second reason which constrains direct comparisons: the inherent differences in the sports industries. Despite the efforts of Congress to exempt American Football from the rigorous discipline of the competitive marketplace, American sport is an industry run on the basis of the profit motive. Its purpose is to make as much money as possible for the participants and, particularly, the owners.

In fact, it is the *ownership* issue which forces the pace of American professional sport. Baseball teams, football teams, basketball teams and soccer teams are not run by boards who act as trustees or guardians of the local interest, baling out the overdrafts of poorer clubs or basking in the reflected glory of the more successful. They are entrepreneurs whose commitment to the local community will, as we have seen, endure as long as a more profitable opportunity does not materialise. The concept of third and fourth division professional soccer clubs, uneconomic because of their location in depressed areas and permanently teetering on the edge of bankruptcy, is utterly alien and incomprehensible. Even college teams, which theoretically are imbued with an amateur philosophy that elevates the game above financial reward, have become increasingly professionalised (influenced largely by the vast sums of money now available for the television rights to college games).

Greater tolerance in the UK for the amateur tradition should not be confused with a less committed attitude to the sport itself. One American academic, in a book which is discussed in more detail later, has tried to demonstrate that this is indicative of a less competitive approach by British teams or players to their sports! According to Joan Chandler, 'the importance of competition is played down' in Britain and there are 'quite different public attitudes to the value of competition'. She quotes Chris Evert-Lloyd, writing about her husband's approach to tennis, which apparently valued the effort involved rather than the result. While this might explain a great deal about John Lloyd's record as a tennis player, it is a gross caricature of how the British play their sports. Anyone who has seen Steve Cram running against Coe and Ovett, Ian Botham bowling to the Australians or the entire Welsh Rugby Union pack piling into their English opposite numbers will not be immediately struck by a gentle air of communal and comradely effort. The determination of these participants to emerge as victors is not diminished by the absence of sackfuls of money.

On the other hand, British athletes are as entitled to the material fruits of their labours as their American counterparts. And to a growing extent these rewards are forthcoming. For although most UK sports have not been the direct beneficiaries of television's increasing interest, the indirect benefits through sponsorship have been huge. The precise relationship will be examined in more detail later, but the financial rewards available to sports which obtain television coverage should not be underestimated. Especially within a broadcasting system whose sports coverage has historically been dominated by two non-commercial channels, the presence of cameras unlocks substantial sums of money from companies eager to have their name promoted on a medium which cannot be bought directly. And there lies perhaps the most critical difference between the two countries. For in America sporting rights have, at least until recently, been bought with 'clean' stadia – that is, no billboards, advertising hoardings or mammoth posters can be displayed in the stadium which might contaminate the commercial messages constantly being promoted by the network's sponsors. Once sports have sold their television rights, that represents their total income for any televised event. Private sponsorship is simply not admissible. It is therefore impossible to make direct comparisons or projections about what sort of income the more successful UK sports might have earned from a fully competitive broadcasting system. Despite the substantial sums earned directly by football and athletics in the 1980s, most sports can probably earn as much from the sale of advertising space around the ground, not to mention shirt, ball and goalpost sponsorship, as they can from television rights.

41

If that is the case, British sport arguably has had the best of both worlds: income derived as a direct result of television coverage, although only a small proportion of it comes from the TV companies themselves; and freedom from interference by television executives who, in return for their substantial investment, demand one or two quids for their quo. Sponsors are not concerned about how the sport is played, as long as the cameras are there. And television is not bothered by hoardings as long as they don't discourage viewers. Viewers, meanwhile, can continue to watch their favourite sports played – more or less – according to unadulterated rules.

3
SPORT IN THE SCHEDULE

For British television, 1989 represented something of a watershed. In February, the medium-powered Astra satellite began operation and by the end of the year it was transmitting seven English-language channels to any British household choosing to purchase a 60-centimetre receiving dish. And British Satellite Broadcasting finalised its plans for a five-channel satellite service to be launched in 1990, and receivable via a 30-centimetre square dish or 'squarial'. Within two years the number of new channels available and relevant to British viewers who are prepared to pay will have trebled.

Sports broadcasting, in particular, is being transformed. For over fifty years sport has been available only as part of an eclectic mixture of different types of programming on channels whose schedules were aimed at universal, rather than specialist, audiences. At each stage of broad-casting's evolution, from the introduction of ITV in 1955, BBC2 in 1964 and Channel 4 in 1982, sport has had to fight for its place in the newcomer's schedules along with drama, news, adventure series, children's programmes and other equally incompatible programme categor-ies. Addicted sports viewers have been subject entirely to the whims of channel schedulers bound to take into account competing demands from other audiences with different viewing tastes.

The extent to which the satellite revolution will make a significant impact on sports viewing is discussed in Chapter 9. Whatever the vastly increased supply in sporting airtime, it is becoming increasingly clear that the short-term effect on viewers themselves will not be dramatic: for the vast majority of viewers, existing terrestrial channels will continue to be the main source of television sports. These four channels have between them carried virtually every minute of television sport watched by British viewers since the beginning of televised sport until the first transmission from Sky's Eurosport (only the tiny proportion of households with access to cable may have watched some of ScreenSport's output in the last few years). In those fifty years, decisions on which sports, at what times of day, for what duration, with what sort of investment, have been the prerogative of very few men (no women have held the relevant positions in the broadcasting organisations). These decisions can have extraordinary effects. They can infuriate the followers of one sport or delight the fans of another. They can provide a financial lifeline for one sport, or devastate another. They can seduce thousands of viewers from a rival channel, or alienate thousands more who defect or switch off.

Such decisions cannot be made in a vacuum. Other programming strands must be accommodated. The relative popularity of the sport or significance of the event must be measured against the responsibilities towards those who are not sports fans and the desirability of different audience profiles for advertisers. It is a mark of the British approach to broadcasting, in contrast to the stark commercialism of America, that different channels have different philosophies and different responsibilities which inform and dictate their scheduling decisions. In that sense, sport represents a microcosm of the broadcasting ecology. Through an examination of how these decisions are made within the different channels, a great deal of light is thrown on the operating principles behind British broadcasting over the last fifty years. In the light of new and rapid developments, the moment is unique; for different pressures and considerations will apply from 1990 onwards.

Sport in the schedule: the facts

Before we look at the influences and philosophies behind the scheduling of sport, some background factual data is essential to set the scene. It is possible to chart the progress and changing emphases of sport in the schedule throughout the 1980s through information available from Sportscan, a service started by the Sports Council and now continued under the auspices of Research Services Limited. From 1980, Sportscan has recorded the proportion of hours devoted to sport in general and to individual sports, as well as the distribution between channels. As an index of the rise and fall of particular sports on television throughout the 80s, this is invaluable.

In its first measurement year, 1980, Sportscan records a total of 1,876 hours of sport on British television which would have included around 200 hours of the Olympic Games from Moscow. These broke down as follows:

	Hours	Proportion
BBC1	723	39%
BBC2	639	34%
ITV	514	27%
	1,876	100%

By 1988, also an Olympic year and therefore comparable, the number of hours of television sport had risen by 73% to 3,243. Only 606 hours, or less than half of the total increase, is attributable to the introduction of Channel 4 in 1982, as the 1988 breakdown demonstrates:

	Hours	Proportion
BBC1	909	28%
BBC2	912	28%
ITV	816	25%
C4	606	19%
	3,243	100%

These figures give the stark statistical truth, that the opportunities for watching sport have nearly doubled in the last ten years. On the other hand, we should be wary of interpreting this as a surge of interest in sports programming at the expense of other programme categories. A large part of the increase is directly attributable to transmissions at times of day which had previously shown nothing but the Test Card. Breakfast television in the UK made its debut on BBC1 in January 1983, and daytime programming gradually established itself on all channels in the following five years. ITV now carries programmes round the clock. In short, while the number of channels has increased from three to four, the television clock has also been expanding.

One way of setting the volume of television sport in perspective is to examine the proportion of sport in each channel's output compared to other programme categories. Since Sportscan does not provide total programming hours, these figures must be culled from the Annual Reports of the respective channels. It is always dangerous to compare figures from dissimilar sources, because it is never certain that the underlying assumptions are identical. These comparisons (see Table 3) must therefore be taken as approximate, though they are instructive.

45

Table 3
1988/9 comparisons of output across the four channels

	BBC1	BBC2	ITV	C4
	%	%	%	%
Feature Films/series/drama[1]	30	21	32	32
Features/documentaries/current affairs	16	22	15	19
News/News Magazine programmes	15	5	13	4
Light Entertainment	9	3	20	11
Schools/College/Open University	2	24	1	14
Children's (not schools)	7	1	8	7
Sport	13	16	8	9
Other[2]	8	8	3	4
	100	100	100	100

1. BBC figures do not separate feature films from series, and include children's series and cartoons. ITV/C4 figures do not separate 'plays' from 'Series/TV movies'.
2. Includes religion, music, weather, continuity and 'Arts' for ITV/C4.

Overall, then, at the point when the amount of television sport is about to increase substantially, it constitutes around 11% of total television time. Its contribution to BBC2, at 16%, is significantly higher than to any other channel, and the BBC overall includes a good deal more sport in its schedule than the two commercial channels. Sportscan figures for 1988 (which overlap most closely with the 1988/9 annual reports) demonstrate that the BBC channels between them showed 56% of all televised sport. Channel 4's Olympics coverage helped to narrow the gap: in the last non-Olympic year, 1987, the two BBC channels accounted for 63% of all sports output.

It is tempting to draw conclusions from the comparatively high figure for BBC2. Does it, perhaps, depend on sport as a cheap source of domestic programming, thereby maintaining low costs for what is after all supposed to be a minority channel? In fact, these figures only reflect the types of sport being covered – in 1988 nearly half of BBC2's sports output came from just three sports (see Table 4).

This table demonstrates graphically why any statistical figures on output should be treated with caution. Cricket, snooker and golf are all activities which span many hours and which viewers will rarely watch from beginning to end. They are, except for the most dedicated fanatic, 'dipstick' sports which may accumulate audiences for exciting climaxes but will sustain overall fairly low viewing figures. They are therefore ideal material for a second, minority, channel which can accommodate many hours of low audiences while the more popular channel can pursue more high-rating programmes. As we shall see, this relationship between the two BBC channels has been instrumental in developing the Corporation's ability to offer live coverage of major events without undue disruption to mainstream regular broadcasting; and in maintaining a long-time sporting supremacy over its commercial rival.

There is another, even more pressing reason why such figures should be treated with caution. Overall increases in the availability of sports programming cannot be examined in a vacuum. They have to be seen, as with all broadcasting, in the context of the available audience. Showing baseball at three in the morning, as ITV has done, is fine for expatriate American insomniacs or video owners but very few of us will see it. In other words, an increase in television hours at the margin of existing schedules provides little additional *accessible* programming. What really counts is sports output at times when viewers are most available to watch – the peak viewing hours of evenings and weekends.

Although there is no systematic enquiry into levels of peak-time sports programming, it is generally acknowledged that since the sporting heyday of the 1950s and 1960s, only exceptional events will make it into the 7–10.30 p.m. viewing slots. As one sports programmer has said: 'Peak-time scheduling has got harder and harder to break into. There's no slack space any more.' It is not so long ago that showjumping featured

Table 4
Top Ten sports on BBC2 during 1988

	Hours	% of BBC2 sport
1. Cricket	205	22
2. Snooker	139	15
3. Golf	101	11
4. Tennis	83	9
5. Bowls	71	8
6. Horse-racing	56	6
7. Winter Olympics	52	6
8. Rugby Union	35	4
9. Darts	29	3
10. Motor-racing	27	3

Source: Sportscan.

prominently in the BBC schedules, or that *Sportsview* was established in the peak-time Wednesday evening slot. Both were important elements of the BBC1 schedule. Perhaps the most recent and most long-standing casualty is *Match of the Day*, which used to dominate Saturday evenings, generating audiences of 10–12 million on BBC1 and providing a scheduling cornerstone. More recently, there has been a tangible decline in the level of sports coverage during those crucial peak hours, as more programme categories and different audience demands vie for attention. Increasingly, it seems, recorded weekday sport or midweek sports specials can be found between 10.30 p.m. and midnight, sometimes later, destined for those with particular sporting predilections but unlikely to pick up the casual viewer.

This relegation of sport in the schedule has important repercussions. Casual 'window shopping', where viewers will settle down to an evening's viewing and watch whatever happens to be on, has arguably been responsible for introducing a great many viewers to types of programme they would not have actively chosen. Evening television is frequently a 'default' activity, a means of relaxation which involves little effort beyond the pressing of a few buttons. For such viewers, unless positively repelled by a particular programme, television is capable of rendering popular and likeable something which was previously unfamiliar. Such considerations are as relevant to sport as to drama, documentaries or any other type of programmes where viewers are not certain what to expect and therefore make no special effort to watch. A classic example in the annals of British television is the story of showjumping.

Before the war, interest in equestrian sports was confined almost exclusively to farmers and the agricultural community, a rich person's sport of little interest or relevance to the vast majority of ordinary people. After the war, two things happened. First, in 1945 Colonel Mike Ansell organised a National Victory Show Jumping Championship at the White City, using a revolutionary course which he had designed while in a prisoner-of-war camp. White City owners, perceiving this as a potential crowd-puller, revived the International Horse Show in 1947, producing not only crowds but a rapid improvement in British showjumping standards. Secondly, London's 1948 Olympic Games provided the perfect foil for advertising the regeneration of a once exclusive sport. Immediately prior to the closing ceremony came the showjumping. 80,000 spectators in a packed Wembley stadium were treated to the sight of a British bronze medal in a sport which the vast majority would never before have seen. More importantly, the triumph was seen in cinema newsreels, and for the first time on television.

It was the beginning not just of a highly successful period in British equestrianism, but of a very fruitful relationship between equestrianism and television. Four years later it was sealed dramatically. At the 1952 Helsinki Games, the equestrian team won for Britain its only gold of the Games and returned home as heroes. A few weeks later, the televised Horse of the Year show at Harringay climaxed in an enthralling jump-off between Colonel Llewellyn on 'Foxhunter' and Pat Smythe on 'Finality'. Dorian Williams, established from the beginning as the voice of BBC showjumping, described the scene some years later: 'There were no less than four jumps-off, and when eventually, to the almost hysterical delight of the audience, they rode in together and shook hands showing that they had decided to call it a tie, the TV cameras were still operating, although the programme had overrun by more than an hour.' In front of several million peak-time viewers, showjumping had arrived. Williams himself wrote that he was in no doubt about the significance of that single telecast: 'I have always considered that it was this event that finally set the seal on the popularity of showjumping with the general public.' It was a popularity which lasted throughout the 50s and 60s and whose effects are still reverberating.

Technology and circumstance combined to elevate showjumping in the public perception. At a time when television was still experimental, cameras were unwieldy and outside broadcasts were complex and expensive to mount, here was a simple sport with a history of British success in international competition. Coverage was relatively simple because, as Williams put it, the screen could contain everything that was essential – the horse, the rider, the fence. All the ingredients for successful sports television were present: rules were simple and easily comprehensible; the stadium was easy to cover; it involved horses; and the image was untarnished with any suggestion of doping or nobbling. The reciprocal benefits produced ratings which in the 1960s frequently exceeded 10 million viewers.

It is impossible to envisage any repetition of similar circumstances. Occasionally, there may be a sport which captures the public imagination through television exposure at the margins of the schedule. Snooker, which made its debut on BBC2 in 1969 to illustrate the benefits of colour television, is often cited as the modern equivalent to showjumping. Certainly, it is the archetypal TV-promoted sport whose players twenty years ago were languishing unpaid and unrecognised in obscure clubs throughout the country. But even snooker now rarely appears in peak time on the two major channels, relegated usually to late-night viewing or afternoons on BBC2.

Another snooker is conceivable, but unlikely. Even given a dramatic British breakthrough in a previously obscure event, and even if such an event is eminently suitable for television, there are simply too many conflicting pressures on peak-time television and plenty of other outlets for promoting new and different sports. There will, of course, be live coverage of major events which happen to be scheduled at peak times: Olympic Games, soccer World Cup qualifying matches, Wimbledon into the early evening, major snooker championships. None, however, will consistently occupy a mid-evening schedule and thereby be afforded the opportunity of accumulating followers from the ranks of the uncommitted.

Peak-time scheduling, therefore, is critical and any overall trend analysis of sport in the schedule must be treated warily. Within these limitations, the trend throughout the 1980s provides a fascinating portrait of the ebb and flow of certain television sports. Chapter 4 will analyse how these variations may have influenced audience taste; this chapter is concerned with how the emphasis on different sports in the schedule has evolved throughout the decade. A straightforward comparison of the most frequently broadcast sports in 1980 and 1988 is given below.

Table 5
Top Ten scheduled sports in 1980 and 1988*

	1980 Hours	%		1988 Hours	%
1. Cricket	370	21	1. Cricket	339	12
2. Horse-racing	290	17	2. Snooker	307	11
3. Soccer	215	12	3. Horse-racing	272	10
4. Tennis	162	9	4. Soccer	219	8
5. Golf	122	7	5. Golf	157	6
6. Snooker	120	7	6. Tennis	150	5
7. Equestrian	61	3	7. American Football	89	3
8. Rugby Union	50	3	8. Bowls	87	3
9. Wrestling	37	2	9. Athletics	79	3
10. Boxing	32	2	10. Motor-racing	71	3

*Figures exclude Olympic coverage for both years.

On the face of it, not a great deal has changed. The top six sports have rearranged themselves, but the bulk of television sport seems to have been the same for nearly a decade. A closer look, however, produces a slightly different perspective. The top six sports in 1980 supplied nearly

50

three-quarters of television sport; in 1988, they supplied just over half. Both these figures exclude the Olympics, which provided three times the number of hours in 1988 compared to 1980. If these are included, the difference becomes even more dramatic.

This rapid decline in the proportion of major sports in the schedule – from 73% to 52% of all televised sport – has important implications. It is not enough to point to the inexorable rise in television airtime since 1980. While this has clearly been instrumental, there is ostensibly no reason why expanded television time could not be exploited to provide expanded coverage of all sports, including the top six. In fact, with the notable exception of snooker, the table demonstrates that the absolute number of hours devoted to these six sports has either declined or remained roughly static. Part of the explanation is undoubtedly Channel 4. With a remit, explained in more detail below, to be innovative in all programme areas it was obliged to apply this philosophy equally to sport. Even so, of Channel 4's non-Olympic coverage in 1988 a total of 38% was devoted to horse-racing alone. The new channel is only part of the reason why major sports now take up a considerably smaller proportion of sports broadcasts.

An inescapable conclusion is that expanded television airtime has provided an opportunity for increased coverage of minority sports which traditionally have had little exposure. The figures confirm this trend: ice hockey, which received a grand total of one hour's television in 1980, had eleven hours in 1988 – none on Channel 4. Basketball was up from four hours in 1980 to nearly thirty hours in 1988; cycling from five hours to twenty-six (mostly on Channel 4); yachting from half an hour to twelve hours; hockey from two hours to nearly ten. And there are others. Any temptation to stay with the mainstream sports (and there is much more cricket, soccer, snooker or golf which could be covered) has been resisted in favour of more minority activities.

To some extent, this pattern will reflect an assumption by sports schedulers that certain events have reached viewer saturation point. It also reflects the more marginal times at which these new sports are being telecast: no channel would waste a popular snooker game or soccer match on breakfast-time or late-night audiences. It is also, however, a reflection of the BBC's deliberate policy (as well as Channel 4's) to offer some airtime to sports which may not be immediate or even potential ratings successes but which command passionate support from a small but dedicated band of followers. Outside the peak-time periods, BBC television need not be entirely occupied by the size of its audience. The increasing scope and variety of television sport through the 1980s is the first manifestation of

A trend towards minority sports: Channel 4 covers basketball

how the BBC's public service mantle can embrace more marginal sports as well as more marginal programmes in other categories.

It is therefore outside those first six sports that the real changes have been occurring. A glimpse of the radical nature of these changes in the rest of the sports schedule is provided by numbers 7–10 in the scheduling hierarchy, which have undergone a complete transformation in those eight years. Out go equestrian events, no longer swept forward by the momentum generated in the 60s; in comes American Football, entirely created by Channel 4's commitment to new and unfamiliar sports. Out goes wrestling, once the staple diet of ITV's Saturday afternoon *World of Sport* and another perfect foil for the limited technology of twenty years ago; in comes bowls, condemned by one American commentator as 'the most funereal sports event I have ever seen' but managing to combine drama and tranquillity within a setting ideally suited to television cameras. Bowls, perhaps better than most other sports in recent times, illustrates the ebb and flow of sports coverage – and how fickle television can be. In 1980, there were just over ten hours of coverage, which rose to a peak of 178 hours in 1987 (when the level of exposure even exceeded soccer's). Then the BBC started to withdraw some support, and coverage was almost halved to 87 hours in 1988 and fell again in 1989.

Both the remaining sports which made 1980's top ten listing illustrate how increasing airtime has created the restructuring below the top six sports. Although neither feature in 1988's top ten, both boxing and Rugby Union now have more television time than eight years ago: Rugby Union up from 50 to 58 hours, and boxing more than doubled from 32 to 70. That even more hours have been allocated to new sports is demonstrated by Rugby Union's position behind not only bowls but even baseball, which in 1988 received 61 hours of coverage. This comparison is a good example of the potentially fallacious nature of straight airtime comparisons: much of rugby's coverage is on Saturday and Sunday afternoons while baseball tends to be confined to late-night and early-morning television.

One postscript to the table above is required to complete an accurate picture. By taking evidence from the first and last available years, both coincidentally Olympic years, the proportion of airtime usually devoted to athletics is underestimated. In 1987, the last non-Olympic year during the period, there were 153 hours of athletics; at over 5% of total sports coverage, this placed it easily among the 'major' television sports. Figures for 1985 and 1986 are comparable, establishing athletics as an important ingredient in television sports. This is partly due to the exclusive contract for British athletics, cemented in 1984, which encouraged ITV to devote a good deal more airtime to track and field events. At the same time the BBC continued to televise events abroad, thereby raising the profiles and coverage of a sport previously under-represented on television.

Sport in the schedule: the philosophy

Traditionally, a variety of factors in British broadcasting influence programme scheduling decisions. There is often an assumption, especially by those raised on or committed to principles of the free market and deregulation in broadcasting, that a public service system is too unaccountable to its audience and too vulnerable to the subjective whims of programme controllers. According to this philosophy, programme ratings are the only certain guide to popularity, the only reliable means of maintaining contact with the television audience.

These have not been the sole guiding principles of British television, in either the public or the private sector. The Reithian doctrine which has formed the cornerstone of BBC philosophy for over sixty years is well documented: programmes should not only entertain, but should educate and inform as well. As a general explanation of what constitutes public service broadcasting, this is a simplistic and unsatisfactory definition. Before we consider its application to sports programming it is important to appreciate the ethos of public service broadcasting, for many people tend to dismiss it as an outmoded example of Reithian paternalism. Six guiding principles can be identified:

1. Range: there should be a diversity of programmes so that audiences have access to both relaxing and demanding programmes, arts and science as well as soaps and quiz shows.

2. Quality: production values should be maintained, whether in the creation of a new soap opera, the serialisation of a classic novel, or the production of a half-hour news programme.

3. Innovation: programme makers should sometimes seek to lead, rather than follow, audience tastes. Experimentation should be encouraged.

4. Minority programming: programmes should be available for a range of minority groups and interests, whether cultural minorities, demographic minorities, or those with minority tastes. These programmes should be accessible, not relegated to the margins of schedules.

5. Distance from vested interests: programmes should be subject to neither political nor commercial pressure, and editorial control should rest entirely with programme makers.

6. Cultural identification: programmes should reflect and enhance Britain's cultural richness and diversity, even though domestically produced material may be substantially more expensive than imported material.

These requirements are embodied in the BBC's Charter and, while ratings still constitute an important yardstick for assessing the success of programmes (especially on BBC1), the public service factors will often influence programming decisions.

54

In this respect, the BBC does not operate in a vacuum. For commercial television, although run entirely on income from the sale of advertising airtime, has been as vital to the maintenance of a public service system as the BBC. Because the independent television companies have been overseen by the Independent Broadcasting Authority (IBA), and because they have been obliged by their licence agreements with the IBA to follow certain tenets of public service broadcasting, ITV has itself made a positive contribution to the quality and reputation of British broadcasting.

The regulations applied to the commercial sector would be anathema to free market broadcasters, for they have been in many ways every bit as prescriptive as the BBC Charter. In return for their regional monopolies on advertising airtime, ITV companies have been obliged to limit imported programmes to four hours of peak-time television per week; subscribe to Independent Television News (ITN) and transmit its 'Ten O'Clock News', limit advertising to seven minutes per hour overall; and plough back a reasonable proportion of their profits into original drama and factual documentaries. Renewal of their highly lucrative franchises has depended ultimately on a proper fulfilment of these obligations.

Finally, Channel 4. This most recent addition to British terrestrial television was born out of the 1981 Broadcasting Act and started transmitting in November 1982. Although a second commercial channel, it represents the quintessence of regulation applied to the commercial sector in pursuit of programming objectives deemed to be in the public interest. Assiduous lobbying by the advertising industry failed to convince the then Home Secretary, William Whitelaw, that a second commercial channel should compete for advertising with ITV. It should, he decreed, be able to marshal commercial resources to provide a positive addition in variety and style to existing channels. In an ingenious legislative structure, Whitelaw established the channel on a publishing basis: editors would be responsible for commissioning programmes from independent producers according to a remit laid down by Parliament that the channel should develop 'a distinctive character of its own'. Its airtime would be sold by existing ITV franchises, thereby maintaining the advertising monopoly; in return, each ITV company would hand over 17% of its gross revenue as Channel 4's financial guarantee. Insulated from the market, and therefore liberated from the straitjacket of mass audience programming, the new channel was given the structural support through which it could fulfil its statutory responsibility to be different. Channel 4 was the last piece in the public service jigsaw of British terrestrial television.

This is the fairly complex legislative and constitutional environment in which British broadcasters work, and which has had a major impact on the philosophy they bring to making programmes. Since practice is not wholly dictated by reference to last week's ratings, there is considerable scope for discretion. Producers must be responsive to audiences and use both ratings and audience research as a guide. They must also, however, be concerned with trying new approaches and ideas; with making sure that minority tastes are covered; with providing a range of offerings within their programme genre; and with promoting essentially British material. Although the concept of 'public service' might seem less appropriate to those responsible for television sport than, say, to makers of drama or comedy, decisions on sports programming within the four channels in fact owe a great deal to the history and constitution of each of those channels. Each needs to be examined separately.

The BBC
Since BBC decisions are not predominantly dictated by ratings, the Corporation can afford to spread its sports portfolio. In fact, as part of its public service remit, it is arguably obliged to allocate some of its schedule to the less popular sports. On the other hand, lines have to be drawn: while curling or arm-wrestling might excite a small minority, the BBC would risk ridicule if it spent time and money on extensive coverage of such sports. How to decide? One rule of thumb is a World Championship status. According to Jonathon Martin, 'If it's a World Championship and it's in Britain we will try to cover it.' That decision is, to a large extent, irrespective of the popularity of the sport or how extensively it is played. Although it commissions a great deal of research, the BBC will not leap for the statistics on the popularity of, say, rowing before deciding to televise the World Rowing Championships. The event's status, and the knowledge that there will at least be some interested viewers, is sufficient to justify coverage.

A case in point is the 1986 World Hockey Cup. Despite qualifying late for the finals of the Los Angeles Olympics in 1984, the British team had done well. And despite a fairly unglamorous location for the 1986 world tournament – in Willesden, North London – Martin succeeded in persuading Director of Programmes Michael Grade that this was an important sporting event which ought to be televised. By the end of the event, Grade was asking for highlights. In this case, the decision was influenced by England's success in 1984, but hockey is not a mainstream British game. Its appearance on British television was a combination of responsibility to an improving national sport, instinctive feelings that it would make stimulating television, and the BBC's public service responsibility to provide the growing number of devoted hockey fans with the cream of their sport.

This last reason is probably the most difficult element in the equation. A universal licence fee payable by every television household clearly carries with it a responsibility to cater to all sporting tastes. And of course it hardly needs repeating that there is no such thing as the 'sports audience', just an aggregate of several minorities of viewers interested to varying degrees in a number of entirely unrelated sports. Martin acknowledges the burden this imposes on licence-funded broadcasters: 'You hope that at some stage in the 52 weeks you're satisfying *all* parts of the sports audience; so when a world championship comes to Britain, small though the audience may be, that's their big moment. They may have waited 25 years for that, so the BBC can hardly ignore them.' But even for a public broadcaster with national responsibilities there must in the end be a bottom line where the equation of cost and audience is simply too unbalanced: 'You can't spend £2.5 million for 200,000 people every night.' This dilemma becomes particularly acute when events of national significance but limited appeal are staged abroad. When the England cricket team visited West Indies for a much publicised Test series in 1986, the logistics, even for the country's national broadcaster with a duty to cover a national sport, were prohibitive.

Decisions like these must rely on the discretion of those who manage limited technical resources on a limited budget. They are open to criticism because there is no objective measure by which they can be evaluated. This, however, will always apply to channels which do not schedule strictly according to ratings. Sport is a perfect illustration of how ratings as the sole yardstick will prejudice the opportunities for minor sports, and the ability of followers of those sports to watch them on television. Since the sports audience comprises an aggregate of scores of minorities, judgment by ratings alone condemns most of those minorities to television oblivion. In promoting an eclectic sports schedule, therefore, a national broadcaster funded through a universal system of payment fulfils two important public service functions. First, such a responsibility enables sports programmers to satisfy the multifarious sporting demands of a disparate audience: it can satisfy public service principles of providing exposure for a range of sports which will cater for several viewer minorities. Secondly, it can help to capture the sense of national pride and national significance attached to sporting achievements by British teams and participants in almost any sport with a following in the UK. By making cameras available at international events, and by justifying expenditure through the significance of that event within the sport rather than through the number of viewers it attracts, the BBC can foster interest in and support for British successes in the less obviously popular sports. This is a valuable contribution to cultural identification which should not be underestimated.

In pursuit of these aims, the BBC is fortunate to have one major advantage over other UK channels and over most broadcasters world-wide: a second channel. When a third terrestrial channel became available in the early 1960s, disillusionment with commercial television was at its peak. The Pilkington Committee, reporting in 1963, was unequivocal about its views on ITV's poor standards and on the need for a second BBC channel to redress the cultural balance. The Conservative government concurred with Pilkington's analysis, and BBC2 began broadcasting in June 1964. Its contribution to the overall strength of BBC programming has been enormous. Without jeopardising its ratings base, and therefore undermining the justification for a universal licence fee, the BBC has been able to exploit the second channel to build audiences for new, experimental programmes and cater for minorities, while simultaneously providing more popular and familiar fare on its first channel.

The significance of BBC2 for sports programming has been equally fundamental. For one of sport's unique characteristics when contrasted with all other programme categories is its duration. While a few events may last for less than thirty minutes – horse-racing and track athletics are obvious examples – the vast majority take a great deal longer. It could be eighty minutes for a rugby match, ninety minutes for soccer, two hours for a tennis match, three hours for a Formula 1 Grand Prix, five hours for a snooker match, or six hours for each of the five days of a Test Match. For these sports to be shown live in their entirety demands a great deal of a channel's schedule time. With just one channel, such a disproportionate emphasis on any one sport would be intolerable for the majority of viewers with different tastes in both sport and television. With the exception of the most obvious high-rating and prestigious events, complete live coverage would be virtually impossible.

Cross-scheduling has for twenty-five years provided an ideal solution. By switching coverage from BBC1 to BBC2 during the course of a day, thereby allowing one channel to maintain its regular programmes, the BBC has avoided alienating those with no appetite for the particular televised event, while simultaneously satisfying its responsibilities to the followers of that sport. Six hours of cricket, golf, tennis or snooker coverage would be unsustainable for a single-channel public broadcaster and unprofitable for a single commercial channel. Blessed with the

58

flexibility of two-channel coverage, the BBC has been able to satisfy most of its sports fans, its other licence payers, and – just as importantly – a commitment to major sporting bodies to provide full uninterrupted coverage of their sport. It has not always succeeded, since decisions will frequently be a difficult matter of balance between competing demands. It does, however, have the flexibility and manoeuvring space to achieve a proper compromise between high-rating sports and minority interest sports.

ITV

By contrast, ITV has laboured under twin disadvantages during the whole of its thirty-five years. Not only is coverage restricted to a single channel, consisting of regional companies bound together in a somewhat uncomfortable and not always harmonious alliance; at the same time, it must accommodate commercial breaks. In a country where for many years the dominant broadcaster – and in particular the dominant *sports* broadcaster – has been non-commercial, the audience has required some careful marshalling through these initially unwelcome interruptions.

At the same time as coping with a commercially untrained audience, ITV companies encountered initially a chary attitude from sports promoters. In characteristically British fashion, as we have seen, some governing bodies were a little suspicious of these arrivistes who regarded television as an excellent prospect for lining pockets. With this sort of handicap, it is scarcely surprising that ITV has found some difficulty in challenging the BBC's supremacy. Whereas in other fields, such as drama, news and current affairs, the independent sector has developed its own tradition to rival and sometimes exceed the quality of the BBC's output, sport has been a continuing struggle. A victim of this struggle has been ITV's contribution to the public service commitment in sport. While in other programme areas the IBA's regulatory strictures have ensured a proper sharing of public service responsibilities, ITV sport has simply not been in a position to adopt the mantle. Much to the irritation of the BBC – but understandably given all ITV's encumbrances – ITV sports policy has rarely focused on any but the most popular and manageable sports. In contrast to the BBC, ratings and audience profiles have been dominant factors in the ITV scheduling equation. The history of ITV's involvement in football illustrates its approach.

From the very beginning, it was entirely logical that ITV should target soccer as its primary objective. Even in a period of apparent decline in soccer's popularity, ITV's former Head of Sport John Bromley believes that ITV is right to stick with it: 'Soccer is still the national game. It is still the number one spectator sport and the most popular sport in the country – as judged by the number going through the turnstiles, as judged by interest, and as judged by instinct.' After the abortive attempts in the late 50s to obtain coverage of League matches, football made its ITV debut on Anglia in 1962 with recorded highlights of local matches. But it was not until London Weekend won the franchise for London's Saturday and Sunday programming that significant steps were made to challenge the BBC. Jimmy Hill, himself an ex-professional player turned manager, was appointed as Head of Sport and presentation of televised soccer was revolutionised. London Weekend invested £60,000 in a slow-motion machine ('an absolute fortune in those days,' says Bromley) and initiated *The Big Match* on Sunday afternoons, featuring (like the BBC's *Match of the Day*) recorded highlights of one of the previous day's top games. For the first time, British soccer viewers were given the benefit of expert analysis to complement the action. Even at this stage, commercial television was hampered by its regional structure: *The Big Match* was a London Weekend production, which was never seen in the Granada, Yorkshire or Central television areas.

By the World Cup of 1970, when national interest was high and England's chances of retaining the trophy supposedly even higher, ITV had discovered its 'formula'. A panel of provocative experts would enliven intervals and post-match discussions through a mixture of informed comment, passionate debate and outright abuse. Malcolm Allison, Bob McNab, Derek Dougan and Paddy Crerand ('the two goodies and the two baddies') attempted to establish ITV's credentials as a legitimate alternative to the BBC in bringing national sport to television.

Despite their attempts at originality, creativity and additional invest-ment in production, ITV throughout the 60s and 70s could never quite discard their secondary image. Production values were as professional as the BBC's. But come the FA Cup Final, soccer's blue riband and highest-rating event broadcast simultaneously on BBC and ITV, the commercial channel would be consistently outrated by margins of 2 to 1 or more. Throughout this period there had been no problem with negotiating rights. Football was discovering the lucrative potential of sponsorship, and sponsors needed airtime. Consequently, the Football League was happy for both networks to carry football, and the networks were delighted to avoid the pitched battles of exclusive rights negotiations. Although ITV soccer audiences tended to rate lower than the BBC's, they were sufficiently profitable. Relative harmony reigned.

In 1979, the peace was shattered. In their determination to overcome a long-standing and irritating subservience to the BBC's soccer coverage, under Michael Grade's stewardship as Director of Programmes at LWT, ITV decided to break ranks with the BBC and secure exclusive rights to League football coverage. If the BBC could not be beaten within the ruling spirit of co-operation, the spirit would simply have to be sacrificed. Behind closed doors, and unknown to the BBC, the deal was signed and announced to an unsuspecting public. Uproar ensued. While the contract was perfectly legal, and entitled ITV alone to coverage of English League soccer matches, it was somehow not fair play to exclude the country's national broadcaster from showing the country's national sport. Representations were made, strings were pulled, even the Office of Fair Trading was asked to intervene. What in America had become a customary feature of the television sporting landscape created in Britain a furious backlash which ITV was unable to withstand. 'In the end,' says Bromley, 'we had to concede it – we couldn't sustain the deal.'

Having considerably upped the stakes, the real beneficiaries were the Football League. For their part, ITV had at least achieved their most pressing short-term objective: forcing the BBC to surrender their exclusive hold on Saturday night football and to agree a system of rotation. For alternate seasons, one network would be entitled to Saturday evening, while the other would have Sunday afternoon. ITV looked forward to attracting the 10–12 million audiences on Saturday that the BBC had traditionally accumulated for *Match of the Day*, and to having the same focal point around which other Saturday evening programmes could be scheduled. It was not to be. Following the dislocation of two decades of British television sporting tradition, the audience for recorded Saturday night soccer highlights started to dissolve. It is conceivable that a declining interest in recorded soccer happened to coincide with the end of the BBC's exclusive hold on that Saturday night slot. But Bromley for one believes that somehow ITV and Saturday night soccer were incompatible and contributed significantly to the audience drift: 'It was probably taking *Match of the Day* out of the system that really rocked the boat. It never really fitted properly into ITV. *The Big Match* on a Saturday night on ITV – there was something about it that just didn't feel right.' Declining audiences for recorded soccer ushered in a new era for televised soccer in Britain. Live matches may have been a familiar feature of American television for years, but in the UK live soccer coverage beyond World Cup matches and the FA Cup Final started only in 1984. Neither ITV nor the BBC had any intention of cutting back on their total coverage. It was simply the form of coverage that was to change.

ITV's determination to include soccer as a centrepiece of their sporting schedule was undeterred by the arrival in 1988 of their satellite rival,

British Satellite Broadcasting (BSB). It simply cost them a great deal more. When BSB announced itself as a serious competitor, just as ITV had done thirty years earlier, by slapping down an offer of £200 million for the rights to League football over ten years, ITV were forced into an immediate corporate decision. Either accept the presence of a third force, and the existence of enough soccer to be shared among three networks; or treat them as a dangerous threat and blow them out of the sky with a one-off pre-emptive deal for exclusive rights. The significance of soccer to the ITV sports schedule is reflected in their decision to take the second – and vastly more expensive – route. ITV's offer of £44 million over four years, buying exclusive live and recorded coverage of League matches, was orchestrated by Greg Dyke, LWT's new Director of Programmes. It was met with astonishment. Most commentators agreed, and John Bromley subsequently confirmed, that the offer represented less a proper market price for the sporting commodity than a definitive attempt to remove BSB from the competitive equation. Whatever else, it assured soccer a prominent place in ITV's schedules at least until 1993.

Such a dramatic increase in rights fees had a secondary effect on ITV's attitude to soccer coverage, as well as depleting the network coffers. Although the emphasis had switched to live football in a conscious attempt to arrest declining audiences, no systematic effort had been made to invest money in larger-scale or more extravagant productions. ITV were determined to exploit their £11 million per season investment, and promised a revolution in televised soccer.

When Everton played Manchester United on 30 October 1988, the first match of the exclusive contract, the pre-match publicity had little to do with the relative merits of the teams or the possible outcome. ITV announced their plans with a flourish. There would be ten cameras instead of the usual four or five: one on each of the 18-yard lines, one inside each of the goals, a reverse-angle and a roving camera with trackside reporter Jim Rosenthal. In addition, there would be interviews with personalities and players, more sophisticated graphics and on-screen information, and touch-of-the-button instant replays. For the time being, at least, there would be no dressing room interviews with players at half-time (according to Dyke, 'the atmosphere at half-time would be too charged'). This latest intrusion of television did not find universal endorsement within the Football League, whatever the price: at least one notorious First Division manager made it abundantly clear that any demand for live interviews would result in the swift dispatch of producer and equipment into the neighbouring river.

The press speculated. Could this much-vaunted production process

In 1988, ITV introduced new techniques of live soccer coverage. (Cartoon courtesy of the *Listener.*)

KenPyne

'We'll play the first half with the TV cameras facing us!'

really make any difference, or was the television audience for football in terminal decline? Greg Dyke may have been greatly influenced by coverage of American Football, but neither he nor John Bromley was under any illusion about where the entertainment value would come from. Bromley was optimistic as long as the players delivered: 'I don't see any problems as long as football itself provides the meat. We can provide three-dimensional replays but we can't provide the match.' In the event, despite disappointing ratings at the beginning of the season, a sensational climax in the last minute of the last game of the season provided some respite from accusations of squandering network money. Even given a spectacular finale with spectacular ratings to match, ITV could not shake off the sense of controversy and criticism which had accompanied this deal from the beginning. As Chapter 6 explains, the amounts of money now at stake meant that soccer suddenly had to face a reality it had never known: television starting to call in its debt and dictate terms.

While soccer has represented the focal point of ITV's sporting schedule, the network has tackled other sports. In its infancy, when competition was confined to one BBC channel, ITV took advantage of Wimbledon's protected status by exercising its option on parallel coverage. Co-operation with the BBC was requested but declined, so they competed head to head, sometimes showing the same match. As soon as the BBC was granted the second channel, the experiment died. Competition could just about withstand commercial breaks, and a faint British misgiving that somehow tennis on anything other than the BBC just wasn't tennis. Against two non-commercial channels which could cover both main courts, cross-promote and cross-schedule, the battle wasn't even worth fighting. Wimbledon is still the event which Bromley perceives as perfect for ITV, should the listed events provision be repealed: clean, exciting, guaranteeing audiences, and appealing in particular to the young high spenders so cherished by advertisers. But it would have to be an exclusive deal.

It is this notion of live exclusivity which now underpins ITV's approach to scheduling sport. Given the BBC's head start and domination in most areas, the number of opportunities for implementing this strategy have been limited. It was only as recently as 1984 that ITV succeeded in its first real breakthrough, securing its first exclusive contract in a sport where the BBC had held undisputed supremacy. Four ITV companies combined to make an irresistible offer for exclusive rights to British athletics. All the available evidence suggested that athletics was the perfect foil for a new ITV philosophy in scheduling sport. Audience research demonstrated that it was popular throughout all sectors of the population: while many sports are watched predominantly by men, athletics had a mixed following. It was clean: no scandals (the drugs scare was yet to make an impact), sound family entertainment, events to suit all ages and interests. It was achieving consistently good audiences on the BBC. Most important of all, there were British stars coming through: Sebastian Coe, Steve Ovett and Daley Thompson were all world-class athletes and Olympic medallists. Steve Cram was a new and exciting middle-distance prospect.

Athletics was therefore an eminently saleable commodity. While editorial decisions are generally taken independently of the sales departments, commercial judgment on these issues inevitably plays a part. A sports department tired of the BBC's constant shadow was buoyed by the prospect of wresting away a prestige contract, but the euphoria would be pointless if no one could sell the airtime. Consultation is easier given the traditionally cordial relationship between sport and sales – not a particularly common or necessary characteristic of British commercial television. In the event, editorial judgment was supported by commercial judgment. ITV's offer of £10.5 million over five years to the Amateur Athletics Association and the British Amateur Athletics Board was accepted, and for the first time domestic athletics was off the BBC's schedule.

Again, an exclusive contract won by commercial television was dogged by criticism. There were accusations of over-commercialised coverage, not assisted by a heavily promoted 'celebrity' race between Zola Budd and Mary Decker-Slaney, billed as a grudge match after Budd's inauspicious (but accidental) tripping of Slaney during the Los Angeles 5,000 metres Olympic final. ITV were accused of ignoring the efforts of mainstream British athletes in their desperate search for a good story. Traditionalists hated it; and 11 million people watched on television. In the first twelve months of its contract, ITV screened twenty-eight domestic events. As the sudden influx of wealth began to be distributed, as Chapter 6 shows, new criticisms were heard about the increasing emphasis on material gain in an officially amateur sport.

Apart from the accusations of over-commercialism, athletics did not turn out to be the exclusive triumph which ITV had planned and paid for. Many of the more spectacular races, including Cram's record-breaking runs, took place outside the UK where the BBC continued to dominate. These events enabled the BBC to maintain its presence in athletics, and to provide a constant reminder of the contrast in coverage between the two channels. All these difficulties were reflected in the new athletics contract which was sealed in October 1989. Far from escalating costs created by competitive bidding, ITV retains exclusive rights to domestic meetings for a *reduced* fee of £7 million over four years, beginning in April 1990. In return, they will cover only six outdoor and three indoor meetings annually plus two cross-country races. It is not a contract which will lose the BBC much sleep, given its continued guaranteed access to major European athletics outside the UK. It does, however, help to continue ITV's maturing strategy of establishing reputations in a few select sports rather than spreading its net. Triumphantly, in furtherance of this strategy, ITV announced in 1989 a significant victory in securing exclusive coverage of the 1991 Rugby Union World Cup to be held in the UK.

The corollary of this strategy is a systematic removal from the schedule of those sports which no longer fit. From its earliest days, ITV was quick to recognise the Saturday afternoon audience for sport and developed its own eclectic recipe of sporting entertainment. For twenty years, ITV faced BBC's *Grandstand* on Saturday afternoons with its own *World of Sport*. Its staple diet tended to centre round horse-racing, wrestling and a sports results service, but a range of other sports was also covered. *World of Sport* faced the perennial ITV problem: it could never match the consistently higher ratings being achieved by *Grandstand*, with its longer tradition and more prestigious events. In October 1985 it was axed. Still unable to dislodge the BBC from its sports pedestal, ITV companies

65

decided on a different strategy which would abandon the studio-linked format in favour of discrete sport and entertainment programmes. Wrestling would be followed by general entertainment, which in turn would be followed by live coverage of an event exclusive to ITV. Gradually, the range of those exclusive sports has been whittled down. Wrestling, gymnastics, bowls and darts have been dropped from the schedule, snooker greatly cut back, and horse-racing turned over to Channel 4. For the first time in over twenty years, ITV did not cover the 1989 Cup Final, preferring instead a series of films billed explicitly as 'The Cup Final Alternative.' For many within the network's sports departments, the final ignominy was ITV's withdrawal from the 1992 Olympic Games in Barcelona. How, they asked, could a channel which was seriously trying to establish itself as '*the* athletics channel' withdraw from the pinnacle of international athletic competition?

Amid speculation of low morale and frustration within ITV sports, 1989 saw two significant departures. In August Dickie Davies, who for twenty-one years on *World of Sport* and its successor had presented the face of ITV sport, resigned, leaving observers in no doubt about his reasons for going: 'ITV sport did so much in the past – it is sad to see it cut back now. Something very special has become mediocre.' And in October, John Bromley himself left to become chairman of an independent production company specialising in sports. Loyal to the last, Bromley was not prepared to concede that ITV had essentially surrendered to the BBC. He told the *Independent*: 'There's been a definite change of policy and philosophy. But if it is quality and exclusive, sport still has a place on ITV.'

ITV's definition of quality, according to critics, has little to do with the intrinsic merit of individual sports and everything to do with the purchasing power of respective audiences. The network is accused of becoming obsessed with the demographic profile of its viewers, and marketing to a 'yuppie' audience, thereby prejudicing a great many fans of other sports. For its part, ITV claims it has found the right formula with continued emphasis on live exclusivity in soccer, athletics, boxing and now rugby. But despite all its best efforts, ITV has been unable to overcome its subordinate position. Hampered by a regional structure well suited to certain types of programming but too unwieldy for effective planning of national sports coverage; faced with cross-scheduling over two channels by the BBC; and obliged to include the commercial breaks which still constitute for many viewers unwelcome interruptions in sporting events, it must now look forward to an even tougher competitive environment. Until it has defined its new role and established some

66

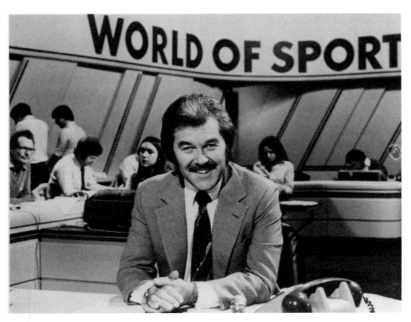

Declining standards at ITV? Dickie Davies, presenter of *World of Sport*, who resigned in 1989 following a change of policy

financial security against new commercial competitors, continuing uncertainty will have a disproportionate impact on the commercial network's sports department.

Channel 4

While the fourth channel was established as a constitutionally separate entity with a different remit from ITV, its financial relationship with ITV offered an irresistible opportunity in the sports field. Although the new channel was still disadvantaged in terms of the BBC by the need to include commercials, there was at least the potential for complementary scheduling to match the BBC's twenty-year-old two-channel advantage. According to Adrian Metcalfe, 1964 Olympic silver medallist and Channel 4's Commissioning Editor for Sport from 1982 to 1989, the channel's brief to provide new and different programming was interpreted more flexibly when it came to sport. 'The IBA took a slightly different view about the role of sport. There was an opportunity now for the commercial television system to negotiate for large contracts which had hitherto been pointless with a single channel.' The challenge to be innovative was

67

certainly not ignored, as we shall see. But a more co-ordinated operation did allow Channel 4 to schedule, for example, six or seven of the twenty-five athletics meetings to which ITV had committed themselves. Some of the burden of fulfilling their obligation to the sport was therefore lifted from ITV, there was again the opportunity for cross-promotion and cross-scheduling, and ITV was provided with additional ammunition in their negotiations for other sports.

Horse-racing is perhaps the prime example of how the relationship could be exploited to the advantage of both channels. With far too much racing for any single channel, BBC and ITV have effectively shared it: for example, ITV will take the Derby and Newmarket, the BBC the Grand National and Ascot. In 1985, some pressure was exerted on Channel 4 to adopt a proportion of ITV's racing which, with initial reluctance, it accepted as part of its responsibility to the sporting calendar. While racing was not a natural contender for Channel 4 coverage, given the extensive exposure elsewhere, it did constitute part of the special flexibility exercised in sports programming. It was also justified by the channel's Chief Executive, Jeremy Isaacs, on somewhat more dubious grounds. He wrote in 1989: 'I wanted an outdoor feel to the channel, and liked the idea of the green of the track, the most restful of colours, on our screens in the afternoon. Besides, if pluralism counted, the horsey interest also deserved to be catered for.' Having accepted the 'horsey interest' as part of its sports schedule, Channel 4 decided to make the best of it. It now covers all the classics exclusively, including major international races like the Arc de Triomphe and the Breeders Cup. By the end of his tenure, Metcalfe was convinced that Channel 4's authority surpasses the BBC's and that the channel has established itself as providing 'the best racing coverage in the world'.

Second only to horse-racing in its contribution to Channel 4's sports schedule, and present from the channel's very beginning, is American Football. American Football represents for many the quintessential example of a minority channel fulfilling its brief not just to encourage diversity of output but to innovate in production and presentation techniques. With average audiences of around 3 million, rising to a staggering 5–6 million for a live Superbowl which starts just before midnight, Channel 4 is directly responsible for developing a cult following for a new and unfamiliar sport. Its British television origins lay in Adrian Metcalfe's own passion for the sport and his conviction that he had 'never met anyone who didn't enjoy it once they'd seen it'. Choosing a sport with potential popular appeal was, however, a small first step. Channel 4's different philosophy in bringing sport to the screen dictated an approach which was almost revolutionary in British sports coverage: starting from an assumption of ignorance and taking viewers through detailed explanations of rules, tactics, and the culture of the game. It was an approach which, from the very beginning, eschewed any undue emphasis on individual personalities, grudges or hostilities and attempted to introduce the viewer not just to another sport but to a little bit of America.

Metcalfe's determination to develop a new approach was illustrated graphically by the choice of presenters for the very first series. 'We didn't want American Football to be seen as part of this ghetto of the masonic, white middle-class, middle-aged, blazer brigade. So we decided to have a 7-foot black professional basketball player and 5-foot Jewish disc jockey to introduce the show as a way of saying, without taking the mickey out of it, that anybody can enjoy this.' Nicky Horne, the undersized disc jockey, was particularly well qualified since he had never even seen a game. He was, however, a lover of American music, familiar with American culture and adept at conveying atmosphere and feeling. As for the rules and tactics, Metcalfe describes his involvement as 'a deliberate let's-all-grow-up-with-this-together'. And grow up they did, taking with them an increasingly committed, young and upmarket audience which turned an instinctive experiment into a successful money-spinner. Presenters since the second year have reflected a growing familiarity and sophistication among the viewing audience; the approach is now a little more technical, and assumes that the audience has 'grown up' in its level of understanding.

A more recent addition to the experimental portfolio also created a following of its own, and at one stage was graphically featured on a Channel 4 poster campaign to promote public awareness of its distinctive style. Sumo wrestling again started with Metcalfe's own conversion after visits to Tokyo. He was fascinated by the 'strange ritual of a brutal and foolish sport which still had the same grandeur of bullfighting'. Even more than American Football, Sumo represented a fascinating insight into a different culture as much as a sport in the traditional sense of athleticism and competition.

It is indeed a fierce contest in which one competitor will try to outwrestle another, in a small arena in front of paying spectators, within a set of tightly defined rules. But it is a contest embedded within a series of rituals as fascinating as the event itself. It was, of course, important to convey the excitement and tension of the physical struggle between two enormous men. But for Metcalfe it was equally important for a proper appreciation of the sport to convey and explain the surrounding ritual:

A different culture: sumo wrestling from Japan, a Channel 4 innovation

how they cut their hair, what they eat, how they train, the significance of the clothes and the folding of the belt: 'We built up a sort of mosaic and then built that up into an actual event, so you saw these warriors as people. There's a continuity, a sort of dramatic drive to the tournament which gave it an energy and a direction.' The reward for those who watched was not just half an hour of sporting entertainment, but appreciation of some aspects of Japanese culture.

It is not just foreign cultures which have provided the inspiration for Channel 4's approach. Minority sports in Britain, which have traditionally had little exposure on the established channels, have been well represented on Channel 4 from the start. As well as the staple diet of American Football, the channel's first full year in 1983 saw coverage of angling, badminton, volleyball, Irish hurling, Gaelic football, and cycling. Metcalfe is particularly enthusiastic about the special coverage given to cycling, practised as a sport by relatively few people but an activity which everyone can relate to. 'We started city-centre cycling as a whole new concept. Nobody had ever actually closed the roads of major cities and put on a terrific race with some of the world's best riders. And then developed it into the professional tour of Britain which has 20,000 people standing on mountain tops in the North of England cheering these blokes over the pass.' It is cycling's accessibility which earned it, and other sports like it, a place in Metcalfe's affections and Channel 4's schedule. Even granted a guiding principle that, some sharing with ITV aside, there was no place for the mainstream sports of soccer, cricket and rugby, a large number of possibilities still remained. Just as fundamental was the principle that Channel 4 should confine itself to affordable and inviting activities – 'sports you can do with a pair of shoes'.

For this reason, motor sports or anything with an engine have never made an appearance on Channel 4, while a great deal of effort and expenditure have gone into sports like volleyball and basketball. As we shall see, the impact which televised volleyball has made on participation has been dramatic and has more than vindicated Metcalfe's golden accessibility rule. Basketball has been less successful, and illustrates that Channel 4 scheduling is not simply dependent on a statutory remit interpreted on the whimsical preferences of one commissioning editor without reference to the audience. While ratings certainly are not the dominant yardstick, as Metcalfe says, 'It would be perverse to do something time and again which only 20,000 people wanted to watch.' Despite money, ingenuity, effort and a peak-time Monday evening slot, basketball never really captured the British imagination. Whether because audiences were uncomfortable with a sport involving consistently heavy scoring (and therefore too 'easy'), or for lack of appreciation of the skills involved, the audience drifted away and Metcalfe acted accordingly. 'We cut back on our basketball coverage for the reason that if people weren't watching it then we should be spending our money on other sports.'

It is a difficult balance to achieve. At what point does a minority audience become an unacceptable minority? Since there is no direct commercial pressure, decisions are not dictated by absolute numbers or by the disposable income and buying power of each sports television audience. On the other hand, limited resources and schedule time require a sensitivity to audience requirements and the exercise of discretion based to some extent on audience research. Surveys have been used, for example, to establish sports which women would find congenial; skating and gymnastics have both featured as a result. Audience research does not dictate the schedule. It is, however, one element in an equation which has attempted to bridge the gap between mainstream sports with plenty of exposure and minority sports with no television tradition at all.

Ultimately, some sports will not make it to television, despite Channel 4's best efforts, because their translation to the screen simply does not work. As part of the Channel's commitment to the television untried, it launched in 1987 a series called *Challenge to Sport*. It offered technical advice and facilities for an eight-minute video to any sport which felt it could make the grade as a regular sporting feature. The results were to be televised in a series of half-hour programmes, each featuring three sports. Despite technical ingenuity and ambitious scripts, some sports found it difficult to make an effective transition. However slowly one operates the slow-motion action replay during an archery contest, the flight trajectory of an arrow is almost impossible to follow. In eight minutes, it is difficult for the most skilled of directors to convey the drama and excitement of Orienteering. On the other hand, tug-of-war, ten-pin bowling and karate are all easy to follow and provide good pictures. They will not all achieve their own series; but they have all had an opportunity, albeit a small one, to present themselves to a television audience with little previous knowledge or understanding of their sport.

More than anything else, it is perhaps that assumption about the audience which underpins Channel 4's scheduling approach. As long as the main public service channel is obliged to provide full coverage of major sports, and the fully commercial channel is governed by its quest for ratings and a marketable audience, there is no room for experimental forays into the dozens of less familiar sports which – if given a chance – audiences might find captivating. Channel 4's philosophy of sports programming has provided more than an opportunity for a number of sports to promote themselves and achieve a higher level of participation. It has added a new dimension to television for those who may not regard themselves as obsessive sports fans but who enjoy the spectacle of competition within an array of different settings and frameworks. In Adrian Metcalfe's words: 'I think there's an audience out there that isn't a passionately committed sports fan, but if approached and entertained and talked to intelligently is more than interested, more than prepared to say I'll give you a bit of my time.'

A different television perspective: the USA

If British television is dominated by a public service tradition, American television represents an utterly different philosophy. In a country committed to the enterprise ethic, where interference in the operations of a free market is regarded with undisguised contempt, it was only natural that American broadcasting should be driven by commerce from its very beginning. While contributions from state funds were limited to providing educational programmes which could never offer adequate return for the commercial channels, mainstream American television was driven entirely by the need to sell airtime to advertisers. Since advertisers measure their return almost wholly in terms of sheer numbers, the driving force in American television became the ratings. Ratings now constitute the currency and life-blood of American commercial television, the only means of evaluating performance in markets where stations compete for the same sources of funding.

It is claimed by proponents of the free market model of broadcasting that unbridled competition and absence of regulation is the best guarantee of fulfilling audience requirements. According to this argument, there must be greater accountability to the audience if the ultimate test of a programme's worth is the number who watch; it must be a more valid test than the arbitrary and unpredictable whims of a programme controller combined with a pinch of audience research.

Two studies, undertaken in Britain by the Centre for Television Studies at Leeds University, have demonstrated the programming consequences of an unregulated private sector in broadcasting. The first, a straight comparison of programme schedules over three days in Europe, Australia and the United States, demonstrated the complete absence of serious or minority programmes from Australia's Channel 10, Italy's Canale 5 and every one of the American commercial networks. For those three days, the American, Australian and Italian free markets produced a schedule almost entirely dependent on a diet of news, adventure series and advertisements. By contrast the European channels, including the British commercial sector, produced a diverse menu of entertainment, adventure series, current affairs, original drama and documentaries. A second report, devoted specifically to the United States, is more revealing. Through detailed interviews with senior network executives, it documents the pressures and tensions which govern the decisions of American producers and schedulers. It is plain that programmers themselves acknowledge how creativity, innovation and experimentation are squeezed out by the increasingly voracious demands of advertising agencies. Commercial imperatives are innately conservative: advertisers demand the safety of last year's successes rather than the uncertainty of an untried playwright, an unfamiliar format, or an experimental idea. The words of one executive summed up the spirit of the free market: 'We don't want the young comer, the untried. We want the bankers. There's too much at stake ... we can't afford to do anything else.'

American broadcasting is therefore founded on a very different set of operating principles. Its tradition is firmly entertainment-based within formats which are assiduously researched and designed to appeal to mass audiences. The very concept of regulating for diversity, for minority

73

programming, for innovation rankles with free market principles. Many influential Americans have despaired of the consequences and baulked at what one former Federal Communications Commission Chairman called the ensuing 'cultural wasteland': in the words of Chester Simmons, ex-President of NBC Sports, American television represents 'an abyss, a black hole into which tens of millions of dollars have been thrown without any visible cultural, entertainment or creative benefits, and with few if any redeeming features'. According to Simmons, however, the one area in which television has been exploited as the ideal medium is sport. In fact, American network television has approached sport in much the same way as other areas of programming: a valuable programming tool at peak viewing times within an entertainment framework designed to attract more viewers than entertainment programmes on any other channel.

Perhaps the best illustration of how American networks make use of sport is the history of one of those networks, ABC (now Capital Cities/ABC). In 1941 NBC, a subsidiary of the huge RCA corporation, owned two very profitable radio networks: the 'Red', which featured popular music and comedy; and the high-prestige but lower-rating 'Blue', which featured current affairs and discussion programmes. Strict FCC regulations against communication monopolies forced NBC to divest itself of one network, and they chose the Blue. Bought by ABC for $8 million, it emerged with the unfortunate tag of 'NBC's sacrificial lamb': weaker, with fewer affiliates, and discounted by major advertisers, it urgently needed, in the words of one commentator, 'attention-getting, popular, reasonably inexpensive programming'.

Sport provided the perfect foil. As the television ratings race developed during the 1950s, ABC trailed a poor third behind NBC and CBS. Its opportunity came in the later 50s when it picked up the Friday night boxing contract which had been surrendered by NBC – and the entire $8.5 million Gillette advertising budget which accompanied it. Assisted by what was at that time a stupendous amount of money, ABC was suddenly in a position to bid both for major league baseball and for the jewel in the 1950s sporting crown: college football. In 1959 it won exclusive rights to the baseball play-offs for the National League pennant. And in 1960 this upstart network staged a remarkable cloak-and-dagger coup to seize that prestigious college football contract. Auctioning of television rights to college football took place in public. It was widely known that NBC, the traditional home for these rights, went into the bidding with two envelopes: one with a lower bid in the absence of any challenge, and one with a higher bid to be submitted if a competitor's representative were recognised at the auction. In March 1960 it was assumed by NBC that, with CBS committed to professional football and ABC an impoverished nonentity, the floor would be clear for their lower bid. It was certainly true that, in any bidding competition, ABC could not hope to match the resources of its erstwhile parent. Come the appropriate moment in the Royal Manhattan Hotel, NBC's representative could see no recognisable challenger and stepped forward with the lower price. He was not to know, but immediately discovered, that ABC's Director of Sports Tom Gallery had meticulously briefed an unknown junior executive to wait for the NBC submission and only then produce the ABC counter-bid. This was set at just over $6 million, correctly anticipating an NBC lower-level bid of around $5.5 million. To the College negotiating body's chagrin, to everyone else's astonishment, and to ABC's undisguised delight, they had succeeded in wresting the prize and announcing themselves as a serious third network.

By 1970, ABC had begun to establish its reputation as the major force in television sport. This reputation was enhanced when the professional National Football League, looking for additional revenue, first approached ABC with a revolutionary suggestion: football during prime time. It was novel because live sport had traditionally been restricted to weekend afternoons when male-oriented programming was less damaging to ratings. The danger of weekday evenings was the alienation of a considerable number of women, who would be more attracted by mainstream entertainment available on other channels. ABC decided to adapt the format to this wider demographic range, and agreed to pay $8 million for thirteen games. On 21 September 1970, a tradition was born which became part of American television folklore: live Monday night football.

Meanwhile ABC were intent on exploiting an even more potent sporting weapon: the Olympics. Even in 1968, it seemed that neither NBC nor CBS were awake to the potential of Olympic Games coverage in the schedule. While they slept, ABC snapped up exclusive rights to both Summer and Winter Olympics, and began to consolidate their reputation as the channel for sport. Their persistence was rewarded in gruesome style after they had won rights to Munich's 1972 Games: huge ratings, albeit generated by circumstances unrelated to sport, began to convince other networks that the Games were worth pursuing. It was 1976, however, which clinched both ABC's sporting hegemony and the Olympics as a television spectacle without peer. Another clean sweep for ABC, with friendly time-zones in Montreal and some spectacular images in ice-skating and gymnastics, it was widely acknowledged as a sporting and television triumph. Both its rivals were keenly aware that ABC now regarded the Olympics as personal property. Far more importantly, those two sporting weeks lifted the network from third place in the ratings to a clear first, a position which it maintained for the rest of the decade. For that reason, it mattered little whether revenue for those two weeks exceeded expenditure on rights fees and production costs. Through its access to such a high-status event, the stature and image of the network was elevated. In the words of American authors Klatell and Marcus, the real significance of the Olympics was not the bottom line but 'as an unmatched promotional soap-box for the rest of the network's entertainment programming'.

Eight years later, ABC were again prepared to pay ridiculous sums for access to that soap-box. After NBC's debacle with the 1980 Russian Olympics, ABC achieved another clean sweep with successful bids for both Sarajevo and Los Angeles. Their determination to maintain a sports reputation was confirmed by the $75 million margin between their $225 million bid and that of the runner-up, CBS. Exclusive Olympics coverage was the one area where promotional and image values even superseded the ultimate criterion of programming value: financial return. Despite losing $65 million on Sarajevo, ABC still produced their staggering $309 million for the Calgary Winter Olympics.

Tolerance of such a loss-making potential is strictly limited to the Olympics, which fulfils a vital function as a network showpiece in compensation. In virtually every other area of American sports coverage there is only one rule which dictates which sports reach the screens: can the total network outlay be recouped by selling the attendant advertising space? If insufficient numbers of viewers are prepared to watch or – even more critically – insufficient opportunities exist for inserting those crucial commercial breaks, the sport falls by the wayside. This last consideration is fundamental to understanding the influence which television producers attempt to exert on sports administrators. The fewer the pauses during a game, whether natural or contrived, the smaller the likelihood of attracting sufficient advertising money. This combination of ratings with opportunities for commercial messages will decide which sports are televised, and with what frequency. It explains why some sports have succeeded while others have tried desperately to accommodate their rules to television. Hockey simply did not attract sufficient numbers of viewers and was a network loss-maker. Soccer was doomed by its unbroken 45-minute per half duration, which meant sacrificing commercial revenue or missing part of the game while commercials were shown. Meanwhile, American Football – as we shall see – adapted itself at every conceivable opportunity to the dictates of the television market in order to safeguard its prime-time coverage and therefore its huge bargaining power.

In particular, American Football was prepared to understand and absorb the entertainment tradition of American television. Roone Arledge, longtime Head of ABC Sports and described by Benjamin Rader as a 'television sports impresario without peer', founded his approach to college football coverage squarely on the need to get the audience emotionally involved: 'If they didn't give a damn about the game, they still might enjoy the programme.' American Football was happy to oblige because it wanted the prime-time sports whose focus was pure Hollywood-style entertainment and show business. If some sporting authenticity had to be sacrificed in the process, it was a small price for the additional viewing converts and the considerable extra cash generated as a result. Howard Cosell led a commentary team whose primary purpose was to ensure that an audience not entirely convinced of the joys of American Football would find the programme irresistible. In his own words: 'There is no damn way you can go up against Liz Taylor and Doris Day in prime-time TV and present sports as just sports.'

In parallel with its influence on existing sports, the irresistible drive for ratings through entertainment promoted some intriguing new initiatives. Although categorised under a sports heading, they owed little to any traditional code of playing rules and much more to the exigencies of commercial television keen to attract viewers. Commonly known as synthetic or 'trash' sports by their detractors, these events served the dual of purpose of attracting reasonable audiences and providing a cheap source of recorded programmes ready to transmit at any time. Some weird and wonderful sports have been featured, many on ABC's *Wide World of Sports*. These include wrist-wrestling, rattlesnake hunting, a Big League gum-blowing championship, World Championship Buffalo-Chip-Tossing (*sic*), barrel-jumping and fridge-carrying races. Sports producers are unapologetic: one from CBS is quoted as offering the following explanation: 'People want the human interest stuff. . . . A guy lifting a barbell, that's boring. But the same guy lifting a refrigerator, a car, barrels of water, that's human interest.' But we need not worry about their imminent appearance at the Olympic Games, since this producer at least is happy to concede the hybrid nature of such activities: 'I don't call them trash sports. I call them entertainment features within the anthology format.'

Perhaps the most obvious sports derivative which has featured regularly on American television is sporting challenges involving superstars or celebrities. In the former, top athletes compete in specialities other than their own or may combine with celebrities at their own sport (pro-am golf tournaments, for instance). In terms of ratings successes, however, nothing can contend with celebrity tennis matches: a match between Farrah Fawcett-Majors and Bill Cosby drew 49% of the television audience. Years before, in 1973, Billie Jean King had accepted a television fee of $100,000 to take on the incurable chauvinist Bobby Riggs in a so-called Battle of the Sexes. In front of over 30,000 spectators and millions more on prime-time television she routed him 6–4, 6–3, 6–3. The catalyst for that match had been a similar challenge earlier in the year between Riggs and Margaret Court, which Court had lost but which had drawn a higher television rating than the men's World Championship Tennis Finals played on the same day. Ultimately, it will count as legitimate television sport in America if enough people want to watch to make it profitable.

It is invidious to compare two completely different television environments and try to evaluate which best serves the sports viewer. In their approach to sports scheduling, British producers arguably cater for a greater variety and wider scope while trying to remain faithful to sporting traditions. In doing so, they may be less likely to attract the casual non-sports viewer. American producers will try to provide some Hollywood razzle to lure even the most anti-sports viewer. In doing so, they may distort both traditional sports and the traditional concept of competitive games. They also afford minority sports less opportunity for exposure and therefore valuable publicity.

This contrast is of more than academic interest. As long as television is interpreted according to the entertainment model, providing viewing enjoyment for the greatest possible number of people, the opportunities for those sports whose visual appeal is not immediately obvious will be limited. This has dual consequences: less scope for minority sports to promote themselves and therefore expand, and few opportunities for the followers of such sports to indulge their tastes. Ultimately, the concentration on one or two sports with a proven track record and a proven ratings value is likely to result in a disproportionate following for those sports at the expense of sports afforded less television exposure. On the assumption that television must take some responsibility for structuring tastes and preferences in sports as in most other areas, we can hypothesise that the British appetite for sport on television covers a wider spectrum of sporting activities than the American equivalent. A better understanding of sporting preferences on television can be achieved through an examination of audience figures and research.

4

SPORT AND THE AUDIENCE
A View from the Couch

What is the most popular sport in Britain? Such a simple question deserves an uncomplicated answer, but the simplicity is misleading. As with any statistical question, it all depends on definitions. We might answer the question by looking at participation. Those sports which attract the greatest number of active participants have legitimate claim to popularity. But participation itself raises problems of definition. Does one include only regular participants (say, at least once a week)? Or also occasional participants, in which case we have to define some measure of time (once a month, perhaps, or once a year)? And what of all the sports fans which this criterion must necessarily exclude? The elderly may have given up rugby but still love watching it: similarly with disabled people. Squash enthusiasts may have limited or no access to necessary facilities. Only the most privileged showjumping fans can afford their own horse. If participation is the yardstick, many sports with a popular following will be disadvantaged.

Perhaps, then, we should take attendance as the most appropriate measure. After all, a willingness to travel, to pay, and in many instances to brave the British elements must be some testimony to popularity. But then there is the same problem with frequency. Do we include only regular spectators, say once a week? Or, more realistically, at least one paying visit over a year? Some sports, like soccer, offer many more spectating opportunities than others, like gymnastics or showjumping. Those living in outlying areas are less likely to have access to competition stadia, and therefore may have no means of fulfilling their sporting preferences. And again, reluctance among certain sectors of the population to attend events may be unrelated to their enthusiasm for the sport: women may be deterred from attending soccer matches by fear of violence, or older people by the inevitable chilliness of many outdoor

79

events. Once again, if spectating is the yardstick, many popular sports will be excluded.

What, then, of watching sport on television? Most of the disadvantages of participation and attendance are immediately overcome, since 98% of households have television. The old, sick, disabled, fearful or just plain lazy will have access to most of their favourite sports through television. Indeed, one might reasonably ask what still motivates long-standing loyalists to endure the crowds at Wimbledon, the umpires waiting interminably for a cloud to pass at Lord's, or the biting wind and imperfect view at Twickenham, when there is a comfortable chair and perfect view in the warmth of their own homes. And more enticing refreshments than a stale hot dog and a cold cup of tea. But judging popularity by reference to television viewing carries its own problems, because watching television is itself a complex activity. For many years, mass communications researchers have studied what people watch, how viewing choices are made, what categories of programme are preferred by different people, and the effects of scheduling. One conclusion is inescapable: many people will watch a television programme for reasons which have nothing to do with liking it or deliberately choosing to watch it.

This concept is central to any analysis of television preferences, and applies to sport as much as to current affairs, soap operas or drama. Ratings are an accurate guide to which programmes attract most viewers, but conceal all manner of considerations which ultimately determine the size and nature of a television audience. This problem is exacerbated in an area which encompasses many varieties of viewing experience and decision-making. The difficulties are best illustrated by reference to specific examples. Table 6 lists the highest-rating sporting events during 1988 and 1989. There is remarkably little consistency in either the events which have made the top ten or the audiences they attract: only the Grand National, the Wimbledon Ladies' Final and the FA Cup Final are common to both years. It is not audience sporting tastes fluctuating wildly from year to year but the critical nature of other intervening factors which creates the unpredictability. For instance, why should the premier UK tennis match, the Wimbledon Men's Singles Final, which attracted nearly 12 million viewers in 1989, not even make an appearance in the 1988 top ten? In this case, the reason is one of scheduling: persistent rain on the Sunday afternoon resulted in postponement of the 1988 final to the next day. Because of work and school commitments, most potential viewers are simply not able to watch television on a weekday afternoon and audiences are therefore depressed. It is a tribute

Table 6
Top-rated sports programmes 1988/9

1988

Programme	Channel	Audience
1. Horse-racing: Grand National	BBC1	14.3m
2. Snooker: UK Professional Final	BBC1	13.2m
3. Athletics: London Marathon Highlights	BBC1	11.0m
4. Snooker: Benson and Hedges Final	BBC1	10.8m
5. Boxing: McGuigan *v* Miranda	ITV	10.6m
6. Tennis: Wimbledon Ladies' Final	BBC1	9.7m
7. Soccer: Match of the Day (21/2/89)	BBC1	8.9m
8. Olympics Today (29/9/88)	BBC1	8.8m
9. Rowing: Oxford *v* Cambridge Boat Race	BBC1	8.4m
10. Soccer: FA Cup Final	BBC1	7.8m

1989

Programme	Channel	Audience
1. Boxing: Tyson *v* Bruno (recorded)	BBC1	14.3m
2. Horse-racing: Grand National	BBC1	11.9m
3. Tennis: Wimbledon Men's Final	BBC1	11.7m
4. Soccer: The Match (Liverpool *v* Arsenal)	ITV	10.3m
5. Soccer: FA Cup Final	BBC1	10.3m
6. Soccer: The Match (Everton *v* Liverpool)	ITV	9.8m
7. Boxing: McGuigan *v* McDonnell	ITV	9.6m
8. Tennis: Wimbledon Women's Final	BBC1	9.5m
9. Snooker: Mercantile Credit Classic	ITV	8.5m
10. Skating: 100 Great Sporting Moments	BBC1	8.3m

to the event's attraction (and possibly to a certain British ingenuity in finding a means of watching television during working hours) that 7.4 million still watched on the Monday afternoon.

This illustrates one of the most important determinants of television watching: availability of viewers. In a series of systematic studies called *Daily Life in the late 1980s*, the BBC has shown that there are only limited times during the course of a week when substantial numbers of people will be in a position to watch television: that is, not at work, out of the house, asleep or engaged in other domestic or leisure activities. The most available parts of the day are, of course, the so-called peak viewing times of mid-evening – from about 7.00 to 10.30 p.m., with around half the population watching at any one time. Sports transmitted live at this time,

81

or whose recorded highlights are scheduled for this window, will automatically attract more viewers than sports scheduled at less popular times. A particularly vivid example of this from the table above is the comparative ratings for the London Marathon highlights: from 11 million viewers in 1988 to 3.4 million in 1989. Although there may have been declining interest in marathon running, scheduling was a vital factor: from a peak-time slot in 1988 to a marginal 11.00 p.m. slot in 1989, when the BBC research shows that only around 21% of the population will still be viewing. For the same reason, of course, numbers available to watch are subject to seasonal variations: there will be fewer potential viewers during summer peak-times compared to winter peak-times.

For live sport these considerations have severe ratings implications. Test Match cricket does not feature in the top tens, suggesting that it might not be sufficiently popular to warrant ball by ball television coverage. But cricket happens by day, and for four days out of five on weekdays. Available audiences are small and there is therefore only limited potential for accumulating numbers. Snooker finals, on the other hand, are deliberately planned to coincide with the largest available audience – not only in peak-time, but invariably during winter and early spring. In the United States in particular, the peak-time television audience has increasingly become a more important consideration than paying spectators, as we shall see.

There are three other reasons why ratings comparisons are an unreliable guide to relative popularity. First, it is not generally appreciated that a crucial influence is the channel of transmission. British viewers with no pressing choice of programme for an evening will be drawn to a particular channel rather than individual programmes, and will generally fight shy of the two minority channels, BBC2 and Channel 4. Because of this 'channel loyalty' factor, an identical programme scheduled on BBC2 rather than BBC1 will get a substantially smaller audience. An excellent illustration from sports programming is audiences for the Derby from 1982 to 1989:*

1982	1983	1984	1985	1986	1987	1988	1989
3.2m	4 .3m	4.0m	4.4m	1.7m	1.5m	2.0m	2.4m

Why should audiences be halved from 1986 for an event which in the horse-racing calendar is second in importance only to the Grand

* These figures start from 1982 since this was the first year of metered measurement. Methods of collecting data have been consistent since that year.

National? The answer is not in some dramatic loss of interest in the race, but in the transfer of television coverage from ITV to Channel 4 from 1986 onwards. This suggests that, despite gradual gains on Channel 4 over the last three years, the Derby attracted a somewhat fickle and uncommitted body of viewers. Can we therefore assume that a certain proportion of viewers to all sporting events are marginal and will not follow that event to a minority channel?

That theory is exploded by audience figures for the British Grand Prix. From 1983 to 1985, this was shown on BBC1; it was then transferred to BBC2. Audience figures were as follows:

1983	1984	1985	1986	1987	1988	1989
3.2m	2.8m	3.7m	4.4m	4.9m	4.8m	3.0m

What should we conclude? It is unlikely that a transition to BBC2 actually served to increase the audience artificially. Part of the increase in ratings can be explained by Nigel Mansell's success, and his British win in 1987. Whatever the other reasons, these figures are evidence that there is no uniform equation which can be applied to compensate for channel effect. Different sports, and no doubt different events within the same sport, will command different levels of commitment from the television audience. There is no reliable method of separating out those who deliberately chose to watch a sporting event from those who chose to watch whatever happened to be on a particular channel.

The second reason for mistrusting the ratings is suggested by statistical analyses of viewing figures undertaken by the London Business School, which concluded that there was irrefutable evidence of an 'inheritance effect'. That is, audience ratings for a particular programme will be materially affected by the programme scheduled both immediately before and after. It is not an uncommon technique for broadcasters wanting to boost a new or unfamiliar series to 'hammock' an unpredictable programme between two proven winners. A graphic illustration from the table above is event no. 10 from 1989: a 15-minute repeat showing of one of Torvill and Dean's memorable ice-skating performances. Despite being unscheduled, it drew over 8 million viewers. Part of the programme's popularity was, certainly, appreciation for a stunning sporting achievement; but a major contributory factor was that the programme followed immediately after *That's Life*, which rarely drops below 10 million viewers. *100 Great Sporting Moments* inherited a large number of Esther Rantzen's fans.

Finally, of course, there is the competition. No realistic comparison of

The BBC's cameras at Becher's Brook in the 1960 Grand National. Always an exclusive BBC event, the Grand National has in recent years attracted widely fluctuating viewing figures (© BBC)

ratings over time can ignore the critical factor of competitive scheduling which will ensure that, even if one other channel is doing its best to provide a complementary schedule, two others will be seeking to lure away the less committed sports fan. An identical sporting event on the same channel at the same time with the same level of popular interest will return radically different figures if the alternative is a James Bond movie one week and a religious programme the next. We must add to this the vagaries of the weather, which is liable to add or subtract several percentage points to an average audience, and any particular excitement or interest generated by the particular event. An international athletics meeting with substantial British interest; or a Football League match poised to decide the First Division Championship, or a snooker match featuring a particularly popular (or notorious) figure, is perfectly capable of generating a significantly larger audience than its predecessor. These fluctuations do not allow us to draw conclusions about trends in the popularity of a particular sport over time.

Two examples of the capricious character of television audiences come from two events which might be expected to demonstrate consistency and stability over time. The Grand National is always held at 3.20 on a Saturday afternoon in April; it is always promoted as the racing event of the year, and rarely features a horse or rider of unusual prominence to attract higher than normal viewing figures; and, although a listed event, it is always televised exclusively on BBC1. Viewing figures over the last eight years reveal anything but consistent audience levels:

1982	1983	1984	1985	1986	1987	1988	1989
10.8m	12.9m	10.6m	16.9m	15.4m	12.2m	14.3m	11.9m

Even the Grand National's popularity could, arguably, be subject to the waxing and waning reputations of individual horses and jockeys. For an event which encapsulates the essence of an identical contest, it is hard to beat the annual Boat Race. Held over the same course, at the same time on a March Saturday afternoon every year, between the very same university teams, almost the only intervening variables for television viewers are the weather and competition from other programmes. These are the ratings for the last eight years:

1982	1983	1984	1985	1986	1987	1988	1989
6.2m	8.8m	6.2m	8.8m	11.0m	8.5m	8.4m	6.5m

There is a simple explanation for these audience inconsistencies: that watching television is increasingly a default activity. Some viewers, certainly, will examine the schedules and make positive, discriminatory choices on what to watch; some will methodically plan an evening's viewing, switching the set off during programming lacunae. For many, however, the television could easily be connected to the living-room electric light switch: both are switched on simultaneously, with equal indifference about what emerges as long as it bears some resemblance to light and sound. When there is nothing else to do, TV takes over. Those with remote controls might switch around to see what appeals to them and settle for the least unappetising programme; those without will simply allow the channel of first choice to wash over them.

This is not just impressionistic hearsay about viewing behaviour. While it is almost impossible to quantify accurately some scale of commitment or the extent of positive programme selection, qualitative work in the UK has revealed some insight into the dynamic process of television watching. Research using both observers in viewers' homes and remote cameras situated on television sets has confirmed that, while the set may be switched on, its images will frequently provide a mere backdrop for newspaper reading, ironing, domestic tiffs, telephone conversations, etc. Predictably, this phenomenon of distracted viewing applies particularly to families. According to one IBA research study: 'Individuals in families do not view continuously but share their viewing with other activities; of five families studied, between one-quarter and one-third . . . of time in front of the set was spent doing other activities.' In short, a ratings figure actually tells us little more than the number of people in a room at the time a television set is on. But, to complicate matters further, the ratings figure itself is an oversimplification. The industry needs to quantify viewing in order to set advertising rates and make scheduling decisions; a single programme measure is therefore valuable. But this simple average measure conceals a hive of activity during the course of a programme which can sometimes result in twice as many people having seen some part of it as are recorded in the final rating. In other words, ratings cannot record the scale of any audience turnover during a programme.

This has particularly serious implications for sport, where less committed sports fans will not be enthralled by the prospect of a complete game but might want to witness the excitement of the last few minutes and the final result. These viewers will artificially swell the final ratings figures, even though most of the match was watched by a considerably smaller audience. For short competitions or races – middle-distance athletics or horse-racing, for example – the issue does not arise. But for live matches of any length, such as soccer, cricket or rugby, it can have a considerable impact. Analysis of audience figures for the memorable final match of the 1988/9 soccer season demonstrates this phenomenon. The match achieved an overall rating of 10.3 million; Table 7 tracks the movement of audience figures at 15-minute intervals. According to analysis of another live game by advertising agency BMP Davidson Pearce, '90% more people watched the last five minutes than watched the first fifteen minutes'. This is disturbing for ITV, because it has implications for advertising revenue before and during the game's first half. But it also adds another dimension to the complex assessment of what constitutes a popular television sport. For any televised event, there will be a dedicated nucleus of viewers who will settle down to watch from beginning to end; what proportion of the average rating this nucleus represents will vary from game to game and from sport to sport. Again, no consistent equation can be applied to achieve a more accurate measure.

In summary, then, a television sport rating will be an accumulation of a multitude of conflicting factors, many of which have little to do with a viewer's appetite for watching that particular sport. It will depend on the season, time and channel of broadcast; on the weather; on what is on rival

Table 7

Audience Flow for Liverpool v Arsenal, 26.5.89

8.00 p.m.	7.4m	(Programme starts)
8.15	9.5m	
8.30	9.8m	
8.45	10.1m	
9.00	10.2m	
9.15	11.0m	
9.30	11.5m	
9.45	12.5m	
10.00	9.5m	(*News at Ten*)

Source: BARB.

channels; on what other social and domestic activities might be happening simultaneously; on what other members of the family want to watch; and on the propensity of the less enthusiastic to sample a small part of the event. To put it succinctly, we can make only the most tentative deductions about the popularity of television sports on the basis of how many people actually watch.

This presents a dilemma. If participation, spectating, and television watching figures are all dubious indicators of popularity, what might constitute a legitimate measure? Given increasing pressure on schedules from sports which have recognised the value of TV airtime and vie for a slice of the television cake, accurate and reliable data are essential to inform the decisions of sports programmers and justify those decisions to the dissatisfied losers. When cricket audiences consistently fail to break the three million barrier, we need to know how far these figures are related to daytime, weekday transmissions rather than growing disillusionment with the sport. A mistaken decision to withdraw coverage could have far-reaching consequences for both a public and a commercial broadcaster if they are perceived to be losing touch with their sporting audiences.

How to solve the dilemma? A long-standing means of gauging the public appetite for television has been the fairly simple expedient of survey research: if you want to find out what people like, ask them. One considerable advantage of audience research through surveys is that responses need not be limited by the constraints of available time or someone else's scheduling. Those who enjoy watching golf can say so, even if they missed the previous night's Open Championship highlights because another member of the family was watching something else. This approach, too, has its limitations. First, reliable data collection is an expensive process, and is therefore often restricted to occasional *ad hoc* surveys to answer specific programming problems. Second, questions are rarely standardised and even a small alteration in wording can create substantial differences. Asking people what sports they 'tend to watch' on television will elicit different responses from asking what sports they 'enjoy watching' or 'would like to see more of'. Third, size of sample in survey research has important implications for accuracy; most tend to involve no more than a thousand respondents, adequate but accurate only within 3 or 4 per cent either way. Finally, and most serious of all, responses will always be sensitive to time of year. Questions asked during late summer, with Test cricket and Wimbledon tennis fresh in viewers' minds, will provoke more positive responses to those sports than soccer or rugby. A particularly exciting or high-profile event in the recent past will have a disproportionate effect on viewers' opinions about watching that sport.

An ideal set of data for examining the relative popularity of TV sports and their shifting trends over time should therefore have the following characteristics: sample size of sufficient magnitude to guarantee a high degree of accuracy; consistent questions over a period of years, covering a wide range of different sports and asking for preference rather than behavioural information; and interviews spread throughout the year to eliminate the seasonal or special event bias. Although it has never been analysed in any systematic way, this information has in fact been collected since 1969. A leading British market research agency, British Market Research Bureau, has for twenty years collected information on leisure pursuits and consumer purchases which are then compiled into several volumes of statistical data available to prospective purchasers. Called the Target Group Index (TGI), it is one of the informational bibles in the world of marketing strategy. Information is derived from a substantial questionnaire which is given to a representative sample of 1,000 respondents most weeks throughout the year. Respondents are asked to return the completed document by post (there is a response rate of around 60%). At the end of each one-year cycle, the aggregated data from nearly 25,000 respondents are analysed. Since 1969, with occasional very minimal variations on wording, the following questions have been asked:

'Which of these a) do you take part in or play *yourself* these days? b) have you paid to watch in the last 12 months? c) do you like to watch on TV, if it's shown?'

These questions are followed by a list of sports which, over the years, has been adapted and expanded to take account of new trends and interests. Respondents are invited to tick the sports appropriate to them.

It is by no means a foolproof method. Postal questionnaires always achieve a lower than average response, and there is no way of knowing quite how unrepresentative the non-respondents are. Nevertheless, comparison of TGI data with government figures suggests that it is a generally reliable and representative guide. For our purposes, it fulfils three vital criteria: consistent questioning over time; a TV question which taps interest rather than behaviour; and data collected throughout the year rather than over an unrepresentative period of time. Furthermore, the additional questions on participation and spectatorship allow us to compare how the same people can manifest their enthusiasm for sports in different ways. We can, with substantial accuracy, match the profiles of those who play, with those who pay to watch, with those who like to watch at home *when they have the opportunity*. More than anything, these data afford a unique insight into how the British taste for sport on television has evolved, diminished or stabilised over a substantial number of years.

Before we examine trends, two simple lists derived from TGI data will demonstrate the substantial shift in sporting tastes which has taken place in the space of twenty years. Table 8 shows the ten most enjoyed TV sports in 1989, compared with responses to an identical question in 1969.

Table 8

Sports most enjoyed on TV, 1989/1969

1989		1969	
	%		%
1. Snooker	43	1. Football	52
2. Athletics	37	2. Showjumping	49
3. Tennis	30	3. Athletics	45
4. Football	29	4. Skating	44
5. Boxing	27	5. Wrestling	44
6. Skating	25	6. Swimming	43
7. Darts	24	7. Boxing	43
8. Cricket	23	8. Tennis	38
9. Motor-racing	23	9. Skiing	35
10. Skiing	22	10. Horse-racing	33

Source: TGI.

Changes in the rank order are in themselves an interesting reflection of changing tastes. Even more intriguing is the substantial decrease in levels of absolute interest: the third most enjoyed television sport of today, tennis, would twenty years ago not have made the top ten. There seems to be irrefutable evidence of a major decline over twenty years in viewers' enjoyment of the so-called major sports. Reasons for this apparently universal decline are discussed below, although one important dimension of change is not conveyed by the table above: as we shall see, viewer interest in a number of traditionally less popular or 'minority' sports is growing. This illustrates one limitation of the TGI approach, since only a small number of sports were included on the questionnaire during the early years.

There is, however, no doubting the overall trend for the nation's most popular sports, and the following linear graphs demonstrate some spectacular falls in popularity over the last twenty years with few compensating rises. The first graph deliberately contrasts two extreme examples: a sport whose popularity has almost trebled meeting, on the way down, another whose popularity has more than halved. Snooker's much chronicled rise, with a slight dip in 1976/7, carried it in the mid-80s to the 50%

Figure 4.1

Trends in TV sport: snooker and showjumping

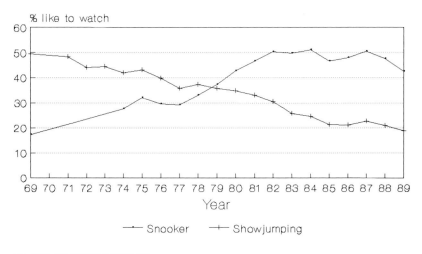

No data for Snooker 1970-73
No data for Showjumping 1970

90

mark occupied twenty years ago by showjumping. But this graph also illustrates how the audience appetite for snooker has almost certainly passed its heyday, and is now starting to slide: the 1989 enjoyment figure, at 42.6%, is the lowest for ten years. An extraordinary World Championship final in 1985, when Denis Taylor and Steve Davis went to the last ball of the last frame to settle the match well after midnight, may have served to bolster flagging interest for a short while. 1988/9 saw no such games. Meanwhile the wave of enthusiasm for showjumping, initiated in 1952 by 'Foxhunter' and 'Finality' and enduring for two decades, seemed until recently to be in terminal decline. In fact, since 1985, enjoyment of televised showjumping appears to have bottomed out at around 20% of viewers. While unlikely ever to regain its former popularity, it cannot yet be consigned to the lower status of a minority sport. Apart from providing television entertainment to over a fifth of viewers, equestrianism consistently offers good British Olympic prospects which in turn will serve to maintain interest and enthusiasm.

Most countries tend to be characterised as having 'national sports'. These can represent both strong cultural traditions and a history of national success and hence popular interest. America, of course, is dominated by baseball and American Football; China by table tennis; Japan by judo and karate; Russia by gymnastics and ice hockey. Britain, defying its level of international success, is still generally perceived as the home of soccer and cricket. England's World Cup soccer victory in 1966 was perhaps the pinnacle of both achievement and interest in the national sport. It was the first time international soccer had been featured so heavily on television since set ownership became widespread in the mid-to-late 50s. It was also the first time that British soccer could truly be said to have proved itself in the international arena, following a 6–3 drubbing by Hungary and a humiliating defeat by the United States in the not too distant past. The combination of international success and viewing opportunities provided a television impetus which, in 1971, saw enjoyment of televised football rise to nearly 60%. From 1970 onwards, there has been a slow but steady decline.

Cricket, meanwhile, has not been subject to the same process of disillusionment (nor experienced, it has to be said, the same scent of international success). Audiences for the nation's traditional summer sport have been reasonably consistent, with definite signs of renewed interest since 1985. Given this virtual stability in the potential audience for cricket, Figure 4.2 shows how the popularity gap between Britain's two national sports had narrowed in 1989 to a position of virtual parity.

Figure 4.2

Trends in TV sport: soccer and cricket

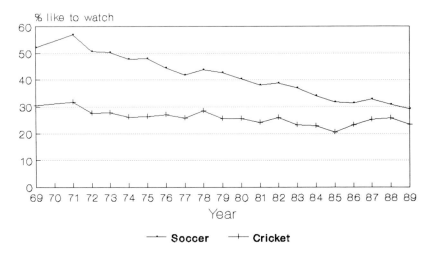

No data available for 1970

As we have seen, ITV's machinations in 1979 to secure a share of Saturday soccer from the BBC were widely assumed to be the major cause of the subsequent audience decline for soccer. Disruption of well-established viewing patterns may have been a contributory factor. But potential audiences for soccer were steadily shrinking anyway. 1979 was in the middle of an almost uninterrupted process of viewer disillusionment with soccer which has seen its potential audience almost halved in less than twenty years. Declining enthusiasm has, predictably, coincided with both declining soccer ratings and declining gate receipts, leading to speculation that this quintessentially British sport is facing a consumer crisis of disastrous proportions. It is an unnecessarily pessimistic prognosis, given that diminishing enthusiasm has been a feature of most traditionally major sports. Football has certainly suffered a disproportionately greater fall, but then it started from a considerably higher base. Most trend analyses, whether of viewing or spectating, tend to start from the very point in British sporting history when soccer was king. It would be unreasonable to expect it to maintain the same position of supremacy during a fallow period when both national teams and club teams in international competitions were faring considerably worse than in the 1960s heyday. Whatever problems soccer may face, its detractors should accept that enthusiasm for the televised game still stands at nearly one-third of the viewing population.

Cricket, however, seems to have succeeded in bucking the trend. Starting from a lower base of television popularity, and therefore perhaps less vulnerable to peaks and troughs of international success, it attracted in 1989 only 7% fewer viewers than twenty years ago. Far from becoming increasingly marginalised and relegated to a minority sport, it has improved its relative position considerably – from 12th most popular TV sport in 1969 (behind even the far less accessible activity of skiing) to 8th in 1989.

In order to establish the proper context for viewing preferences, we need to examine a few other sports. Figure 4.3, which traces enjoyment levels for three more of the 1969 top ten sports, presents further evidence of a quite dramatic slump in television popularity of some major sports.

Figure 4.3

Trends in TV sport: swimming, skating, horse-racing

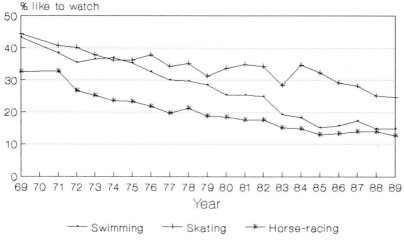

No data available for 1970

All three sports have suffered, but the impact on swimming in particular has been remarkable. In less than twenty years, it has lost two-thirds of its popular support and now shares with badminton and squash the distinction of a sport with higher levels of active participation than enthusiasm for passive television viewing. Horse-racing has fared little better, losing over half its potential audience in a slow but almost uninterrupted decline which shows no sign of abating. Skating, meanwhile, though not entirely escaping the downward trend, has succeeded in maintaining a better profile. It is a particularly vivid example of how the popular fortunes of a sport, and especially one in which the live spectating opportunities are limited, will fluctuate according to the success and profile of particular personalities. Skating's decline is punctuated by two bursts of increased popularity, one from 1979 to 1981, the other in 1984. They coincided with a dramatic revival of British fortunes in European, Olympic and World Championships: starting with John Curry's figure skating gold medal in the 1976 Olympics and continuing with Robin Cousins' victory in the 1980 European Championships, the renaissance culminated in the 1984 Winter Olympics with a thrilling performance from Jayne Torvill and Christopher Dean whose ice rendition of Ravel's 'Bolero' captured viewers' hearts and Olympic gold. Almost certainly, the World and Olympic champions were entirely responsible for the 6% rise in television popularity of their sport between 1983 and 1984. Since then, there has been no equivalent talent or imminent success in British skating; in parallel with this vacuum, viewers' interest has started to wane.

Two sports which featured particularly heavily in the early days of less sophisticated technology were the indoor stadia competitions of boxing and wrestling. The latter in particular was a staple diet of ITV's Saturday afternoon coverage. As the next graph shows, ITV's decision to axe wrestling in 1989 came at the end of a long period of declining popularity. It is a little easier to understand the relative decline of sports whose original popularity was promoted by their accessibility to TV cameras. Once outside broadcasts, slow-motion replays, lightweight cameras and colour television had vastly increased the number and variety of sports which could be effectively translated to the small screen, the attraction of relatively colourless ring-bound competitions started to fade. Allied to this, wrestling has never attained international recognition as an orthodox competitive sport, and is generally (and probably accurately) perceived as belonging to the entertainment school of sporting activity. Boxing, on the other hand, is certainly recognised internationally. As with any other sport where Britain competes in the world arena, the nation welcomes and glorifies its heroes. Boxing provides champions, personalities and continuing television interest. For that reason, its rapid decline in television popularity from 1969 to the early 1980s is less easily understandable.

It becomes more explicable if interpreted in the same light as soccer:

Figure 4.4
Trends in TV sport: boxing and wrestling

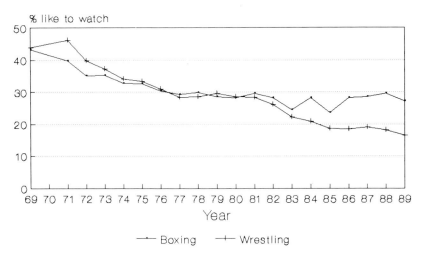

% like to watch

Year

—•— Boxing —+— Wrestling

No data available for 1970

that the base-line for trend information, by taking 1969 as its starting point, may unwittingly have exaggerated popular enthusiasm. For the first time in many years, Britain had produced a heavyweight contender to challenge one of the most colourful and talented world champions of all time. When in June 1963 Henry Cooper floored Cassius Clay at the end of round four, the nation counted in unison. That moment created a hero whose reputation survived a second defeat by Clay in May 1966 and was confirmed when Cooper regained his British title and won the European Championship in 1970. Throughout the late 60s and early 70s one man developed an immense popular following which would certainly have been translated into viewing figures. Even if only partly true, this thesis would explain boxing's apparent revival since 1983 while wrestling continues its demise. In 1985, Barry McGuigan became world feather-weight champion, followed in 1986 by Lloyd Honeyghan's world welter-weight title. Meanwhile another pretender to the heavyweight throne was being elevated to the status of national saviour: Frank Bruno. His single shot at the world title, in February 1989, was widely perceived as one of boxing's most stupendous mismatches. Given the number of title shots by British champions, it scarcely mattered. Britain has become adept at making martyrs of its losing challengers, and even the most

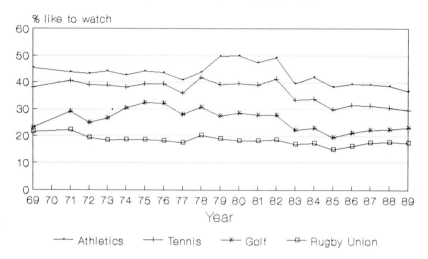

Figure 4.5

Trends in TV sport: athletics, tennis, golf, rugby union

% like to watch

Year

—•— Athletics   —+— Tennis   —*— Golf   —□— Rugby Union

No data available for 1970

committed detractors of a much-reviled sport have grudgingly welcomed Bruno as the acceptable face of pugilism.

National success, or at least national failure at the highest competitive levels by telegenic people, may therefore be a vital prerequisite of boxing's continued television popularity. One sport which seems to have survived both the widespread downward trend in popularity and a conspicuous lack of British success is tennis. It is one of four very different sports, shown in Figure 4.5 (above), which demonstrate a remarkable consistency in television popularity over the twenty-year period. Viewer enthusiasm for athletics was stable throughout most of the 1970s, including the Olympic Games years of 1972 and 1976 which might have been expected to stimulate interest. A sudden and steep rise from 1977 to 1979 was then maintained throughout the early 80s with a falling back in more recent years. In this case, national success provided a clear stimulus. During precisely those years, three British athletes provided a series of world-beating performances unlikely to be paralleled for many years. By the end of an astonishing four weeks in 1979, Sebastian Coe became the first man to hold simultaneously the 800 metres, 1,500 metres and mile world records. At the Moscow Olympics, Steve Ovett took the 800 metres gold medal and Coe the 1,500 metres, while Daley Thompson established himself as the world's number one in the decathlon. The following year, Coe regained his world mile record from Ovett, then lost it to Ovett, then won it back again. It was enthralling competition, unique in British sporting history, and magnificent television. No wonder ITV wanted a part of it.

Tennis, of course, has provided as much British glory in recent times as skiing, without the personalities to match; yet it has suffered only a marginal fall in popularity over the years. The one significant British victory, Virginia Wade's Wimbledon title in 1977, was probably responsible for most of the six-point rise in interest at that time and provides some indication of tennis's potential should Britain ever find its heroes. If the country ever develops even a shadow of its athletics presence in tennis, we can confidently expect television enjoyment figures, and consequently ratings, to soar.

Less easily explicable in terms of domestic triumph is the apparently steady rise in golf's fortunes through the mid-70s. In between Tony Jacklin's British Open Championship in 1969 and Sandy Lyle's victory sixteen years later, there was not a tremendous amount of British interest. In fact, interest declined again in the early 80s and has only recently begun to climb – helped by the success of Nick Faldo and three historic Ryder Cup victories in 1985, 1987 and 1989. It is not impossible that the mid-70s surge was partly a reaction to Tony Jacklin's triumph, which several years earlier did trigger a new curiosity in a sport which had provided little drama for some time. But a second explanation is more plausible, and allows greater consideration of the medium than the sport itself. Golf is traditionally the hardest of sports to televise. Courses are spread over a wide area, and little white balls have a habit of disappearing into the most inaccessible greenery. A poor shot into the bushes may have unfortunate consequences for the golfer; for the cameraman, it can be a positive nightmare. Not only must cameras be able to second-guess almost any permutation of mishits, they must repeat the process at least eighteen times while attempting to keep sight of the smallest ball in all major sports. As long ago as 1964, the BBC's golf commentator Henry Longhurst wrote: 'People like to see the ball as it flies through the air, and this is only feasible if you can find camera sites where the ball comes almost directly to or away from the camera. Trying to follow it cross-wise with a television camera is as difficult as with the wrong end of a telescope.' By the early 70s, coverage of golf had improved considerably. Screen images were clearer, leader boards were more quickly updated and comprehensible, and the widespread availability and use of colour sets enhanced the viewing experience of a sport dominated by green images. While Jacklin's success will have spurred enthusiasm, it required important technological advances in the medium to exploit viewers' new-found enthusiasm. More than for almost any other sport, it was probably television itself which contributed to the higher level of enjoyment for televised golf.

Finally, what of Rugby Union? Compared to every other sport, it shows the most consistent level of television popularity throughout, with scarcely any evidence of significant fluctuation. As a team sport, it does not rely on personalities. More importantly, with a World Cup only recently inaugurated, the most important event of its annual calendar is the Five-Nations championship involving England, Ireland, Scotland, Wales and France. National chauvinism is a less manifest issue except for those suffering from acute Francophobia. International matches against Australia and New Zealand provide additional sparks, but generally little has changed in the game's appeal. Possibly, the four-yearly World Cup will generate a few extra converts, but there appears to be a bedrock of support which is stable while resisting any major increases or decreases.

Is there any underlying pattern to this apparently haphazard collection of trends? Without wanting to develop a definitive model of viewing preferences, it is possible to summarise these trends succinctly. First, with one notable exception, every major sport has experienced some decline in television popularity over the years – and even that one is on its way down. And second, this downward trend has been mitigated either by national success, or by the emergence of individuals of particular merit and personality, or by improvements in television coverage itself. In addition, the 1969 measurement base may have unfairly exaggerated viewer enthusiasm for some sports at the peak of a successful phase.

Why is it that consistently fewer viewers seem to be enjoying sport on television? There can only be three possible causes: changes intrinsic to the sports themselves; changes in how sports are covered; or changes in audience behaviour for extraneous reasons. It is fair to assume that, for most sports analysed here, there is little evidence that they have become intrinsically less interesting. It would be a quite fantastic coincidence if every major sport had undergone a significant downturn in the excitement or enjoyment provided for spectators in the last twenty years. We must therefore accept that the almost universal decline in enjoyment of television sports has something to do either with audience attitudes or with the televisual product. It is equally hard to accept that the product has failed. Increasingly modernised technology, lightweight cameras, ingenious locations for both cameras and microphones, sharper sound and vision have all contributed to more professional production values which in turn are better able to convey the excitement of the moment. It is hard to believe, while watching a Grand Prix racetrack through a camera fixed in a car travelling at 150 mph, or a downhill piste through a camera attached to a pair of skis, that viewers are becoming increasingly unmoved by such dramatic pictures.

Which returns us to an explanation centred on the audience. Given the fluctuations both in audience appreciation and in ratings, we can reasonably conclude that at least some of the sports audience is fickle. With what we have already seen about television as a 'default' activity, it could well be that each sport attracts two types of viewer: the committed viewer who, time and family permitting, will watch any programme featuring a particular sport; and the casual viewer whose disposition towards the sport will depend on extraneous factors like competitive programming and special interest generated by an event or personality. In this sense, sport is not much different from other programmes. There will be some viewers devoted to *EastEnders* or *Blind Date*, while others will tune in on a more haphazard basis. What distinguishes sports programming is the likely existence of a third category, the casual viewer not committed to watching a sport whenever it is televised but committed to certain events within that sport. Thus a casual tennis viewer might make a point of watching as much Wimbledon as possible but will not miss *Cagney and Lacey* for the final of the American Open. Similarly, a casual Rugby Union viewer might settle down every year to the Saturday afternoon Five-Nations matches, but is unlikely to leave the pub for Sunday afternoon's *Rugby Special* featuring club matches.

It is likely that the backbone of sports viewing – the sport-committed viewers – is very small for most sports, and that even the event-committed viewers will not add a substantial proportion. Both categories could be expected to respond positively when asked if they enjoyed that sport on television. It is the casual viewers, those whose preferences are often dictated by peak-time scheduling decisions or by unpredictable factors like popular personalities or the prospect of national success, who lie at the heart of fluctuating enjoyment figures. The extent and direction of fluctuations will depend on how the audience for a particular sport is constituted: what proportion tends to be committed to the sport or to an event in that sport's calendar, and what proportion is casually attracted by special but unpredictable considerations. On this basis, we can ascribe the overall decline in enthusiasm for sport to three separate factors: the increasing number of television opportunities which attract considerably lower audiences (for example Breakfast Television, Channel 4, Night Time); diminishing peak-time schedules devoted to major sports; and increasing numbers of minority sports (basketball, cycling) vying for audience attention. In short, variations in enthusiasm can be explained by the ebb and flow of less committed sports viewers rather than by any real disillusionment among the sport- or event-committed.

While additional television choice is welcome, and minority sports exposure is a deliberate and equally welcome policy decision, one question remains. Why should sports, which have clearly demonstrated their ability to capture popular imaginations, be relegated to the relative obscurity of late-night schedules? Different analyses of the TGI data provide the answer. Television audiences, and particularly peak-time audiences, tend to be heterogeneous: representative of the population, containing in their proper proportions young and old, male and female, educated and uneducated. If tastes for the most popular sports were similarly distributed throughout the population, scheduling those sports would create no problems. If, however, tastes vary among different demographic groups, large numbers of people could immediately be alienated from the channel when a sporting event is shown. Competitive scheduling by rival channels against sport would then be easier, since most other programme categories generally attract support from all sectors of the population.

Analysis of the enjoyment questions by different population groups shows exactly why most sports do not lend themselves to competitive scheduling at peak viewing times. TGI data allows us to examine sporting 'Top Tens' for both different ages and sexes. Table 9 opposite compares, for example, Top Tens for the youngest and oldest viewing generations, with some interesting contrasts.

There are similar levels of interest in athletics, football, tennis and darts. Snooker appears in both lists, but with a much higher commitment from older people. And there the similarity stops, leaving five sports in each list which do not compare. The 1988 list for younger viewers told a remarkable tale: American Football had overtaken soccer in television popularity among this group, adding an interesting twist to the phenomenon of cultural imperialism. Soccer's improvement in 1989 is less a function of its own recovery than of American Football's decline, and we must wait for figures over the next few years to see if this is the beginning of a longer-term process. It is a tribute to American Football's telegenic qualities that it should have impinged so dramatically on the young, and the number of British parks sporting gridiron games at weekends testifies to its successful importation. But its apparent declining popularity among the young (with almost no interest from the over-45s) suggests that the national game will not be uprooted quite so easily.

100

Table 9

Sports most enjoyed on TV, 1989: young v old viewers

15–24 year-olds		65+ year-olds	
	%		%
1. Athletics	35	1. Snooker	54
2. Snooker	33	2. Bowls	34
3. Boxing	33	3. Athletics	33
4. Football	28	4. Tennis	32
5. Tennis	29	5. Showjumping	31
6. American Football	26	6. Skating	31
7. Skiing	26	7. Golf	30
8. Motor-racing	26	8. Football	30
9. Motor rallying	21	9. Cricket	30
10. Darts	21	10. Darts	26

As Table 9 suggests, the overall Top Ten will conceal substantial age variations for almost every sport. Figure 4.6 overleaf illustrates these differences in graphical form by displaying the age profile for each of these Top Ten sports. The more universally popular the sport, the more evenly segmented each vertical bar should be. It proves why scheduling sport can be so difficult: only athletics and, to a lesser extent, snooker and darts appeals across all age groups. Of even greater scheduling importance are preferential differences between the sexes. One can, with some anxiety, alienate one or two age groups within the viewing population since it still leaves a residual majority. To alienate, at a stroke, half the viewing population would be verging on the suicidal. For that reason, incompatibilities between male and female preferences create serious dilemmas for sports programmers. Table 10 (on page 103) reveals that while men and women may not be beyond reconciliation in their sporting tastes, there are serious inconsistencies.

The 'gender gap' is a familiar concept in political polling, used to describe differential voting patterns between the two sexes. It seems to be just as problematic for sports broadcasters as for political parties. It is not just that, as with the generation gap, only five sports are common to each Top Ten. More significant is the difference in proportions even in those sports for which enthusiasm seems to be shared. Thus while over half of male viewers enjoy watching snooker, the same is true of only a third of women. Golf is enjoyed by nearly a third of men but less than one

101

Figure 4.6
Who enjoys which sports: analysis by age

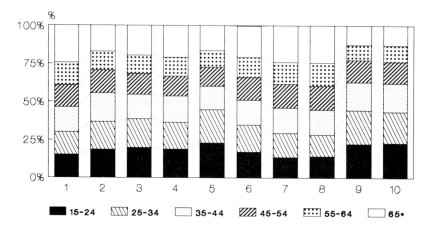

1= Snooker, 2=Athletics, 3=Football,
4=Tennis, 5=Boxing, 6=Darts, 7=Cricket,
8=Skating, 9=Motor Racing, 10=Skiing.

in six women. Even athletics and darts attract, respectively, 14% and 10% less women than men. These differences are positively tiny when compared to those for the other five, more traditionally 'masculine' sports, in the male Top Ten: 13% of women enjoy football, compared to 47% of men; 12% enjoy boxing compared to 44%; 12% enjoy cricket compared to 36%; 10% enjoy motor-racing compared to 36%; and only 7% enjoy Rugby Union compared to 29%. Similarly, men do not share women's enthusiasm for skating or showjumping: only 13% and 14% respectively, compared to 36% and 24% of women. In all, only two major sports achieve any kind of parity: tennis, enjoyed by 28% of men and 31% of women; and skiing, 24% and 22%. What price sports programming for all the family?

As television becomes increasingly competitive, the more ill-advised it becomes to introduce any form of programme into peak-time periods which is unlikely to find favour with nearly half of the potential viewers. And yet the nakedly competitive American system has long featured the more popular sports, and in particular American Football, during prime-time. Are British women simply different in their distaste for television sport, or is it a more universal phenomenon which American networks have somehow overcome?

Table 10
Sports most enjoyed on TV, 1989

Male		Female	
	%		%
1. Snooker	51	1. Skating	36
2. Football	47	2. Snooker	35
3. Boxing	44	3. Tennis	31
4. Athletics	44	4. Athletics	30
5. Cricket	36	5. Showjumping	24
6. Motor-racing	36	6. Skiing	22
7. Golf	31	7. Darts	19
8. Darts	29	8. Swimming	17
9. Rugby Union	29	9. Bowls	15
10. Tennis	28	10. Golf	15

American preferences for TV sport

Comparison of any cross-cultural survey data is dangerous, particularly when these data are derived from different methodologies through differently worded questions asked five years apart. Nevertheless, it is difficult to find anything more contemporary in America than the comprehensive national study sponsored by Miller Lite in 1982, which addressed a range of issues concerning American attitudes to sport. A national cross-section of over 1,100 American adults was interviewed by telephone about all aspects of national sport. The critical question ran: 'I'm going to read to you a list of different sports. Please tell me how interested you generally are in *watching* each of the following.'

Question-wording is certainly not comparable, particularly since responses were scaled from 'always interested' to 'never interested' (probably a more reliable means of separating the casual from the committed sports viewer). In addition, watching in this context is not defined and will include live spectating as well as television viewing. Whatever the limitations, this is all we have. As a measure of discrimination between male and female preferences, rather than absolute national differences, the information can provide some valuable indicators to the presence or absence of a similar 'gender gap'. Table 11 lists the Top Ten sports for American men and women, after aggregating respondents who say they are 'always' or 'usually' interested in watching.

Table 11
American interest in watching sports, 1983: male v female

Male	%	Female	%
1. Football	69	1. Gymnastics	46
2. Baseball	47	2. Football	41
3. Boxing	44	3. Baseball	41
4. Basketball	38	4. Skating	41
5. Athletics	26	5. Swimming	36
6. Tennis	25	6. Basketball	29
7. Motor-racing	25	7. Horse-racing	28
8. Gymnastics	21	8. Skiing	28
9. Swimming	21	9. Tennis	27
10. Weightlifting	21	10. Athletics	22

Two observations stand out. First, if one excludes the astonishingly high figure of over two-thirds of men interested in American Football, the range of interest in sports is similar between men and women – from around a fifth to almost a half. There is, it seems, a great deal less antipathy among American women towards television sport than among British women. That said, the gender gap *within* each sport is still apparent. Although seven sports are common to both Top Tens, 28% more men are interested in football and 9% more in basketball; conversely, 25% more women are interested in gymnastics and 15% more in swimming. Something approaching parity is achieved by baseball, tennis and athletics. The female taste for horse-racing is fascinating, and it is the only sport where equivalent national scores are nothing like comparable: conceivably, it is displacement for showjumping in Britain, which has no real equivalent on American television.

We may conclude, then, that while American network programmers have a slightly easier task – the absence of any great male/female divide in baseball is particularly fortuitous – the dominant sport of American Football is not universally embraced: over half the female population could be alienated if it were scheduled in prime-time hours. And yet one of the great American television traditions since 1970 has been live, prime-time Monday night football – even to the point of one Florida college introducing a course in 1979 grandly entitled 'Understanding and Enjoying Monday Night Football'.

How could any network in such a fiercely competitive environment first take the chance of instantly alienating one quarter of the population, and secondly make it work? In fact, all three networks were wary and reluctant to gamble. But ABC were vulnerable because the embryonic Hughes Sports Network, which would jump at the chance of some pro football, transmitted mostly on ABC stations. Ron Powers tells how the NFL Commissioner Pete Rozelle – who wanted both more money and greater exposure for the sport he served – exploited ABC's weakness and his own legendary cunning to bounce ABC into accepting a prime-time package. The result was an entirely new concept in sports coverage and sports packaging, designed not just to convey a football match but to stimulate a sense of drama, excitement and energy which would be irresistible to the most obstinate critics of television sport. The product consisted, in Powers' words, of 'state-of-the-art television covering state-of-the-art sport'.

Masterminding this revolution in sports programming was Roone Arledge, in the process of building a career which would take him eventually to Head of both Sport and News within ABC. Some years before, a younger Arledge had written a prophetic memo to his boss outlining his vision of televised sport in the years ahead. He had explicitly acknowledged the gender gap as an audience consideration which had to be addressed:

To improve upon the audience . . . we must gain and hold the interest of women and others who are not fanatic followers of the sport we happen to be televising. Women come to football games, not so much to marvel at the adeptness of the quarterback in calling an end sweep or a lineman pulling out to lead a play, but to sit in a crowd, see what everyone else is wearing, watch the cheerleaders and experience the countless things that make up the feeling of the game.

Patronising as they may sound in retrospect, these sentiments provided the basis for Arledge's philosophy of prime-time television football. Halfway through that memo he had written in triumphant capital letters, 'We are going to add show business to sports!', and that was precisely what he did. By concentrating on personalities, on stories surrounding the teams and their origins, by building up a pre-match atmosphere, by showing all the extraneous glitz that surrounds a big sporting occasion, as well as through creative and ingenious use of cameras and developing technology, Arledge provided something new. As Powers says, 'People came to these telecasts who had never even watched football on TV in any

105

other form: most significantly women.' But he also gives at least one unambiguous reason as to why women might have been attracted: 'Arledge's . . . dwelling on the male athletes' sexual appeal has received almost no comment – but it helped attract women to Monday Night Football, and women provided its margin of ratings success.'

Nearly twenty years later, the same tactic is being applied to a different sport in a different country. Australia's Channel Ten, in an equally fierce competitive environment, has recently acquired the rights to Rugby League, the premier sport in most parts of the country. It is a quintessentially male sport, and therefore requires some judicious 'selling' to the female population. Channel Ten's promotional film is utterly unambiguous in its message to women: slow-motion pictures of bronzed, muscle-bound and scantily clad men indulging in gym exercises which bear little resemblance to activities on the rugby field, interspersed with close-up pictures of fast and furious (and sometimes angry) action on the field of play. In its blatant use of sexual imagery it is as unsubtle as ABC's cameras lingering on cheerleaders' thighs. As an object lesson in closing the gender gap, it may well be equally effective.

Are we likely to see a similar marketing and packaging effort in Britain? We have already seen how scheduling philosophy tends to be dominated on the BBC and Channel 4 by the relative importance of particular events and by the desire to experiment with new activities and new techniques. ITV have, certainly, given a great deal of prominence to both soccer and athletics, even promoting itself as 'the Athletics Channel'. But no channel has yet resorted to blatant packaging of extraneous factors in order to seduce the marginal viewer. Perhaps it is because peak-time sport is becoming increasingly extinct, and British programmers are reluctant to apply entertainment techniques to sport. A more likely barrier is the almost universal consumer resistance which such an approach is likely to provoke. Many American and Australian marketing and promotional techniques are considered brash and inappropriate by British viewers. ITV's heavy promotional campaign on soccer for its exclusive 1988/9 season boasted new, more and better cameras as well as interviews, half-time goal feasts and the latest in new technology; certainly there was hype, but it was strictly football-related hype. Apart from a very British distaste for contrived or exaggerated drama, it might be hard to find any tanned soccer players willing to display their naked torsos for the benefit of putative female viewers.

Conceivably, as cheap sources of domestic programming become ever more scarce, the main channels will find themselves trying to coax unwilling sectors of the population into unfamiliar sports. More likely, sport will remain on the margins of British schedules, with typically restrained promotional techniques. A characteristic reaction to recent American hype exemplifies British aversion to the show-business approach. In an effort to attract more viewers to its coverage of the American Open Golf tournament, one network had produced a three-minute film attempting to capture the history of the tournament and players, with pictures accompanied by scarcely comprehensible voice-over doggerel. *Grandstand* included the film as part of its build-up to the golf coverage. The pace was frenetic, the imagery seductive, the lyrics abominable. At the end of the film, Desmond Lynam raised his despairing head from his hands and said reassuringly: 'It's all right. We're sending Peter Alliss out there.' Viewers knew what he meant.

5

THE KNIGHT IN SHINING ARMOUR

During its short reign, television has been blamed for most of the planet's evils. At various stages of its development, we have been reliably informed that television induces premature short-sightedness; obesity; a decline in sexual morality; murderous rampages by psychotic gunmen; 'copycat' riots in city streets; retarded development in children; distorted coverage of contemporary politics; and a declining birth-rate. Among its lesser evils is the irreparable damage which television is allegedly inflicting on sports. It is variously held responsible for declining attendances, declining enthusiasm for participation, disruption in traditional means of organising events, and, most unforgivably, interfering with the very integrity of sporting processes. Some of these charges, as Chapter 6 will show, are undoubtedly true. But weighed against the potential damage which television is capable of inflicting on sports is its equal capacity for enhancing and enriching otherwise underpractised and moribund activities. For a great many minor sports, television is a White Knight whose powers of resuscitation and rehabilitation are eagerly pursued.

For sporting associations, television coverage can have two unique advantages. First, it can bring otherwise little known or unfamiliar sports to the attention of vast numbers of people. While any number of different factors might be instrumental in providing that crucial spark of interest, television has unprecedented universality. Potential sports participants or spectators have limited time to devote to sports, and their choice would traditionally be conditioned by local accessibility and family patterns of sporting activity. Television makes unknown sports familiar and increases the range of activities from which people choose.

Promoting the benefits of their respective sports is one of the critical functions of sporting bodies. In this respect, publicity is an end in itself rather than a means to money or status. It provides the seeds of interest which every sport seeks to implant and then develop into a more active manifestation of enthusiasm. Familiarity breeds participation which in turn breeds greater demand for better training, better facilities, more competitions and clubs, and ultimately a stronger pool of players for club, county and national selectors. From successful publicity can ultimately come the international representation and Commonwealth or Olympic gold medals which every sport craves.

Exposure, however, also provides sporting bodies with the means to a different end, which is television's second unique contribution: money. Sporting bodies must traditionally rely on three sources of income: fees from participants, including competition and subscription fees; a grant from the Sports Council; and sponsorship. For many smaller sports, total income can be pitifully small – less than a quarter of a million pounds from which to run offices, institute promotional campaigns, encourage and underwrite training programmes, maintain contact with youth clubs, schools, colleges and other institutions where sports will play an integral part. Subscription fees must be kept to manageable proportions to attract participants of all ages and backgrounds. Sponsorship is sporadic, often forthcoming through personal contact at the chairman's level and always subject to the maintenance of good social relations. And Sports Council grants are the object of intense negotiation, the amounts increasingly emasculated as part of a government campaign to discourage public spending in favour of private sector contributions. Even a few minutes of television coverage can unlock substantial contributions to an impoverished treasurer's current account. The source of this television windfall is not, ironically, the television channel which secures broadcasting rights. Television is merely the gold-plated conduit to an Aladdin's cave of riches: the unbounded generosity which private companies like to bestow on sporting bodies in sponsorship money in order to exploit television airtime.

As Chapter 8 explains, sponsorship is particularly valuable in a country where a non-commercial public broadcaster dominates television sport. Opportunities for advertisers who might regard certain sporting audiences as prime marketing targets are limited to specialist magazines and the sports pages of the regular press. But these marketing tools cannot command the instant power of a moving visual image, particularly potent if the product in question is directly sports-related (sports footwear or equipment, for example). Names on a hoarding at the back of a sports stadium may not be the ideal substitute but are better than no exposure at all; and with some judicious placement, in line with the main action camera or adjacent to a scoreboard, there can be enough visual credits during the course of a short broadcast to render spot advertising almost redundant. So a television airing means opening doors. The greater the exposure, the higher the sponsorship; more sponsorship money means bigger prizes which in turn attract the sport's top competitors as well as providing a cash incentive for those at the lower levels to raise their sights. Whatever people's original motives for taking up a sport, the prospect of substantial financial inducements for success in top competitions must help to stimulate and maintain participants' levels of interest. People play sports essentially because they are fun. If their level of skill, competence and enjoyment is heightened by the availability of financial as well as emotional reward, both sport and players benefit.

Governing bodies, we should remember, are responsible for the welfare and promotion of their sport at every level of the amateur game. In their quest for money as a means to this end, they therefore differ substantially from those professional bodies which serve to promote the interests of those whose livelihood depends on maintaining a healthy income from playing the game. A classic example of this dichotomy is the different attitudes displayed by the Football Association and the Football League. The FA, concerned about soccer from school playground to Cup Final, have from the earliest days of television been responsive to its unique ability for positive promotion. Income from Cup matches is exploited at every level to enhance training facilities, encourage junior teams, provide instruction in schools and enrich every facet of the game. Televised soccer assists in those objectives simply by providing exposure, elevating role models and bringing the highest competitive level into the living rooms of aspiring footballers. Money helps, but represents only part of the equation.

Meanwhile, the Football League represents the interests of professional teams for whom the major aspiration is financial success or, more realistically in most instances, survival. While ownership of football clubs has never been a route to instant wealth, managers, staff and players need to be paid; in First Division clubs who wish to retain their reputation and status, they need to be paid well. As long as professional players depended on gate money for their income, the Football League jealously guarded turnstile income and reacted with instant suspicion against an innovation which seemed to threaten that income. With TV-related sponsorship, and escalating costs of TV rights themselves, a potential revenue threat was transformed into a potential goldmine.

How this perspective has influenced soccer's relationship with television, and potentially the organisation of the game itself, is examined in Chapter 6. To appreciate the benefits which sport can derive from television, it is important to understand the different requirements of the professional versus the amateur game. Certainly, there are areas where the distinction is blurred: athletics is a straightforward example of a sport where supposedly amateur participants will be rewarded indirectly for their appearance if not performance. Most minor sports, however, cannot boast the luxury of significant rewards for individuals. Successful players are generally content with the silver trophy which sits on the mantelpiece for a year, and the knowledge that their name will be indelibly inscribed on its base for generations to come. Governing bodies, meanwhile, are often content if they can afford the trophy.

In conversation with some of these bodies, it was clear that television is regarded both as a means to generous patronage, and therefore a financial lifeline for those in parlous financial straits, and as exposure which is good in itself. Some case studies provide concrete examples of how television coverage is coveted, and the disproportionate impact which even the briefest of coverage can make on viewers. The following examples illustrate how the marriage between television and sport can be successfully consummated without spawning undesirable offspring.

Of Great Britain's twenty-four medals in the 1988 Olympics, perhaps the least celebrated was a bronze in the *archery* team event. While not a sport immediately associated with an international reputation for Great Britain, its popular following in the UK is not inconsiderable. Around 20,000 aspiring archers pay their dues to the Grand National Archery Society, a number which has been increasing at a fairly constant rate of 5% over the last six years. Total income is less than a quarter of a million pounds, over half of it from participation and membership fees. Around a third comes from the Sports Council. Out of this meagre income must come all administration costs, plus all coaching fees for training at clubs and youth groups. In addition, costs of participating in international events must be met for national representatives since there are no professionals. With administration costs in the region of £100,000, and travel expenses taking most of the Council grant, investment in training inevitably suffers. For that bronze medal to become the precursor of further British successes, more money must be poured into coaching. As far as archery's governing body is concerned, TV rights are not an issue. It would gladly give them away as a heaven-sent means of earning extra revenue through sponsorship.

It is painfully aware of the obstacles to television coverage. Even for a country scarcely overburdened with Olympic medals, the Seoul bronze received approximately twenty seconds of coverage. Archery is, to be blunt, not a good spectator sport. With arrows travelling at 210 feet per second, and now leaving the bow at a faster speed than bullets from a gun, the most sophisticated slow-motion technology finds it hard to follow. Shooting sessions are long, far longer than the five minutes or so a skilful darts player needs to score 301 on the darts board. But if the intrinsic obstacle of arrow-speed could be overcome, archery would have little hesitation in inventing a TV-specific knock-out tournament with shorter rounds if there were the slightest hint that it might attract the cameras.

The sport's parlous financial circumstances would make it irresponsible not to do so. But money is not the only incentive. Although active participants may well be double the membership levels, every sport craves higher levels of activity, and archery is no exception. When it made its first appearance on Channel 4's *Challenge to Sport*, volunteers were required to man telephones to cope with the enormous viewer response. And this from a programme aired at 6.30 on a Saturday evening with maximum ratings of 1.4 million, sometimes no more than 400,000. Even an article in *The Times*, which can hardly match even the limited visual appeal of a bow and arrow sport in action, provoked forty-four letters of interest within three days. It is undoubtedly true, and was demonstrated by public response to archery's medal-winning achievement in Seoul, that competitive success serves to boost both morale and membership. Even success at the highest international level, however, is no substitute for a television appearance which can make the difference between continued obscurity and national patronage on a massive scale.

One sport which initially reaped some of the benefits of television is *basketball*. In this case, however, the influence was less on participation, which has been growing steadily for several years, than on live attendance. Until the 1970s there were no spectator events, and the sport was limited to school playgrounds and college halls. A National Basketball League started in the 1970s and according to the *Digest of Sports Statistics*, six teams watched by 11,000 spectators in 1972/3 had by 1984/5 expanded to sixty-eight teams with over 300,000 spectators. The English Basketball Association is in no doubt that television coverage has been a significant factor in increasing that live audience. Coverage started in the mid-70s with half an hour on *Grandstand*, and reached its culmination in a four-year contract with Channel 4. This allowed for twenty-six live matches every week from October to April, exclusive to the channel. This period of regular live coverage coincided with the highest attendance figures, even to the point of spectators being turned away from a full stadium. Channel 4's changing priorities – and its doubts about the successful translation of basketball to the small screen – has left the sport with more sporadic appearances on BBC television.

As well as depressing attendance figures, this abrupt halt to regular slots (albeit on a minority channel) affected sponsorship income. Of the Association's half a million pounds income, around 40% comes from the Sports Council; sponsorship revenue fluctuates between 5% and 15% of the total depending on airtime availability. Although sponsors like the substantial exposure which a BBC spot can provide, the unpredictable nature of coverage makes it a more difficult sales task. This unpredictability has persuaded the Association to sign a contract with the new satellite broadcaster BSB, but it is uncertain how sponsors will react to a new animal with an unproven track record. As we shall see in Chapter 9, satellite television is still an uncertain route to new sports audiences.

Pulling out the cameras does not necessarily result in a wholesale retreat by sponsors. *Bowls* now receives a substantial contribution from sponsorship, amounting to over half of annual income for the English Bowling Association (there are a total of eighteen governing bodies for bowls throughout the UK, so accumulated data are difficult to compile). Much of this is directly related to television, starting with the BBC's *Jack High* in 1978 which transformed the financial state of the game. According to the Secretary of the EBA, 'the game has altered beyond all recognition. Nobody in 1964 would have dreamt of an annual sponsorship income of almost £200,000, nor of top players competing for a first prize of £10,000.'

From 1989, however, the BBC's patronage of bowls was somewhat diminished. It has pulled out of both *Jack High* and another tournament which it was instrumental in initiating only three years before. Ostensibly, the television-linked sponsorship might have been expected to disappear simultaneously; but the governing body was confident that there were sufficient numbers of sponsors who wished to target the playing membership as much as the more remote (and less easily definable) viewing audience. Financial institutions in particular are attracted by the stable (and often substantial) incomes of those 40–60-year-olds who comprise a substantial proportion of players. Television can therefore act as marriage broker: bringing an apparently unlikely sport to a sponsor's attention by providing the incentive of televised credits, and leaving the newly-weds to a (reasonably) happy reciprocal relationship.

More obscure sports wait in the wings, seeking television opportunities but meanwhile courting sponsors who find the participants a more attractive proposition even than potential viewers. *Croquet*, a possible long-odds bet as the bowls of the 1990s, earned £100,000 in sponsorship in 1988, which owed nothing to television and everything to the upmarket and increasingly youthful profile of its players. More than most, croquet encapsulates many of the qualities which render a sport screenworthy: played over a small area requiring relatively few cameras; appealing to both sexes; with apparently the same sedateness as snooker or bowls but actually fiercely competitive; and with rules that do not require hours of explanation.

Much the same criteria can be applied to *table tennis*, with a major additional advantage. With well over 2 million current participants (overwhelmingly aged under 24) and millions more with some distant experience of a relatively simple game, rules need little explanation. Despite all its small-screen advantages, table tennis coverage has been almost non-existent since 1978. It is making a comeback, not least because the English Table Tennis Association is now prepared to accommodate BBC scheduling decisions where previously no attention was paid to television concerns. As a result, the national championships which were to be played in the third week of January 1990, which the BBC could not have covered, were moved to early January. Concessions have also been made to the playing environment. Instead of four tables alongside each other in an auditorium, making life difficult for the viewer and almost impossible for the producer, ETTA has agreed to a special television set with proper markings. From ETTA's point of view, these are small but highly desirable changes, indicative of a more professional approach by a sporting body which was close to bankruptcy in 1986. Such small compromises do not alter the fabric of the game, but allow the Association more freedom to exploit a potentially lucrative source of much-needed income.

There is a further reason for the Table Tennis Association's determination to regain television coverage. While several minority sports illustrate how even the smallest coverage can have an immeasurable impact on interest and hence participation, there are few opportunities to examine the obvious corollary: the impact of heavy television exposure being withdrawn. Prior to 1978, coverage of the sport was regular and comparatively heavy, then halted abruptly until 1988. From the same data source described in Chapter 4 (Target Group Index), it is possible to trace the steady and almost uninterrupted decline in British table tennis playing since 1980. From a peak of 3.2 million in 1980, the number of players has dropped by over a third to barely 2 million in 1988. This precipitate decline cannot be ascribed solely to the absence of television, although ETTA believes it to be a highly significant factor. Demographic factors like a fall in the teenage population, and the simultaneous rise in

114

popularity of other sports, will also have played a part. It is hard to avoid the conclusion, however, that television has been instrumental, and that the new ETTA philosophy will have its reward in a gradual recovery in participation. Despite the difficulty in following a fast and sometimes furious game with a very small ball, table tennis's willingness to make itself available to TV producers – and its relative cheapness to cover – suggests that a strong revival for an old favourite may be another good bet for television sport in the 1990s.

Unlike table tennis, the amount of television coverage for *volleyball* has increased since *Grandstand* covered its 'Hitachi Cup' in 1984. Since then, while the BBC has continued to cover that tournament (which has changed its climax to a Saturday to accommodate the programme), Channel 4 has also carried four one-hour programmes. 1984 therefore marks the watershed year for televised volleyball, and the figures below show the number of affiliated players for the four years before and after that year:

1980	*1981*	*1982*	*1983*	*1984*	*1985*	*1986*	*1987*	*1988*
3,310	3,402	4,460	4,703	5,627	10,134	15,352	17,753	24,606

In the four years to 1984, playing membership rose by 70%; in the subsequent four years, it rose by nearly 500%. It is scarcely surprising that the sport's governing body attributes this huge growth in participation directly to television, and was prepared even to change the final set scoring system so that match times do not impose too much pressure on schedules. Instead of running for close on forty minutes, a fifth set is now more likely to last for about ten minutes. For a sport targeted at young people and which therefore tries to ensure a low subscription fee, television coverage provides a vital opportunity for securing additional revenue through sponsorship. Of £400,000 income, only 12% comes from membership fees with the balance divided almost equally between Sports Council grant and sponsorship. For volleyball, therefore, television coverage has served both objectives: it has encouraged huge numbers of youngsters to take up a sport with which they were previously unfamiliar; and it has helped to supplement the treasury coffers.

In many instances, improved technology allows television access to sports where exciting or creative coverage has traditionally been difficult or impossible. Of the major sports, both golf and motor-racing are obvious examples. Within minor sports, perhaps the most successful transformation has been in *cycling*. Where old-style fixed cameras allowed fleeting glimpses of blurred wheels, coloured shirts and the occasional agonised expression, none of which made for captivating television unless the finish was close, modern lightweight versions can magnify every bulging muscle on to the small screen. Results have been twofold: another success for Channel 4's innovative coverage of a long-standing event; and finances for additional events in the UK in a sport where mounting any competitive event incurs inordinate costs.

Even for viewers who had problems with their childhood tricycle, Channel 4's coverage of cycling's world premier event – the epic Tour de France – has been a revelation. Complex timing rules have been explained, personalities explored and the machines themselves analysed, while cameras mounted on following motorcycles and parallel cars have shown every last grimace. Once again, original presentation and creative camerawork were exploited in 1989 to capture the closest finish in the history of the race, as Greg Lemond rode a spellbinding time trial to wipe out a 50-second deficit and win by 8 seconds. It was television and sport at its most magnificent, seducing in the process over one and a half million viewers.

It is precisely that combination – visually attractive and informative presentation with a sporting contest at its most dramatic – that can stimulate viewers of appropriate age and fitness into participation. The British Cycling Federation reports new membership rising by a steady 4–5% a year after a sharp decline in the 50s and 60s. Just as with volleyball, the Federation is convinced that television coverage has encouraged membership and will continue to do so. It has certainly provided the catalyst for competitions which might otherwise have never taken place: city centre races have been organised and designed with TV cameras in mind, providing for an inside lane giving access to cameras mounted on motorcycles. These races are expensive to mount (the BBC-televised Milk Race costs an estimated £1 million), and provide a series of springboards for British competitors to improve their abilities against international opposition. One can only speculate on the potential impact of British success in a sport whose skills and fascination, appreciated by the French for decades, is just beginning to impinge on a country weaned on the gentler pastimes of cricket and darts. A surprise Olympic medal or the emergence of a Sean Kelly figure in Britain would almost certainly have a dramatic and immediate impact on the profile and participation of what is still a minor sport. When and if this figure should materialise, British television could rightfully claim a substantial proportion of the credit.

It is just this kind of dramatic, closely fought competition which a minority sport really needs to tempt the cameras. But drama is not always possible. Some of the backwater sports like fencing or handball – ever conscious of the huge benefits which can flow from television coverage –

116

Backwater sports can benefit from TV-generated sponsorship. (Cartoon courtesy of the *Listener.*)

'If only we'd known this was going to happen we could have arranged some great TV-sponsorship deals . . .'

tend to offer limited scope for even the most ingenious technology to provide stimulating television. Those determined stalwarts who risk sporting obscurity by taking up tug-of-war – though there were English victories in two classes at the 1989 World Championships – must accept that some additional element of drama will be necessary to catch the eye of TV sports executives. According to a *Guardian* reporter, the case is not entirely hopeless: 'You never know. A luminous rope, fancy gear, and maybe a pool of piranhas separating the teams.'

At the amateur level, where exposure and money for the sport are not the paramount issue, the temptation to accommodate television is easier to resist. Much as these undiscovered sports might covet the television success of volleyball or cycling, they would sooner maintain a life of stable obscurity than make wholesale changes in rules, tactics, tournaments, and approaches. It is when professional teams and players are involved, when individuals' sole source of income is derived from the sport they play, that the role of television and its attendant income starts to loom large. Very often, as we shall see in the next chapter, the consequences for sport can be unfortunate. Sometimes, however, the financial advantages which television can provide at the professional level can – given proper encouragement and co-operation – be exploited at every level of the amateur and even the recreational game. An example of such mutual benefit is tennis, ironically a major sport in which British success has been conspicuously, and consistently, absent.

Of the major tennis Open Championships, Wimbledon is the last surviving event to be played on grass; for many professionals, a Wimbledon singles title remains the most important ambition of their career. The two-week Championship is administered by the All England Club, which is responsible for its promotion and marketing and the selling of television rights. Income to pay for administration and prize money is derived from four major sources: merchandising, corporate hospitality, ticket sales, and the sale of television rights. Although the All England Club prefers not to break its income figures down, and therefore precise calculations are not possible, television fees constitute over half of its total Championship income.

One reason for the unusual significance of television is the virtual absence of sponsorship. While other tournaments gratefully append the names of generous benefactors to cups and trophies, allowing advertising hoardings in strategic and conspicuous areas of the stadium, Wimbledon is determined to retain its purity. Thus low-key and subtle exposure is permitted for Rolex, on the scoreboard, and for Robinsons Barley Water, on the umpire's stand; otherwise, there is not a brand name to be seen on the courts except on the carefully designed clothing of competitors. The reason lies in the unique nature of Wimbledon itself. By preserving the quality and tradition of the tournament, by severely limiting on-court commercial opportunities which might detract from the essence of the occasion – and leave them vulnerable to the commercial demands of sponsors – the All England Club can enhance the value of their own product. In contrast to almost every other major sport, their current policy is therefore to merchandise their own brand rather than attract sponsors. Consequently, television's money becomes proportionately more important. Rights are sold in different packages around the world, the bulk of television income coming – inevitably – from American deals with both Home Box Office for the full fortnight and NBC for the last five days. The deal for non-UK European rights illustrates one of the pitfalls of an increasing dependence on television money.

Until recently, the European Broadcasting Union (EBU) had a virtual monopoly on rights to European sporting events. With the advent of multi-national media empires, spanning many countries and many media outlets, there is now increasingly bitter competition for original television product. World-famous sporting events rank very high on the list of programmes which are not necessarily country-specific and can command exceptional ratings. In 1989, the German-based media conglomerate Bertelsmann made the All England Club an offer for Wimbledon television rights which the EBU could not match. These rights were sold on to television companies throughout Europe; in Germany itself they were passed to Bertelsmann's own subsidiary, the satellite-delivered and subscription-based private channel RTL Plus. While this represented a major coup for an as yet unprofitable satellite venture, it created some controversy. Because RTL Plus is barely accessible to half of German homes, and because the public channels refused to pay what they considered to be extortionate sums of money for peripheral rights, the majority of West German viewers were denied any pictures from Wimbledon – which was particularly unfortunate in a year when both Men's and Women's Singles Championships were won by West Germans.

While the All England Club might be expected to have regard for the non-universal nature of the Bertelsmann interest, the income equation demands that rights fees be maximised. In the UK, the doomed Listed Events provision prevents competition for exclusive rights at the moment. Once it is removed, both ITV (very keen on exclusivity and the upmarket audience profile of Wimbledon fortnight) and satellite channels (desperate for a unique selling point to boost flagging interest) will be in the fight against a severely cash-limited BBC. With UK rights up for negotiation in 1990, the odds on the BBC being able to sustain its traditional stranglehold on the event must be lengthening as the All England Club searches for new routes to increased revenue.

It is the destination of this revenue which creates the umbilical cord between money for the professional tournament and help for the national game. Once all outgoings are accounted for, there remains a healthy profit. Traditionally, all the excess money which is made during the Championship fortnight goes to the Lawn Tennis Association to be ploughed back into the national game. In 1988, this amounted to a massive £7.6 million, which the LTA used to subsidise the British game at every level. This is a phenomenal increase on the eight years since 1980, when equivalent profits were just £420,000. Whatever black jokes one might care to make about the state of British tennis with or without financial assistance from Wimbledon profits, it is a major contribution to the development of the game in Britain. A major factor in that contribution is fees from the sale of television rights.

This vastly increased revenue has not been achieved without some accommodation of television requirements. In particular, the change of day for the Men's Singles Final from Saturday to Sunday was a direct result of American television concerns. A compromise of that sort could scarcely be interpreted as a major restructuring of the tournament. As competition for sporting rights becomes increasingly fierce, the All England Club may have more difficult domestic decisions to make than whether to switch the day of a major final. If outrageous bids are to be made by channels with limited availability, it might be forced to choose: financial benefit to British tennis players through massive subsidies via the LTA, or viewing benefit to the 15 million or so British tennis fans whose only access to the world's most prestigious tennis tournament is through their television screens? It will not be an easy choice.

One far more significant change to tennis was not confined to Wimbledon and was certainly inspired, if not entirely dictated, by the exigencies of television coverage. In the early 1970s, a tie-break was introduced at six games all in order to break the deadlock and ensure a match did not have to continue for long hours. On the one hand, it meant the end of such classic contests as the immortal Gonzales/Pasarell game of June 1969 – at 112 games still the longest-ever singles match. On the other hand, it meant easier decisions for network schedulers who could better predict when tense matches would finish. Although initiated by television, it was a rule change welcomed by players, who – with increasingly hectic schedules – were not displeased at an element of predictability. In this instance, it was a rule change which achieved the unusual distinction of satisfying the voracious demands of television without spoiling the essence of an exciting and demanding game. In other games, particularly long-standing national games with a long professional tradition, television-inspired rule changes were distinctly less sports-friendly.

6

WHEN THE WHITE KNIGHT TURNS BLACK

Whatever the undoubted benefits for the development of less familiar sports and stimulated participation, television's most valuable contribution by far has been to heighten the enjoyment and availability of events previously restricted to the privileged few spectators. This is a two-edged sword. For while sports are developed and organised according to their own internal set of rules, customs and traditions, television operates according to a different set of principles. As competition for viewers increasingly begins to dictate the scheduling and production values of television executives, pressure grows to maximise audiences for sports as for all other programmes.

Given the generally heterogeneous nature of television audiences, as we have seen, programmes of general appeal need to be constructed to attract the widest possible audience. At the same time, channels dependent on advertising revenue must maximise the commercial opportunities available to them. Both these considerations must be passed on to sports which make themselves available to television. Simultaneously, the financial rewards which commercial channels are prepared to offer for popular events ensure that sporting bodies will be willing to adapt themselves to the demands of television. As competitive pressure increases, so do those demands; the question for individual sports is how far they are prepared to go in their willingness to maximise the television dollar. It is, in fact, the dollar which provides an insight into possible consequences. In the United States, competition between three national networks and – latterly – powerful cable consortia, have produced escalating rights fees beyond the imagination of most British sporting bodies. One consequence of the financial rollercoaster has been soaring salaries for professional sportsmen and women which, again, must be the envy of their British equivalents. High earnings for players create a spiral of expectations whereby increased financial demands are fulfilled only at the expense of concessions by the players and participants. These concessions impinge directly on their sports. It is to America that this chapter turns first, to assess how sporting customs, rules and tactics can be transformed under the powerful influence of television money.

Effects of competitive TV in America

American Football is generally acknowledged as the archetypal television sport. From its position of relative obscurity in the 1950s, dominated by the greater excitement, elan and more polished image of college football, the professional game struggled through an embattled and impoverished existence. In 1951, the entire National Football League earned a paltry $50,000 from television. The Colts v Giants sudden death play-off in 1958, which began the process of rejuvenation, coincided with the permanent adoption of a new interruption in play which had been introduced experimentally in 1955. It was agreed that referees could call a time-out in the first and third quarters of play, without request from the teams, if preceded by an unbroken nine minutes of play. It was a rule change which convinced advertisers that pro football was serious about television; from then on, television was increasingly serious about pro football. Not surprisingly, this unscheduled pause became institutionalised as the 'TV time-out'. In 1969 the 'two-minute warning' was a further innovation, allowing breaks two minutes before the end of the second and fourth quarters. In 1982, a drastic measure was needed to bolster worried television executives who saw Monday night football ratings plummet from 37% to 31% of the viewing audience. Since commercial time is sold on the basis of minimum guaranteed viewers, with shortfalls made good through discounts or free spots, networks were in danger of losing money on their NFL deal. To ease the commercial pressure, NFL Commissioner Pete Rozelle persuaded his teams to accede to another minute of commercial time in each game. Given that television revenue now constitutes 60% of income, it dictates what form its commercial product will take.

Consequently, an American Football game which consists of four fifteen-minute segments of playing time will generally last for 3½ hours or more. It may be tedious from the spectating point of view, but then the role of spectators has clearly been superseded. By the end of the 70s, in Benjamin Rader's words, 'To a very large extent, the paying customers . . . didn't matter anymore. If they mattered, it was largely as ambience, as unpaid, in fact paying, extras in the vast super-studios that had once been known as stadiums.' These willing participants in the television extravaganza were treated to pre- and intra-match entertainments which

122

were spurned by the pro footballers of the 1950s, most famously the cheerleaders who now adorn every football game. Such peripheral visual treats were essential not to occupy the attention of spectators during commercial time-outs, but as part of the television razzamatazz which made pro football easier to sell to a television audience consisting potentially of as many women as men.

Arguably, questions about start times and numbers of interruptions for commercial purposes make little impact on the essence of sporting competition. As long as there is no interference in the game itself, a few additional pauses are a small price to pay for increased access to millions of sporting fans. Unfortunately, changes are not confined to the more peripheral issues of timing and pauses. In 1972, a series of minor rule changes were adopted in order to reduce dependence on field goals and increase the number of touchdowns – in effect, to make offensive play easier. When, by 1977, these changes had been effectively counteracted by new defensive manoeuvres, the NFL introduced more wide-ranging alterations to allow both quarterbacks and receivers more protection. The effect on the game was immediate and dramatic. Rader quotes an average game increase in number of yards thrown from 283.8 yards in 1977 to 408.7 yards in 1981. Scores, too, became wildly inflated as offensive players exploited their new-found freedom. One former

American Football (a Superbowl game), whose rules were changed to suit television. The sport now has a wide following in Britain, thanks to Channel 4

professional turned television commentator was outspoken about the consequences and motives: 'They've taken an art form and destroyed it. . . . They look at the scoreboard, they look at the dollar sign. Does this mean happiness?'

It certainly meant happiness for networks as ratings climbed, and happiness for players who watched earnings soar on the back of inflated television deals. As far as sporting tradition is concerned, perhaps happiness is an elusive concept. When sudden-death overtime was introduced in 1974 to decide tied games, it was not a response to any heartfelt pleas from long-standing spectators, who had readily accepted tied games for many years. It was to satisfy a television audience which, it was assumed, would want a result to ensure that excitement was maintained among those who might have only marginal interest in the game. The question of who exactly dictates changes in long-standing sporting traditions and at whom such changes are directed is a recurring theme. American Football's evolution as the archetypal television sport leaves little doubt about the identity of the piper.

Identical pressures have influenced baseball. If happiness in American Football consists of watching the maximum number of touchdowns, the baseball equivalent is home runs. By the mid-60s, both home runs and total runs scored had reached an all-time low. This was, it seems, a direct result of instructions to umpires to enlarge the strike zone so that batters would be more frequently struck out and the pace of an increasingly desultory game would quicken. A more defensive game ensued which saw both gates and, more significantly, television ratings in decline precisely when American Football was staging its spirited revival.

By 1969, baseball's ruling elite decided changes were needed to reverse this trend. The pitching mound was lowered from 15 to 10 inches, making life more difficult for the pitcher; the size of the strike zone was reduced, making life easier for the hitter; and a 'designated hitter' was approved to replace the pitcher when batting. It is easier for British readers to appreciate the full significance of these changes by imagining the Test and County Cricket Board ordaining smaller stumps and the replacement of one pace bowler with a specialist batsman to increase run-scoring opportunities. Altering the balance of the game in favour of offensive hitting did the trick: run totals and home runs increased in the 1970s. In terms of ratings, however, the crucial changes were made not to rules but to match scheduling. Baseball's World Series is the climax to the season and, until the arriviste Superbowl stole the crown, was king of America's annual sporting events. Winners of the two national leagues compete in a best-of-seven match play-off to decide the world champions. Since the game's inception, these games like all other baseball matches had been played in the afternoon sunshine.

For the first time in 1971, midweek World Series matches were rescheduled from afternoon to evening. Given World Series matches' dedicated live following, this had nothing to do with improving the numbers or convenience of live spectators. There was only one justification: to exploit the vastly increased evening television audience. Predictably, ratings for the midweek matches doubled. It was only a matter of time before even weekend games went the same way, and 1984 saw the last daytime World Series game. Ratings comparisons ensured that prime-time games had secured their place for ever: 18.9 for 1984's weekend game, 25.3 for prime-time in 1985, 28.6 for 1986. A prime-time thirty-second commercial could then be sold for $250,000, double the weekend afternoon rate. For the live spectators it meant a night-time, sometimes chilly, vigil under floodlights; for the players, it meant poorer visibility in a game where – like cricket – seeing the ball is the key to success; for the networks, it meant huge increases in revenue to justify payment of rights fees; for the game, it meant the end of a tradition.

Other sports which had survived quite happily until the advent of television indulged in long periods of soul-searching to attract the marginal television viewer. Ice hockey was expected to succeed, given the potent televisual combination of speed and violence, but disappointed. It was too fast, the puck frequently invisible, and there were insufficient pauses to tempt the networks into serious investment. With the game's roots in other countries, hockey's American managers could not unilaterally change the laws, and only the advent of cable has produced regular television hockey on American television.

Basketball had no such qualms, and its division into four periods with frequent time-outs established its network possibilities. But it failed to draw the viewers, not least because the incessant high scoring made the skills and complexities less easily comprehensible to the marginal viewer who tended to switch on only for the climax of the last two minutes. This time, something *was* done: in 1982, the National Basketball Association introduced a new 3 point score for a long-range shot to encourage some variation in an otherwise monotonous display of end-to-end play. Again, the effect was minimal and despite American domination in the international arena, basketball has failed to increase its television appeal.

Perhaps the most depressing example of interference with the fundamentals of a game is the American attempt to adapt soccer to its television viewer. Following the example of American Football, it was decided that draws were unacceptable. Even a 1975 decision to settle all drawn

125

matches on penalties survived only two years; something more dramatic was needed. Inventive rule-makers dreamed up a shoot-out which allowed one player five seconds in which to take on and beat the goalkeeper from inside the opposing half. As with penalty decisions, each team had five such shots to decide the winner. Adulteration did not stop with a determination to resolve matches. The North American Soccer League (NASL) wanted more goals, and were prepared to take appropriate action: they proposed widening the goal, and reducing the offside area from the halfway line to a 35-yard line. Three substitutes were allowed. Extra points were awarded for goals. American viewers expect action and drama, and American soccer wanted the television cameras – even if, as happened on at least one occasion, a goal could be seen only in replay since a team had been sufficiently inconsiderate to score during a commercial break. By 1981, FIFA had had enough (one might ask why it took them so long). The NASL was instructed to restrict teams to two substitutes and abide by international offside rules, to the despair of American club managers. One American coach, quoted by Joan Chandler, responded with a revealing statement about American attitudes to soccer: 'FIFA has a behind-the-times and stick-in-the-mud attitude typical of European soccer. They just can't realise that we are in the entertainment business.'

To a British eye, American attempts to transform a sport considerably older than their own country appear faintly ludicrous. But these pressures for change cannot all be consigned to oblivion on the assumption that television dominates all. An alternative explanation, developed by Chandler herself, should be considered. Since time immemorial there have been changes in the rules and customs governing sports; no sport is entirely ossified, but undergoes evolution and adaptation to a changing social, economic and political environment in order to survive. On this analysis, ever since sports spectating became an activity in its own right – and certainly since spectators were charged for the privilege – sports have been concerned to attract and entertain observers. No professional sport would be prepared to tolerate empty terraces or deserted halls. All that television has done is vastly increase the pool of potential spectators, beyond the wildest imagination of sporting bodies up to the mid-20th century.

It is certainly true that responsible sports administrators will not regard rules and regulations as cast in stone but will review and, after deliberation, change them. We accept four points for a Rugby Union try instead of three, just as we accept three points for a soccer League win instead of two, as attempts to stimulate more entertaining and competi-

126

tive matches. More radical suggestions are sometimes mooted. One highly respected cricket writer and commentator has suggested that the pitch should be lengthened from its statutory 22 yards to take account of the increase in height and strength of the average male today compared to fifty or a hundred years ago. But there is a difference. Alterations have been made over the years to rules, equipment, dress regulations, and competition formats, timing and length. Within each sport, these decisions may well be taken with a view to increasing the excitement and attractiveness of the sport in question. They will, however, also be taken by people with knowledge of the history and customs of the game, people immersed in the traditions which characterise their sport. Certainly, decisions will be taken with the interests of spectators in mind. But every sport has an internal consistency of its own, a logic which rule changes need to respect. It is for precisely these reasons that very few sports are subjected to wholesale transformations, but to tentative modifications which even then are frequently for experimental and limited periods only. There is a chance to assess the impact, to canvass players and commentators, to examine whether there might in the longer term be any irreparable damage to the game's fundamental spirit.

In other words, adaptation under these circumstances is careful and conditional. Adaptation dictated by television, whether or not in the interests of viewer entertainment, is precipitate and imposed by network controllers whose professional concern is not the welfare or internal consistency of a sport but superior ratings for their respective channels. It is an entirely different set of priorities with entirely different repercussions. To understand completely what must occupy the minds of a sports programmer in a competitive environment, we must go back to the concept of a fickle, wavering audience. Most potential viewers will not be baseball enthusiasts or football fanatics, but people who want some light relaxation and are having difficulty deciding between Monday night football and another channel's weekly comedy. It is those marginal viewers, television's floating voters, who make the difference between ratings success and ratings mediocrity.

Marginal viewers used to entertainment-based television are not enthralled by a one-sided game whose result is a foregone conclusion ten minutes into the match, or by games which involve little obvious action or drama. Hence the need to exaggerate the artificial drama, to contrive excitement, glamour and spectacle where none might naturally exist. In such a tenaciously competitive environment as American commercial television, you cannot afford to take chances on size of audience. Any trick, any device, any packaging of the product which will entice another

1% of viewers away from a rival channel is worth pursuing. And if that includes one or two requested rule changes, regard it as just compensation for the astronomic rights fees. For television's influence to dominate therefore requires two conditions: first, that a sport should be substantially dependent on television for its income; and second, that the broadcasting environment itself should be fiercely competitive. The role and significance of competitive television is confirmed, as we shall see, by the emergence of greater competition in the UK and its effect on the dominant British sport.

This otherwise legitimate explanation propounded by Chandler, which certainly has some bearing on changes in the United States, is discredited by her attempt to extend it to the United Kingdom. Lack of wholesale changes in the structure, timing and regulations of British sports to suit television are explained by an absurd (though not uncommon) assertion that the British have some inbred cultural aversion both to profit and competition. Apart from references to John Lloyd's tennis philosophy (see Chapter 3), we are told for example that 'few British adults watch their children compete', so contemptuous are they of the competitive spirit (no empirical evidence is offered). We are told that 'the importance of competition is played down' and that the British have a careless attitude to winning. What is described as 'hysterical rejoicing' at the 1966 soccer World Cup victory is explained as reflecting some kind of re-establishment of paternalistic superiority which was assumed lost forever.

The thesis is that, since British spectators don't care about winning, and since British clubs are uninterested in making money, there is nothing for television to exploit. Furthermore, since television itself is not subject to the discipline of the market-place and is therefore exempted from the need to make its programmes as attractive as possible, it will be under no urgent pressure to maximise the appeal of its programmes. For an American, such uncommercial practices are almost heretical: 'The Royal Wedding was transmitted free of charge,' says a disbelieving Chandler, clearly pained at the pennies which an impoverished Royal Family allowed to slip from its grasp. It is a common American fallacy (indeed, a common political fallacy) that the drive for profit is the only effective guarantee of healthy competition. As successive Director Generals have testified, competition for audiences between ITV and BBC has been intense since ITV's inception in 1955. Within their respective public service frameworks, the two main terrestrial channels still acknowledge ratings and share of viewing as the primary measure of success. What other justification could there be for the main public service channel importing an Australian soap opera, then stripping it across early evening weekday schedules?

As for competition in British sport, any notion of uncompetitive players or club managers in soccer or elsewhere is really too absurd for serious consideration. At both professional and amateur level, sport throughout the world is played with determination and a drive to succeed for a variety of reasons: pride, enjoyment, aspirations of national recognition, money certainly, but perhaps above all a knowledge that prowess in a difficult athletic discipline is one of the most exhausting yet satisfying of human accomplishments which commands universal respect and admiration. Ancient Greeks, like a steadily declining proportion of today's Olympic heroes, did not require material inducements to perform to the very peak of their athletic ability. No generous benefactors offered sackfuls of obols or the latest model of turbo-charged chariot. They were tough, highly trained and determined competitors who coveted the most highly prized possession of all – the winner's laurels.

The crucial difference between Britain and America is that in British sport decisions have not until recently been dominated by the need to secure large television fees, or to satisfy a sports producer's idea of what constitutes dramatic television. But there are changes afoot. Before we examine how similar influences are beginning to make an appearance in the UK, there are three other potential consequences of television which American experience demonstrates. These are not confined to specific sports, but are more generally applicable to the American sporting environment.

First is the blurring between amateur and professional sport. In America, there has always been a strong tradition of amateur sport played at the college level. Until professional football took off in the 60s, it was college football which received most attention, attracting large numbers of paying spectators and television viewers. Like all amateur sport, and much like university sport in the UK, its aim was to foster high athletic ability and enthusiasm in the best tradition of educational institutions dedicated to encouraging physical as well as mental agility. This was the idealism promoted by the representative and co-ordinating body, the National Collegiate Athletic Association (NCAA).

It was the considerable largesse bestowed by networks for the rights to televise, in particular, college football which gradually eroded that spirit of idealism. NCAA agreements tried to ensure that all teams, not just the strongest, had their turn in hosting the cameras and therefore a share of the hand-out. Slowly, amid growing rumours of corruption and bribery by some colleges allegedly determined to entice the top players, the most successful football colleges became restless at this imposed restraint on their earning capacities. A College Football Association was formed in 1976 to represent the interests of those colleges. They were temporarily pacified in 1977 by a four-year contract with ABC worth $30 million annually, but even a huge increase to nearly $75 million in 1981 did not deter them finally from going to court to seek independence from the NCAA. As a result the NCAA was adjudged to represent a 'classic cartel', and could no longer control the rights of member schools. Judgment was finally upheld by the Supreme Court in 1984, the final nail in the coffin of traditional amateurism. Whether television money was the instigator or the catalyst it is impossible to decide, but the result was an irreconcilable tension between, in the words of Klatell and Marcus, 'lofty idealism and hard-nosed reality'. Whatever else motivates American college players on to the football field, the notion of lofty idealism has had its day.

A second consequence of television has perhaps more to do with the medium itself than with the distorting effect of the cash it can make available. This is the elevation of superstars, a magnification of personalities by their constant exposure on the small screens. This is a two-edged sword, as some British sports stars have already discovered. For while athletic prowess beamed into millions of homes can make today's hero out of yesterday's nonentity, it also exaggerates the indiscretions and unpleasantries that inevitably accompany a proportion of sports personalities. Television-glorified stars are a rich seam of instant fodder for the scandal-mongers who wish to sell newspapers and TV programmes, rather than salute achievements on the sports field. Compared to today's stars, yesterday's may have been poorer but they were certainly less vulnerable to instant vilification.

This television-inspired personality cult, not of course confined to the sporting arena, can result in some strangely inverse relationships in team sports. A national hero, the subject of press profiles and eulogising editorials, cannot always find it easy to submerge his ego to the collective benefit of less well-known team-mates – still less to an utterly obscure and distinctly less well-paid team manager or coach. Rader records how one baseball coach, to illustrate the changing relationship between player and manager, suggested the different ways a coach may have addressed a recalcitrant player over the years: 'Go over and stand in the corner.' . . . 'Please stand in the corner.' . . . 'How about if you went over and stood in the corner?' . . . 'How about us talking about you standing in the corner?' . . . 'Why don't I go over and stand in the corner for you?' Clearly, if a club or team manager feels intimidated or playing colleagues feel envious of an emerging superstar's public persona and private wealth, it could eventually prove disruptive for the team and unhealthy for the game. This is a symptom of the television era, rather than solely of the unprecedented cash now available to reward the privileged few. It is also, of course, a consideration only of relevance to team sports; in some athletic events, for example, it is equally conceivable that television's magnification will serve as an incentive rather than a barrier to performance.

Finally, perhaps the most serious impact American television has had, with universal and probably irrevocable ramifications, is on the Olympics. Combining money, a blurring of amateur and professional status, and the elevation of media-hyped superstars, American television has almost single-handedly transformed an idealistic celebration of worldwide athletic achievement into an orgy of telegenic profiteering.

We have seen in Chapter 3 how exclusive coverage of this quadrennial event is regarded as perhaps the most prized television event of the sporting calendar. Unlike the Superbowl, which entitles each network to its moment of glory and glamour (if not necessarily profit) once every three years, there is no Gubbins turn. The Olympic Games have come to be regarded as a trademark, as a sign of superiority, as a springboard for vigorous marketing of a network's image and programming strengths. Such an indispensable factor in the marketing equation have they become that blood and thunder competition for television rights has resulted in quite fantastic sums of money for the International Olympic Organising Committee.

By comparison, revenue from all other sources pales into insignificance. Although the European Broadcasting Union comprises thirty-two member countries with a combined population well in excess of America's 220 million, its contribution to the 1988 Seoul coffers was $28 million for television rights – less than 10% of the $300 million paid by NBC. This was close to parity compared to the chasm in rights payments for the 1988 Calgary Winter Games where the equivalent Canadian time zones made television coverage particularly lucrative. For this privilege, ABC paid $309 million compared to the EBU's $5.7 million and $1.2 million from the Communist bloc (Russia/Eastern Europe/Cuba). Whether frenzied bidding in a violently competitive market-place eventually elicits an event's true worth or a monumentally overpriced millstone is not the issue. No responsible IOOC committee, ever conscious of the mounting cost and complexity of Olympic operations, will decline a gift horse – even if it does turn out to be a descendant of its Trojan predecessor.

In return for providing over 90% of television revenue, America not unreasonably expects and receives concessions. In response to American

131

The Olympics before packaging. A BBC camera films the relatively unadorned opening ceremony of the 1948 Games in London

pressure, the Calgary Games were lengthened from twelve to sixteen days to provide an additional weekend of television coverage. The number of events rose from around 90 to 128, half of them scheduled during prime-time television or at weekends. Demands have escalated to the faintly ludicrous: there is a rumour that during bidding for the Seoul Games, ABC proposed that South Korea move its clocks forward one hour to minimise the impact of a 13-hour time difference. Certainly, some events with special American interest were scheduled at 8 o'clock in the morning, despite the evident and understandable displeasure of some non-American competitors. In similar vein, it has even been suggested that American television considerations impinged on the 1986 soccer World Cup in Mexico; allegedly, referees were asked to end each half after exactly 45 minutes, regardless of any injury time which might have accrued, to accommodate American scheduling and advertising requirements. Even if true, such practice would pale into insignificance compared to the recommendation of FIFA President Joao Havelange for the

1994 World Cup, to be staged in America. In order to capitalise on American television revenue, he told a Brazilian newspaper, soccer should abandon its two 45-minute halves in favour of four 25-minute quarters.

Certainly, the United States through its television money wields inordinate power in its influence over the Olympic movement and competition priorities in the Olympic Games. The huge amounts being charged to – and willingly paid by – advertisers to enable networks to recoup most of their enormous rights fees were instrumental in an unprecedented decision by the IOC in 1986: to hold the Winter Games and Summer Games two years apart after the Summer Games of 1992. There was growing concern within the American broadcasting community that advertisers may no longer be able to underwrite the massive financial demands being imposed on them twice in a single year. Hence a decision to spread the financial load, and a break with long-established Olympic tradition.

For many observers, the most unwelcome demonstration of American domination was not the restructuring or retiming of events, or even mounting pressure on the IOC to choose time zones beneficial to American networks, but the uncompromisingly nationalistic flavour of American camerawork and commentary when providing international feeds. For countries which have the technical expertise and resources to provide their own equipment and personnel, this is less of a problem (although most broadcasters will rely on the host country for at least some event coverage). For less advanced countries, there can be almost complete dependence on host nation or American coverage which invariably exaggerates the achievements and prowess of American athletes at the expense of others.

Nationalistic fervour is believed by American networks to be an indispensable feature of attractive Olympic packaging for the domestic audience. Judging by the extravagant display during the opening ceremony of the Los Angeles Games, this is a fair assessment. And judging by almost universally unfavourable descriptions elsewhere, including references to 'monumental tastelessness', such undiluted celebration of American achievements is not necessarily welcome worldwide. Klatell and Marcus, otherwise critical observers of the overweening American Olympic influence, provide a blunt if slightly chilling justification of the all-American television portrayal: 'American viewers and advertisers are more important to the financial success of the Games than the rest of the world combined, so ABC's single-minded concentration on US athletes can readily be understood.'

Where does it stop? It cannot be healthy for a worldwide competition, designed to promote the highest standards of sportsmanship and to represent a spirit of international unity, increasingly to depend on American dollars for survival. In other parts of the world, especially Europe, new generation satellite broadcasters are challenging the traditional terrestrial hegemony and competition may in the long term force up the cost of sporting rights. But their future is insecure, their resources limited, and there would be political repercussions if coverage of such a universally popular event were to be limited to restricted access channels. It would take a brave government to sanction the removal of one of Europe's most entrenched public service obligations, universal availability of significant events. As American money continues to rise, it is highly unlikely that increased television competition elsewhere will even begin to close the yawning gap in Olympic television revenue.

It is therefore incumbent on the IOOC to resist what is bound to become an ever-growing American demand for their Olympic pound of flesh. This has nothing to do with malevolent designs on world domination or cultural imperialism. It is a simple matter of hard-headed commercial realism and return on substantial investment. And the only way of mitigating an inexorably greater dependence on that investment is to scale down the size and scope of the Olympic Games. They do not need to be television extravaganzas; they should not be do-or-die confrontations which maximise national antagonisms and minimise the original ideals of athletic endeavour and the fulfilment of personal aspirations and achievements.

To some extent, this is a comment on the way in which the Olympic Games have come to be reported and interpreted. But it is also a comment on the IOOC, on their priorities and philosophy, and on the values which they are trying to foster in Olympic participants. The drug scandals of Seoul are only part of a slowly disintegrating structure whose creed is gradually being dominated by profit and sponsorship-backed success. If we are not careful, the Olympic Games could be hijacked by an obsessively competitive American television industry, whose money will eventually corrupt completely the original spirit. If that happens, it will not be America's fault for obeying the rules of its own television traditions; it will be the rest of the world's for not recognising and resisting it.

Effects of competitive TV in Britain

And so to the UK. For fifty years, British televised sport operated according to principles of limited competition. Where both channels wanted coverage, they generally both got it. Direct competition was invariably avoided by ITV, mainly because the BBC always won. In terms of League soccer, there had always operated, if not a cartel, then a spirit of amicable competition between the two main channels. Even before its satellite had been launched, the advent of BSB transformed the competitive scene. For the season ending in 1988, the cost of League soccer to television was £3.1 million. By the time ITV had responded to the intervention of BSB by ensuring their satellite competitor could not get a sniff of League football, their annual bill had risen nearly fourfold to £11 million. British sport has not been accustomed to those sums of money changing hands, and the Football League – or at least the main First Division beneficiaries within the Football League – could not believe the scale of this windfall. But nor has British sport been accustomed to the concept of attached strings. By the end of that first, generously rewarded television season there had been enough tensions and disputes to leave many soccer officials more than concerned at what might emerge from this Pandora's Box.

Even before a television football had been kicked in anger, there were prophetic rumblings of dissent. In the summer of 1988, Ken Jones writing in the *Independent* summoned up images of television's invidious influence on sports: an American soccer referee who had agreed to be wired for sound for the CBS cameras; and a Detroit boxer who tripped on an extended microphone shoved through the ropes, falling on to a terminal left hook. Jones continued: 'It has clearly not occurred to the Football League that there is a distinction between selling football and selling out. If the latter is not entirely a fact, the clubs will find it difficult to resist the pressure which is sure to come from television.' Following the first televised match of the season, Mark Lawson recommended in the *Listener* some rewriting of the traditional rules 'in line with Greg Dyke's requirements'. Among his suggested changes was Rule 3a of the FA code, that 'A match shall consist of two halves of 45 minutes each'. Lawson advised, 'Delete everything and insert: "*The Match* shall consist of 125 minutes of scheduled screen time, preceded by several trailers before *Blind Date*, and shall include at least four commercial breaks, five minutes of pre-match discussion, five minutes of half-time discussion, and five minutes of after-match analysis."' Include half-time film of every First Division goal scored the previous day and that represents an accurate, if slightly uncharitable, description of ITV's mould-breaking entrance into exclusive live soccer. Despite the hype, despite the ten cameras, the live interviews, the graphics wizardry and the focus on personalities, it was essentially the identical product with more expen-

135

Changing the game for the armchair fan? Kevin Macey's comment in the *Independent*

sive wrapping paper. Although Greg Dyke was widely (and inaccurately) reported as looking for 8 million viewers as an acceptable return on investment, initial ratings were – like the football – disappointing. The fifth and at that time easily most popular live match, Arsenal *v* Liverpool, could only muster a 7.4 million ratings figure.

By the end of the year, with seven games broadcast and fourteen to go, Fleet Street commentators were taking their cue from the audience figures and branding ITV's gamble a failure. Richard Bott commented in the *Sunday Express*, 'Save for a few interesting new camera angles and the occasional glimpse inside a dressing room, the presentation has been a huge disappointment.' His diagnosis, a view shared by many observers, was that no amount of technological gimmickry could render live televised soccer attractive to an audience raised on *Match of the Day*: 'Bred on a phoney diet of packaged thrills for years, the armchair fan needs an exceptional contest to hold his attention.' In similar vein, the *Sunday Times* concluded that 'Greg Dyke has been left with egg on his face . . . his exaggerated ballyhoo has left ITV Sport to make a silk purse every Sunday out of a sow's ear.' It dismissed television's ability to convey the full context of the game as cameras struggled to follow the ball at the expense of tactical considerations and player movements elsewhere. Stuart Jones of *The Times* concluded simply, 'The television public has been let down.'

Even while commentators were – prematurely as it turned out – condemning ITV's experiment as an expensive and damaging failure, those who prophesied television's increasing ascendancy over the interests of soccer found their first vindication. Over the next six months, as ratings gradually rose in response to an increasingly fascinating battle at the top of the First Division, three entirely separate television-inspired rows convinced even wavering critics that strings attached to huge television fees would indeed result in irrevocable changes to the long-standing structure and practices of the national game. Although no one could have anticipated that the Liverpool *v* Arsenal confrontation scheduled for 23 April would prove to be the deciding game, it was always going to be a big attraction at a critical point in the season. Even at the beginning of December, it was earmarked as the penultimate live game of ITV's season. Unfortunately, that Sunday was precisely three days before England's crucial World Cup qualifying match against Albania at Wembley. By delaying the match those 24 hours (all televised matches being staged on a Sunday to minimise effects on Saturday's attendance figures), there was for the players significantly greater risk of exhaustion and less time for recovery from injury. The deal had been signed with the Football League, which represents the interests of football clubs rather than the English national team. For this reason, although England's team manager Bobby Robson was not surprisingly unhappy about the decision, he was powerless to intervene.

There followed what in diplomatic circles is described as 'a full and frank exchange of views', which became fuller and franker as the day approached. Robson's reaction was a poignant acknowledgment of the irreconcilable clash between commercial imperatives and national interests: 'It makes a nonsense of our preparations for international games. . . . I realise the ITV deal is a good one for the clubs and that the money is important for the game. But isn't our international success important, too?' A strictly rhetorical question. ITV, meanwhile, were unrepentant both about the League's contractual obligations and their own determination to retain access to major games. As one ITV statement put it, as tactfully as possible: 'We have paid the League a great deal of money to screen live football, and for that we expect their co-operation. We haven't paid that sort of money to miss out on that sort of match.'

Bad-tempered exchanges rumbled on into the Spring, with compromise dates and times being proposed and rejected with well-publicised regularity. ITV's patience started to wear thin when their proposal to show the match live at 5.30 p.m. on Saturday instead of Sunday was rejected by the League management committee, concerned about the effects on Saturday afternoon's attendances of even a delayed kick-off time. John Bromley fumed: 'We gave them the biggest contract ever in British sporting history and for that sort of money there have to be new rules.' In the event, the dilemma was solved by the tragic circumstances at Hillsborough on 15 April when nearly 100 Liverpool fans died during their FA Cup semi-final against Nottingham Forest. Liverpool did not play again for three weeks, and that troublesome League match against Arsenal was transformed into an end-of-season thriller. Whether either party to the contract will have learned from this experience is difficult to gauge. Ultimately, although the incident was the first to emerge out of soccer's new liaison with television, it is unlikely to prove an isolated incident unless more explicit guarantees are built into the legal contract. It dispelled any doubt that, where television's interests clashed with sport, it was money which dictated the resolution.

Meanwhile, the season was through the halfway mark, a few clubs were emerging as front-runners, and ratings were improving slightly if not dramatically. Unfortunately for ITV, not all the clubs in contention for the First Division leadership were the most lucrative in terms of ratings. Norwich, whose undoubted footballing skills were not matched by their crowd appeal, spent several weeks at the top of the First Division while Coventry – as their chairman forcefully pointed out – were consistently in the top six. By the end of March, television had featured Norwich twice while Coventry had been and remained entirely absent from the small screen. This contrasted starkly with the multiple appearances of the so-called 'big five': Arsenal, Everton, Liverpool, Manchester United and Tottenham. By the end of the season, each of these clubs were the main recipients of ITV money. Under the agreed terms of payment, each home team in a televised match received £145,000 and each away team £47,000. In addition, a flat £200,000 fee was payable to every First Division club whether televised or not. A home televised match was worth considerably more than that £145,000, since with vigorous marketing and carefully targeted sponsorship packages a big club could expect to double that fee. By the end of the season, without calculating the considerable extra benefits of TV-related sponsorship deals, those five clubs had netted around £3.5 million, more than 45%, of the £7.5 million which went to the First Division.

ITV justified this discrepancy through ratings figures: viewers, they said, wanted the big five even if Norwich and Coventry were setting the pace; and the ratings gave some credence to their arguments. But

Table 12
ITV live football ratings 1988/89

Date	Match	Ratings (millions)
1988		
30 October	Everton *v* Manchester United	5.9
6 November	Nottingham Forest *v* Arsenal	5.8
20 November	Sheffield Wednesday *v* Tottenham	6.5
27 November	Newcastle *v* Manchester United	6.2
4 December	Arsenal *v* Liverpool	7.4
11 December	Liverpool *v* Everton	6.7
27 December	Norwich *v* West Ham	5.4
1989		
1 January	Manchester United *v* Liverpool	8.1
2 January	Arsenal *v* Tottenham	7.9
15 January	Tottenham *v* Nottingham Forest	6.8
22 January	Millwall *v* Norwich	5.9
5 February	Manchester United *v* Tottenham	6.4
12 February	West Ham *v* Luton	
	(Littlewoods Cup semi-final)	6.2
26 February	Bristol City *v* Nottingham Forest	
	(Littlewoods Cup semi-final)	7.1
12 March	Aston Villa *v* Liverpool	6.0
26 March	Tottenham *v* Liverpool	6.0
2 April	Manchester United *v* Arsenal	7.8
9 April	Luton *v* Nottingham Forest	
	(Littlewoods Cup final)	8.1
1 May	Arsenal *v* Norwich	4.3
3 May	Everton *v* Liverpool	9.8
26 May	Liverpool *v* Arsenal	10.3

Figures exclude Scottish/Grampian regions which did not show English League soccer (except for the last match, whose ratings are national).

Source: BARB/AGB.

decisions were equally likely to have been affected by secret close-season negotiations in which the prospect of a breakaway 'Super League' was actively pursued by the leading clubs with considerable encouragement from an ITV determined to stave off the BSB threat. Although it would cripple the existing structure of professional soccer, leading clubs were quick to understand the financial implications of securing virtually all television's money for themselves. ITV's secret offer of £1 million per club for four years was abandoned when the television contract was finalised, supposedly designed to provide for more equitable distribution as well as avoiding an irreparable split.

In fact, by virtue of the preferential television treatment afforded to those clubs, they almost certainly exceeded that £1 million income during 1988/9. By the end of the season Liverpool and Arsenal had each been televised six times and Manchester United and Tottenham five. Only Everton lagged behind on three appearances, less than Nottingham Forest (four appearances) and equal with Norwich. A damaging Super League may well have been averted, but it was at the expense of a demonstrably unbalanced distribution of television money which reinforced the strength and resources of the original five clubs to the detriment of the remainder. Undoubtedly, television in that first year of live coverage was responsible for shifting the economic balance of power in the First Division. With enhanced economic power comes the ability to buy the best players, mount more successful marketing drives, and build bigger stands to attract more spectators (and corporate clients) who bring in more money. It is not yet a Super League, but as Crystal Palace chairman Ron Noades put it, 'ITV is creating conditions that make the Super League more likely.'

It was a season which ended, after several postponed matches in the light of Hillsborough, with a fairy-tale climax that neither Greg Dyke nor John Bromley would have allowed themselves to dream. It is unusual enough for the very last match of the season to decide the Championship; it is almost unprecedented for the two opposing sides to each have a chance of clinching the title. Add to that a television peak-time kick-off because the season had run out of Sundays (ITV did not even have to ask), featuring probably the two biggest-rating teams, and a theatrical ending is created before a ball has been kicked. It mattered little that Arsenal's prospects of winning at Anfield by the requisite two goals were generally dismissed as beyond serious consideration. What mattered was the ten million rating figure to round off a season fraught with tension and mounting concern about television's evil influence. When Arsenal scored an improbable second goal in the second minute of injury time (in front of a television audience that by this time had climbed to nearly 12 million), £44 million must have seemed a bargain basement price. It had, it seemed, ended happily after all.

Not quite. No sooner had the drunken revelry around Highbury subsided than another damaging row erupted. This time it was the fixture list for the 1989/90 season, which had emerged from the Football

League's computer in the normal way. Unfortunately, the computer had not been programmed to delay key matches until after televising had started in October, and was sufficiently insensitive to pair off Manchester United and Arsenal on the opening Saturday. ITV reacted as one might expect for a company with a £44 million investment: it sent a solicitor's letter to the League suggesting that, in the absence of any co-operation over such a fundamental issue, it might be withholding its next instalment. Insults were traded with increasing acrimony, with ITV adamant that it could not abdicate all interest when such large sums were at stake and the League equally adamant that it could not reorganise its fixtures list to suit television. In the end, both sides prevailed. In return for allowing the League a fig-leaf of respectability – retention of the 1989/90 fixtures as produced by computer – ITV were granted consultation rights for the final two seasons of the contract.

For some observers, this was the final straw; for others, it reawakened or confirmed the niggling fears which had pervaded soccer all season. One question reverberated around sports pages and no doubt many club boardrooms: who is in control? As the 1989/90 season got under way, controversies continued. With the 1989 climax fresh in everyone's minds, ITV asked for the Arsenal *v* Liverpool match scheduled for 24 February to be moved to later in the season, since it clashed with another televised match. The fears of those concerned for the integrity of the game have not been allayed. 'It has become common,' said David Lacey in the *Guardian*, 'for ITV spokespersons to announce changes in the dates of matches in proprietorial terms. . . . English football is now handcuffed to television and nobody can doubt which of the two is under arrest.' Given the financial interests of top clubs, there can be no retreat from existing levels of financial reward. As American professional sport has discovered, competitive television is a much more copper-bottomed source of spiralling revenue than gate receipts, and needs to be milked. As long as ITV is desperate for live football, it will pay the inflationary cost and expect to call the tune. Football is only just beginning to learn the consequences, and more than one commentator agonised about the Football League selling its soul. 'Now,' said Colin Gibson in the *Daily Telegraph*, 'they are discovering what it is like to be controlled by the devil.'

In all the breast-beating and prophecies of doom, one possible silver lining may have been overlooked. During the heyday of *Match of the Day*, when television soccer was at its peak, one or two lone voices were warning against the dangers of packages of soccer highlights which ignored those long uneventful passages of play from which live spectators

141

had no escape. A generation of youngsters, claimed one or two concerned old-timers, was being raised to expect a game of action, excitement and goals without the correspondingly quiet periods so characteristic of many soccer games. These youngsters will be increasingly less likely to pay the requisite entrance fee when they discover that all but the most exceptional soccer matches can include considerable periods of inaction.

We will never know whether these lone voices had any justification. We certainly do know that live attendances declined dramatically throughout the 1970s and 1980s, showing some recovery only in 1987. Could it be that, as recorded highlights are eclipsed by live coverage as the norm for televised football, tolerance thresholds to those dull passages of play are being raised again? It is conceivable, though an untestable hypothesis, that the televising of soccer matches in their unexpurgated entirety will contribute to a resurgence of interest in the game as spectators return to more realistic expectations of live matches. Needless to say, if television is simultaneously creating an unprecedented domination by five or ten clubs, increasing attendances are themselves likely to be confined to those more successful clubs. In other words, televising entire matches will not necessarily benefit soccer as a whole; just soccer played by an elite minority.

Britain's winter national game, then, is in the first stages of what will almost certainly become an unrecognisable transformation as a direct result of more competitive television. What of the summer national game? To support the thesis that a rapidly changing television structure inevitably impinges on major sports, similar rumblings should be forthcoming in cricket. But there is a major difference between the two sports. County cricket, the equivalent of League soccer, is of variable quality and is not sufficiently ingrained in the national consciousness to represent an attractive television proposition. At the international level, however, Test Matches would certainly present attractive prospects for commercial channels. Far more than football, Test cricket contains all the right ingredients for successful and profitable conversion to television. First, it is cheap to cover: once cameras and equipment are in place, up to thirty hours of television are available over five days for a cost per hour which would compare favourably with most strands of programming. Second, the pause of 30–60 seconds between overs is ideal for inserting commercials without in any way interrupting the pace or continuity of the game. Thirdly, the audience is ideal for a commercial channel attempting to interest advertisers in buying airtime: upmarket, predominantly male, light viewers who are traditionally the most difficult to reach. For a satellite channel, in particular, that audience would be an enticing prospect. Those are the very viewers likely to prove most obdurate in their viewing habits and least likely to invest in additional technology and new channels.

One major obstacle has, to date, discouraged commercial broadcasters from any interest in Test cricket at home: its inclusion as one of the ten 'listed events' which no channel can buy exclusively. (Test cricket from overseas, as Sky has demonstrated, is generally covered by anyone prepared to pay for it.) As long as the BBC has guaranteed access to cricket, no commercial channel can hope to overcome the twin disadvantages of entrenched viewing habits (the BBC has always been *the* cricket channel) and complete absence of commercial breaks. For an audience raised on leisurely, uninterrupted coverage, only one course will persuade them to shift their viewing loyalty: exclusive rights being granted elsewhere. As the government prepares to abolish the listed events provision, it is highly likely that both ITV and new satellite channels will be preparing their strategy for wrenching away the BBC's fifty-year-old domination. To understand how valuable cricket can be for television, and what the potential effect may be on the game, it is unnecessary to speculate. Cricket and competitive television have existed together for many years on the other side of the world and provide a very cautionary tale for British viewers.

If cricket is important to British sports fans, it can sometimes represent a matter of life and death for Australians. For years, it was customary practice for the Australian Cricket Board (ACB) to award non-exclusive television rights for Test Matches to the non-commercial, government-funded Australian Broadcasting Commission (ABC). Although this practice was not enshrined in law, as with the UK's listed events, it was a matter of tradition adhered to by the ACB – not least since ABC was the only genuinely national broadcaster which could carry the national sport to all sectors of the population throughout a vast continent. These rights were sold for comparatively small sums: for the three seasons from 1976 to 1979, ABC paid less than A$70,000 per season.

Australian television is as fiercely competitive as American television, although organised slightly differently. Competitive commercial stations are located only in Sydney, Melbourne, Brisbane, Adelaide and Perth. In each city three commercial franchises are available. Before recent relaxation of ownership restrictions, no individual or company could have a controlling interest in more than two commercial stations. Although theoretically these rules were designed to restrict the growth of powerful commercial networks, in practice three competing groups arose as a result of owning franchises in the particularly lucrative metropolitan

143

cities of Melbourne and Sydney, which between them account for around 47% of Australia's population. These three groups, Rupert Murdoch's Channel Ten, Kerry Packer's Channel Nine and the Fairfax Group's Channel Seven, entered into programming arrangements with other channels which produced three *de facto* commercial networks. As in the United States, competition for commercial revenue was vigorous and commercial opportunities were sought after and exploited.

As long as the non-commercial ABC had rights to cricket no commercial channel could compete effectively, even though non-exclusive rights were on offer. ABC had an established reputation, and viewers had become accustomed to televised cricket without commercial interruptions. Bill Bonney, the late Australian academic, recorded how Channel Seven decided to take up the commercial option on rights for televising the 1977 Centenary Test Match and was outrated 2 to 1 by ABC. Despite more extensive coverage with more cameras, despite more resources and determined on-screen promotion, most viewers would not be dislodged from their traditional cricket resting-place. Packer's Channel Nine were acutely aware both of the value of cricket to commercial television and of the importance of *exclusive* coverage to allow full commercial exploitation. In 1976, they offered the Australian Cricket Board a staggering A$500,000 a year for exclusive television rights. When the Board stuck by their non-exclusive commitment to ABC (for a fraction of the Channel Nine fee) and offered Packer only commercial rights, he rejected them. In competition with ABC, cricket on commercial television lost its value.

Kerry Packer was not prepared to surrender to this outdated sense of public service. Since he was not allowed to buy exclusive access to Test cricket, he contrived instead to buy himself exclusive access to Test players. By the middle of 1977, Packer had signed up around thirty-five of the world's top players to play a series of international one-day games for Channel Nine to televise. Their contracts did not exclude players from participating in official matches, but committed them to Packer's World Series Cricket in the event of a clash. When the news broke in May 1977, it created a storm which in the short term devastated world cricket. England's captain and one of the first Packer recruits, Tony Greig, was sacked. A meeting of the International Cricket Conference was convened to find a compromise, and agreed to scheduling arrangements which avoided any clashes between official matches and World Series Cricket. But Packer still wanted exclusive television rights to official matches, and was refused. Talks collapsed, and Packer determined to take his thirty-five players – including a substantial number of the Australian Test team – into an unofficial but profitable wilderness.

144

Night cricket: the first World Series floodlit match, at Melbourne in December 1977. (Photograph courtesy of the Hulton-Deutsch Collection)

From November 1977, Packer introduced some novel elements into international cricket which were entirely dictated by his television interests and made a mockery of the traditional game. There were now fifty players in the Packer 'circus', enough for a three-way Australia/West Indies/The World series of 'Super Tests' and one-day matches. Timing was changed to coincide with a peak-time television audience. Games were played at night under floodlights. A white ball was introduced for better night-time visibility. Traditional cricket 'whites' were replaced by coloured uniforms bearing a striking resemblance to pyjamas, but providing a very resplendent picture on colour TV. Restrictions on fielding positions were introduced in limited over games to discourage defensive play and increase the scoring rate.

Packer's determination to establish World Series Cricket in opposition to the official game took him to extraordinary lengths. Apart from inventing new rules, dress styles and match times, he was forced to create cricket pitches. Established grounds were already in use, and anyway were not especially willing to accommodate him. It was therefore necessary to make artificial cricket pitches in artificial environments, dig a hole in the middle of a rented park, and transport this freshly created turf to its new home. It was a vastly expensive business, not helped by the low attendance figures at matches and the slow take-up by advertisers for television airtime. Bill Bonney estimated that in his first two years of World Series Cricket Packer lost around A$6 million. As always intended, however, it was a wise long-term investment which ultimately had nothing to do with creating a new game. Australia's official team suffered an entirely predictable collapse, having lost most of its established players, and the ACB was under pressure to concede those precious exclusive television rights. In April 1979, they caved in: exclusive Australian television rights for Test Matches were sold to Channel Nine for three years in the first instance. Packer sold his television interests in 1987 for a huge profit, some of which no doubt derived from the exclusive hold on Test cricket which Channel Nine continues to enjoy. It was a historic and successful coup which for two years split the world of international cricket and rendered Australian cricket virtually comatose. It was not television alone which created this paralysis; it was competitive commercial channels whose owners perceived cricket as simply a unique vehicle for conveying large numbers of upmarket viewers to advertisers. For Channel Nine, cricket was never a sport; it was a priceless commodity.

While the game reverted to its more sensible incarnation – played during the day, with a red ball, by men wearing whites – there was a more permanent legacy. Packer's intervention established not only the popularity but also the profitability of one-day games. These matches contained all the ingredients which cricket lacked for the less traditional follower: played over one day instead of five, with each side restricted to the same number of overs; upwards of 400 runs in a day instead of the average 200–250 for a Test Match; guaranteed wickets, where Test cricket can sometimes provide only a few; and most important of all, a virtually guaranteed dramatic finish where most Test Matches end in anti-climactic draws. While Test cricket continued in front of half-empty stands, the one-day game packed them in – both live at the ground and in their armchairs at home. It was perhaps inevitable that one-day games should then become an indispensable part of the international cricket calendar, in some cases preceding, in others interspersed with Test Matches. Test cricket may still represent the connoisseur's ideal, but both players and national teams are increasingly conscious of the financial benefits of the one-day games. In itself, the proliferation of one-day games is unremarkable, even if at least one tour has seen a Test Match scrapped in favour of two one-day games. The problem is the influence on the traditional game.

Opinions differ on whether and to what extent techniques and tactics appropriate only for limited-over matches have started to invade five-day cricket. Some old-timers, brought up on patience, occupation and accumulation at the crease, are horrified by what they see as wanton strokes of aggression when solid, watchful defence is required. They bemoan the increasing rarity of attacking spin bowlers prepared to toss the ball up and tempt batsmen into a rash shot. These are direct manifestations, they say, of batting designed to achieve as many runs as possible in the shortest possible time, and of bowling designed to minimise scoring opportunities but increasingly unconcerned about taking wickets. According to the pessimists, the traditional game's terminal decline is attributable entirely to the proliferation of its one-day progeny. Certainly, there are differences. There are enough amateur statisticians, and enough variations on statistical manipulation, to demonstrate both sides of the case. Sheer instinct, however, as well as observations from some of the game's shrewder practitioners, suggests that the rigours of one-day techniques have made some impact. On the minus side, attacking spin bowlers do seem thin on the ground, and wilder shots seem more frequent. On the plus side, most observers agree that the standard of fielding today is immeasurably better than it was twenty years ago. Overall, cricket has probably not suffered irreparable damage from the Packer intrusion, and perhaps the greatest casualty is the type of coverage now provided for Australian viewers (discussed in Chapter 7). Should commercial television in the UK be allowed Channel Nine's opportunities, it is the effects on translating the game to the screen rather than effects on the game itself that are likely to prove most disruptive.

Cricket and soccer have one feature in common. In their modern versions, both are essentially professional games involving players whose income is earned entirely from either playing the sport or from sponsorship and promotional deals associated with their playing. Like most working people seeking to maximise income from their work, they will gratefully seize on additional sources of revenue which allow them to improve their own and their family's standard of living. Another sport which has experienced considerable television-related tensions in the UK has until recently survived on an almost entirely amateur basis. With the advent of commercial television money, it is rapidly changing.

Athletics was always going to be irresistibly tempting to commercial television: a year-round sport, attractive to male and female viewers, with Britain recently in the forefront of world success. Names like Coe, Ovett, Cram, Tessa Sanderson and Fatima Whitbread would always produce audiences, especially with some promotional hype and carefully orchestrated head-to-head races. When the British Amateur Athletic Board struck its exclusive deal with ITV in 1984, it received an unprecedented financial boost: the £10 million over five years nearly quadrupled its turnover overnight. 1984 annual income of approximately £750,000 was transformed by 1989 into £5 million of which around 90% was derived from television and television-based sponsorship. With sponsorship still increasing, and ITV insisting on a lower rights settlement for the new contract starting in 1990, the balance between the two is shifting rapidly towards sponsorship as the primary source of revenue. Sponsors will only continue their considerable financial investment as long as there is television exposure; to maintain its revenue, British athletics is now heavily dependent on television.

Certainly, there have been positive consequences from this relationship: a substantial cash injection, and more television exposure for a sport which many viewers enjoy watching but would never attend. But there have, too, been less beneficial consequences for the conduct of athletics, which observers have directly attributed to the substantial amount of television money suddenly available to traditionally amateur participants. Until the 1980s, although payments for athletes were not uncommon, it was a messy and unrewarding business: stories abounded of queues in hotel corridors for brown envelopes with expenses money, and haggling over the real cost of air fares and hotel rooms. In an attempt to resolve this slightly grubby procedure, but still wanting to avoid the outright professionalism of golf or tennis and the advent of prize money, the sport legalised cash payments in the form of appearance fees. These 'subventions' are paid into trust funds, which athletes then draw upon for expenses incurred for training and travelling. As a mechanism to circumvent the professional tag, it is a very fine distinction: expenses for full-time athletes will include all living expenses, house, car, trips abroad etc. Pseudo- or closet professionalism is therefore now the norm, despite the studious avoidance of prize money. These arrangements have ensured that, while a façade of amateurism is maintained, many top athletes are professional in all but name and will therefore seek to maximise their income through appearances at top competitions.

Unquestionably, television now has an enormous influence both in raising the appearance fee stakes and in deciding what constitutes a top competition. According to a table published in the *Daily Mail*, international performers like Carl Lewis and Said Aouita can expect £20,000 or more for a single race, while Steve Cram and Sebastian Coe can earn upwards of £10,000. In addition, of course, these athletes will earn considerable sums from endorsement of sports goods and advertisement appearances. Television is prepared to offer these substantial sums to attract the big names for specially designed spectaculars or head-to-head clashes. The arrival of big money has meant unparalleled living standards for the top athletes (although the vast majority are still unpaid amateurs). Television's interest has, unfortunately, created a new set of considerations and a new set of ethics for athletics meetings which have little to do with sporting ideals. A vivid example occurred at the British Kodak National Championships on 13 August 1989.

For weeks, one race had dominated the headlines. For the first time on a British track, Steve Ovett and Sebastian Coe were to meet in the 1500 metres. After their Olympic (and Olympian) battles, their record-breaking runs and their more recent struggles for fitness, the race was heralded as one of the great television sporting events of the year. In the event, Coe overcame a mid-race collision to win his first AAA 1500 metres title, while Ovett came in a disastrous ninth. Television may have been the catalyst for this event being staged, but it was also instrumental in its destruction. For what defeated Steve Ovett was not lack of training, fitness or ability but a bitter row which preceded the race and which left him in tears during a live post-match interview. It was a strange row, symptomatic of new priorities within athletics. Ovett had learnt that an appearance fee which he had been promised before the race was not being offered to Coe. As an honourable competitor, he was distressed about the blatant inequality of offering cash incentives to one half of a paired attraction but not the other. Event organisers insisted that no payments had been offered; Ovett insisted that they had, and threatened to withdraw unless Coe was similarly treated; and ITV were worried. During a pre-race meeting, at which ITV had no reason to be present given the nature of the dispute, they made their own pitch: that the race had been heavily promoted on the basis of Ovett's long-standing rivalry with Coe, and that withdrawal would be particularly embarrassing since he was employed as an ITV commentator. Clearly affected by the dispute, but persuaded in particular by those who said he would be 'crucified' by the media if he failed to appear, Ovett ran. It was an unedifying episode. Television cameras caught the drama, from an uninspired race to the dramatic post-match allegations. But those same television cameras were ultimately the instigator, the reason why stakes had been raised to unprecedented levels, why the price of withdrawal on a matter of principle was too high. A five-man inquiry was set up to investigate whether money had indeed been offered, but the problem goes substantially deeper than a single allegation about unequal payments.

There are wide-ranging issues affecting the future of athletics which many top-level competitors would like to see examined. To what extent is television now dictating both scheduling and participants in athletics meetings? And is the predominance of track events at the expense of field events due to the latter's less telegenic qualities and therefore less interest for television viewers? If either consequence is even partly true, the effect is to elevate marginal television viewers into a position of influence on the sport which cannot ultimately be in its own best interests. From the top of the athletics tree to the bottom, competitors and administrators are aware of the dangers and are keen to arrest this growing wave of influence. Ovett himself expressed a desire for the AAA investigation to cover all the issues surrounding the sport's promotion. As John Rodda wrote in the *Guardian*: 'These are the questions which would make any campaigner popular among club athletes – and treasurers – throughout Britain.'

There is a widespread feeling that the root of the problem is not the growth of television's power, but the steady erosion of ideals of amateur sporting participation. That somehow, when the rewards of success are transformed into the wholly material, the spirit of the game is changed. Whether for better or worse is a matter for subjective judgment, but it becomes increasingly difficult to find examples of major sports retaining an amateur status at every level. Perhaps the archetypal example, and the last bastion of amateurism in UK sports, is Rugby Union.

Writing in the *Observer*, Mick Cleary quoted the captain of New Zealand's 1987 victorious World Cup rugby side, David Kirk: 'The attainment of a sporting goal involves a much purer sensation when money is not present, because the drive to succeed has come entirely from within. It has not been prompted by artificial concerns such as money.' The English Rugby Football Union has set its face firmly against any kind of payments for players, believing that even the slightest concession could open the commercial floodgates. As a result of long-standing contracts with the BBC to televise the Five-Nations championship, and the ensuing sponsorship deals, it can plough substantial sums of money back into the game. When the contract was being renegotiated in 1988, the RFU made known its dissatisfaction with the BBC's existing coverage; but this had as much to do with the commitment of time and resources for televising club matches as with the amount of money on offer. Given the perceived decline of Rugby Union as a school sport, the RFU is conscious of television's power to attract participants, and wishes to promote club as well as international rugby. Its attitude to television is reminiscent of those amateur minority sports seeking both the promotional and sponsorship advantages of TV cameras for the greater advancement of their sport. To date, it has nothing to do with increasing the standard of living of a few high-ranking players.

How long a major sport can continue to resist the blandishments of lucrative commercial contracts is a matter of conjecture. In many areas, Rugby Union has traditionally been dominated by the middle classes, able and willing to support themselves financially and working in environments accustomed to or tolerant of absences for training and touring. Those in a less fortunate position find it increasingly difficult to justify mounting expenses with no offer of financial help from a governing body growing increasingly cash-rich. One result is the loss of high-class Rugby Union players, like Jonathon Davies of Wales, to the professional Rugby League circuit on lucratiiive contracts which prove irresistible to those with high earning capacity. Television will be making still larger sums of money available to Rugby Union, especially with the new-found interest of commercial channels attracted to the upmarket audience profile. As more players surrender to the lure of a highly paid Rugby League contract, pressures will mount to allow a measure of flexibility and adopt some kind of halfway house. A repeat of the athletics saga is a strong possibility.

While those who spectate, either from the stands or their armchairs, may decry the downfall of amateurism, is it fair to blame participants for wanting to capitalise on their skill, training and dedication? There is, after all, nothing to prevent those of us who wish to indulge our sporting whims from continuing to do so as a means of leisure and enjoyment. In our professional lives we will all attempt to secure for ourselves an adequate income. Why should those who pursue their sporting preferences to the highest levels not also be entitled to exploit new-found sources of income to their material betterment?

One reason, of course, is that the sport can itself become so distorted as to affect adversely the game played by millions for pure enjoyment. Squash is the archetypal leisure success story of the 80s, growing remarkably from an exclusive game played by just a few thousand to one of the most popular participant sports in the UK. But squash does not translate well on to television. Even with transparent walls to allow good all-round access to cameras, the ball is difficult to follow and rallies will frequently end in inconclusive net calls. It is difficult to achieve different camera angles, and the speed of the game makes analysis of shots and explanation of tactics difficult to sustain. When televised, it will rarely achieve ratings of more than 2–3 million, and as currently played cannot therefore tap into the television coffers. For the handful of professional players, this is a barrier to a potentially vast increase in earnings. Having been told that its current form is unsuitable for television, they have attempted to institute experimental changes in the rules which would make the game more telegenic: a different scoring system to ensure more decisive rallies, and a lower tin on the front wall, with an artificial maximum of fifteen strokes per rally being imposed. Players have apparently been advised that, if successful, their version of the game could dramatically increase the value of the game to television. New players seeking to take up the game would, inevitably, take their cue from the television version which would gradually insinuate itself into all the amateur squash clubs and leisure centres, thereby permanently transforming the game at every level. It might be more entertaining to watch through a camera; but as a participant game, it would clearly lose some of its excitement and pleasure.

At a much more intangible level than material damage to the essence of a sport, there are perhaps good reasons for regretting the demise of amateur principles. We come back to the very basis of sporting competition, the enjoyment and fulfilment derived from both the act of participation and the act of spectating. Are competitions which patently lack material inducements, and are therefore indulged in purely for their own sake, somehow more worthy or honourable than competitions which bestow upon successful competitors cash as well as kudos? It is difficult to look at the increasingly desperate lengths to which competitors are prepared to go in the pursuit of victory, and avoid the feeling that somehow the virtue of athletic endeavour, of striving for athletic and competitive achievement, has been irrevocably tarnished by the arrival of huge sums of money. The drug scandals of Seoul, widely acknowledged to be the tip of a well established iceberg, were not the result of athletes concerned with competing to the best of their natural ability. They were not about gold medals, but about the enormous leap in the marketable value of a successful athlete. Winning, in other words, becomes a means to an end rather than an end in itself.

This is why the English Rugby Football Union is so determined to keep money out of rugby. And this is why Bernard Levin, writing a characteristically trenchant column in *The Times*, was hoping that the 1990 Commonwealth Games in Auckland would – as had been threatened – be cancelled. He anticipated what he hoped, with just a tinge of hyperbolic licence, would be 'the end of *all* international sporting events, productive as they now are of nothing but cheating, drug-taking, money-grabbing, racial hatred, political statements, advertising, hooliganism, envy, litter, selfishness, vanity, corruption, intolerance, defamation, sexual excess, robbery, drunkenness and, from time to time, murder'. This litany of disgrace did not even, apparently, include spectators who would require 'an entirely new thesaurus of condemnation'. In one respect, at least, Levin was right: the Auckland Games, while in most respects a model of sporting decorum, did provide another drug scandal.

Every generation will seek to blame the evils of its time on whatever modern fad or invention is perceived as changing contemporary social behaviour and social mores. Without accepting Levin's apocalyptic view of the advent of professionalism, it is impossible to ignore the increasing tensions within sports which seem to be focused on the payment of large sums of money. As long as sports spectating was limited to the number of people who could fill a stadium and be charged an affordable price at the gate, the rewards available to competitors would always be limited. But television has created a massive source of additional revenue. Numbers of spectators are now almost unlimited, their value as an audience rising in direct relationship with the number of channels competing to deliver the largest segment of the population to advertisers. With the arrival in Britain for the first time of channels competing for advertising revenue, audiences will become an increasingly priceless commodity. The sporting event which delivers that audience will therefore carry a proportionately escalating price tag. And the money suddenly made available to competitors will create a spiral of expectations from which there is no return. Once in hock to television there is no release – only more demands. American commercial television has signposted the road, and it would be a brave crystal-ball gazer who could predict that British sport will be better equipped to resist competitive television's voracious demands.

7

FROM STADIUM TO SCREEN

On a dull Friday morning in August 1986, England's cricketers were playing New Zealand in the third and last Test Match of an unremarkable series. It would have been an unremarkable day, had it not been for a long-awaited come-back by the country's cricketing legend of the 1980s. Ian Botham had been suspended for several matches following confessions about drug-taking in his youth, but had been reinstated at the earliest opportunity. His tally of Test Match wickets had been agonisingly stuck during his suspension on 354, just one behind Dennis Lillee's all-time record. Finally, much to the relief of an expectant Oval ground, he was given his opportunity as first-change seam bowler. To the first ball of Botham's resumed Test career, a very ordinary outswinger outside off-stump, a mesmerised Bruce Edgar waved his bat; after some tantalising juggling the catch was finally taken by Graham Gooch at first slip. It was a typically theatrical entrance from England's self-appointed miracle worker. Just eleven balls later, he had become the world's leading wicket-taker of all time.

Watching from the long on boundary, it was almost impossible to see or hear that fateful snick as tentative bat made contact with ball, let alone appreciate the full drama of a catch only made at the third attempt. In the electric atmosphere that surrounded and followed that incident, however, its details were immaterial. For the live spectator, it was sufficient to have been there, to have experienced in person the tension and unbelievable drama of one of the world's great sporting moments. By contrast, cricket followers watching live through a television screen could see in vivid detail the ball delivered, the edged catch, the juggle, and the jubilation that followed. But not even the most ardent cricket fans sitting in their living rooms could have captured the momentary pause of wonderment shared by nearly ten thousand people, followed by the roar of recognition and acclamation.

Much the same point was made by David Lacey, reflecting in the *Guardian* on television's influence on live soccer attendances. Lacey recalled that final sensational moment of the 1988/9 season: 'Domestic football will continue to thrive on the fans' desire to witness great events first-hand. Nobody fortunate enough to be at Anfield when Michael Thomas won the League championship for Arsenal with that assured flick of a shot past Grobbelaar will forget the barely perceptible pause of disbelief before pandemonium broke loose. This was not captured by TV.' In other words, sport on the screen is an entirely different experience compared to sport at the stadium: not simply because a living-room is a different environment from stands and terraces, but because the event being witnessed goes through several processing stages before reaching the screen. The live spectator will be free to move, to turn the head, to absorb many different pictures, sounds and smells simultaneously, and will therefore stay master of his or her own interpretation. The television viewer is a prisoner to sports producers, directors and commentators, with sound and vision subject both to technological and to resource limitations as well as to the whims of one person in a control van. In front of the screen, the event is interpreted on our behalf, in ways which can make the living-room experience utterly different from live experience of the identical event. Viewers may lose out on uniquely atmospheric moments of sporting drama, but their perspective is enhanced in other ways which can make live spectating a humdrum experience.

This process of translation can be divided into three essential components, each of which serves to transform the television experience: the visual, the aural, and the contextual. In each case, the technology employed, the techniques applied in deploying that technology, the decisions made by producers, and the personnel who translate the game through commentary, are instrumental in creating an armchair version of sporting events. Of this trilogy, the visual component is ostensibly the most important. In a very short space of time, blurred and fuzzy black-and-white images of competitors bearing a striking resemblance to Martians at play have been transformed into crystal-clear colour close-ups, and a significantly more enhanced view for the armchair viewer than for the live spectator. In an even shorter space of time, the pictures transmitted from one or two unwieldy cameras mounted in fixed positions have given way to several flexible and lightweight cameras transmitting from a variety of angles, again providing considerably more mobility of vision to the TV viewer compared with the fixed perspective of live spectators. But the most revolutionary development for armchair fans is undoubtedly the most recent: the facility for seeing again, almost instantly and in slow-motion, any dramatic incident or passage of play.

It is the increasingly sophisticated use of replay technology which has transformed not just the visual element of watching sport on television but the very essence of watching sport live. Nearly every live spectator has experienced that uncomfortable but involuntary sensation, having watched a try or goal being scored or a wicket fall, of waiting for the action replay. The world of sports spectating is being turned upside down as, increasingly, stadium spectating mimics the living-room rather than the reverse. As portable television sets become more affordable and more portable, their appearance at matches being televised live – along with picnic baskets, scorecards and six-packs – becomes less remarkable. And for those who have not yet succumbed to the lure of microchip technology, the stadium itself is increasingly prepared to adopt the role of surrogate television producer; it cannot be long before the large electronic screens which dominate sports grounds in America and Australia, showing instant replays of dramatic moments, become an indispensable feature of British stadia. In Australia, instant replays are not the only diversion. Reporting in the *Guardian* from Sydney on the Bicentennial Test Match between Australia and England in 1988, Terry Coleman was bemused by the extra-curricular visual entertainment: 'Don't come here and expect to see leisurely cricket. There is no breathless hush, and no peace between overs either. The huge Mitsubishi TV screen on the scoreboard, when it isn't showing instant replays from five angles of poor Taylor being hit on the head, is advertising Coca Cola or the Action Bank, or else showing flashing, almost subliminal, images of bails flying, cars racing, horses racing, and girls surfing – anything rather than that there should ever be an empty moment.'

Through increased number and flexibility of cameras, the sharpness and variety of the pictures they deliver, and advanced replay techniques, dramatic and entertaining pictures can be delivered from almost any sport, thereby enhancing the television experience – at the visual level – several degrees above the live spectating experience. Whether it is cameras behind the left ear of Formula One racing drivers, cameras inside goals, cameras driven in jeeps alongside race-tracks or in helicopters over boat races, on motorbikes following Tour de France cyclists, or underwater to capture the turning techniques of champion swimmers, technology has made a vast array of sports come alive on television. What cameras can never do, of course, is legislate for drama that is not there. If a match is tedious, or a race is all but won with fifteen laps still to go, even the most sophisticated camerawork cannot instil drama where none exists. Many sports, perhaps the majority of sporting

Extra-curricular diversions: the electronic scoreboard at Lord's, here stating the obvious

events, are not intrinsically or even consistently exciting. This is acceptable to paying spectators who, given their interest in the sport and as long as periods of inaction are tolerably short and irregular, will be able to appreciate skill and subtlety without always being unduly concerned about outcome. It is less acceptable to the majority of television viewers who have not made a special effort to attend, may have only rudimentary knowledge of the game and marginal interest in it, and have at the touch of a button easy access to other kinds of television diversion. In these circumstances, forms of enhancement other than the visual play an important role.

Enter the commentator. There are other peripheral sounds which require transmission to complement the visual, such as cheering crowds, ball hitting goal-post, or anguished cry of a beaten competitor. But none of these can compare with that element of television sport which places the viewer in a substantially more privileged position than the spectator: a voice-over accompaniment to describe, explain, analyse and predict the event as well as to contribute an occasional dramatic embellishment which the game itself may lack.

While it may seem absurd on first reading, there is both anecdotal and scientific evidence that for television viewers it is the commentary which defines their level of involvement and enjoyment rather than the pictures of what is actually happening. To some extent, this will be the result of television viewers being less committed to the sport and therefore more dependent on background explanation for appreciating the contest. But even the most committed fans, regular spectators who will also become glued to the screen if attendance is impossible, find enjoyment enhanced by the accompanying commentary. Most television sports now have their established 'voices' whose characteristic tones are almost irreplaceably wedded to their respective games. No Rugby Union Five-Nations championship has really begun until Bill Maclaren's unmistakeable accent announces the first kick-off. A Formula One Grand Prix would be unthinkable without the breathless declamations of Murray Walker. Wimbledon without Dan Maskell, Test Match cricket without Richie Benaud, boxing title fights without Harry Carpenter would for most viewers lose a great deal of their television impact. Even ITV's exclusive contract for domestic competitions has scarcely dulled David Coleman's reputation as the television 'voice of athletics'.

These are reputations forged over a considerable time-span. When Peter Dimmock decided in 1964 to produce a book to help viewers understand this relatively new phenomenon of televised sports, he brought together contributions from fourteen specialist commentators. Twenty-five years later, it is astonishing that half the contributors are still commentating on the same sports (David Coleman, Harry Carpenter, Alan Weeks, Dan Maskell, Bill Maclaren; Brian Johnston has moved to radio, Murray Walker from motorcycles to cars). No commentator can hope to appeal universally to every member of the audience, and many a furious pub row has featured trenchant disagreement among committed sports fans about the relative merits of a particular practitioner. The balance between description and embellishment is a difficult one which has prompted much discussion over the years inside broadcasting organisations as well as pubs.

Those twenty-five-year-old reflections on a difficult and much-criticised art shed some fascinating light on the underlying traditions of British television commentary, particularly as developed by and practised within the BBC. They illustrate graphically what might be termed the great commentator's dilemma: to speak or not to speak? Neither the nature of the dilemma nor its means of resolution seems to have changed much since Harry Carpenter wrote in 1964: 'The cardinal sin of TV commentary is to talk unnecessarily.' Analysis and biographical details

158

can be provided for the non-expert, but essentially 'don't talk unless you can add to the pictures'. Much the same advice was advanced by the legendary Henry Longhurst, who counselled against the declamatory style in golf commentary, adding that he generally worked on the assumption that he was talking to a couple of people – which, he suggested modestly though not prophetically, 'I suppose is the size of the average television audience'.

Even in slow-paced sports like cricket, the sparing approach was recommended. The Brian Johnston of today is not renowned for his restraint in the radio commentary box, but twenty-five years ago he advised that 'the commentator's remarks drop like stones on a still pond' when accompanying pictures. Like all the others, he was aware of the mixture of experts and non-experts in the audience and summed up the insoluble problem: 'The [television] cricket commentator must try to strike the happy medium knowing that there is really no such thing.' Dorian Williams believed that this medium shifted gradually as the sport became better known through television exposure. As showjumping became increasingly popular and widely watched during the 1950s, it 'became necessary for the commentator to contribute increasingly less in the way of description, biography, detail'.

In general, the principles followed by modern British commentators do not appear markedly different. While visual techniques are exploited for maximum impact, the underlying philosophy of commentary is still to allow the game/race/event to speak for itself while adding dramatic or descriptive embellishments where appropriate. It would be invidious (and inaccurate) to generalise this philosophy across every type and class of sport, and there are natural differences in the approach of, say, Richie Benaud to cricket and Murray Walker to motor-racing. Such differences, however, are more attributable to the nature, pace and dramatic content of individual sports, rather than characteristic of entirely different approaches. Generally speaking, a certain body of knowledge is assumed. Critics have attacked such an approach as too elitist, failing to cater for less committed viewers who comprise a large proportion of the television audience. Unfavourable comparisons are made with American television sports where commentary is exploited as an integral part of a sports programme. Channel 4, in particular, has tried to overcome such criticism by developing a more distinctive and instructive approach, entirely appropriate for introducing untried sports to an unfamiliar audience. In one novel experiment during the 1989 British ice-skating championships, it even asked viewers to vote between a sequence with commentary and a following sequence with no commentary (results

159

David Coleman, now British television's 'voice of athletics', here in a previous incarnation as presenter of the BBC's long-running sports magazine, *Grandstand*

showed a slight majority of the 4,500 votes cast in favour of the silent version). But even for Channel 4, the dilemma remains: to risk annoying committed fans through explanations of basic rules and tactics? Or to risk alienating those with a passing interest who might become seduced by a more accessible commentary?

Cricket coverage provides an excellent illustration. Two victorious Test captains, one Australian and one English, alongside two articulate ex-professionals, interpret, analyse and speculate with the insight that only seasoned internationals can bring to a game. Commentary is sparing and expert; slow-motion replays are used to demonstrate the grandeur of an immaculate cover drive or the lightning athleticism of a reflex slip catch; frequent pauses, particularly during quiet phases, allow committed viewers to appreciate the mellowness and subtlety of the game. For the connoisseur who simply cannot make it to the game, it is a privileged vantage point greatly enhanced by the inside knowledge of ex-professionals. For the uninitiated, however, the jargon almost certainly confuses. Given cricket's live hours of transmission, spanning late morning and afternoon schedules, audiences are more than usually dominated by young children, pensioners and housewives quite likely to be bamboozled by talk of googlies and chinamen. Switching on to hear that an

160

England spinner is bowling with a slip and two short legs, less familiar viewers could be forgiven for assuming they were party to some obscure ritual. There is little in the way of explanation or illustration to help non-specialists understand technical terms, tactics or simple regulations.

While some criticism may therefore be justified, it frequently confuses two very different characteristics of a more pro-active television commentary: the instructive and the entertaining. Both feature greater involvement than is generally forthcoming from British commentators. But while the descriptive or instructive mode might foster a greater sense of awareness and comprehension among viewers, the dramatic mode often serves only to lift humdrum action into melodramatic excitement. When genuine drama exists, this can constitute a vital element of the programme's impact and enjoyment. But when real drama is lacking, there can be an irresistible temptation to invent it, to contrive a fierce competitive battle in order to heighten artificially a programme's entertainment value.

There is sound programming logic for succumbing to such temptation. Experimental evidence from the United States demonstrates how effective contrived drama in television sports commentary can be. In 1977, Cominsky, Bryant and Zillman reported the results of a panel study which tested reactions to two recorded segments of an ice hockey match: one with a fairly normal sequence of play and containing little in the way of violent action or incidents (described as normal-action); and one more overtly violent, containing hard body-checks and other manifestations of roughness (rough-action). Accompanying commentary, however, was inverted: on the normal-action video, announcers apparently gave the impression of an aggressive contest 'with the action threatening to turn into fisticuffs at any minute', even though action was actually at a premium. On the rough-action segment, by contrast, announcers 'let the action carry the game with little commentary of a dramatic sort'.

Experimental groups of students watched these segments in order to test two specific effects of commentary on viewers: first, to what extent can a dramatic commentary influence perceptions of a sporting event, independently of the actual nature of the game? Second, to what extent – if any – do altered perceptions evoke greater enjoyment of the programme? Results were unequivocal. The normal-action sequence with racier commentary was perceived as rougher, more dramatic and more violent than the rough sequence with more even-handed commentary. More significant is the apparent effect on enjoyment: commentary which *stressed* roughness of play created more entertainment and more enjoyment of the sporting event than a sequence of play which was in fact considerably rougher. With some understatement, the authors conclude: 'It appears that, to a high degree, the sportscaster is a critical contributor to the spectator's appreciation of televised sports.' Appreciation in this sense is, of course, related strictly to the *dramatic* content of commentary. One could reasonably suggest that similar segments of play with variations in the *descriptive* content of commentary would be unlikely to make an equivalent impact. As we shall see, these findings have considerable implications for the 'aural' factor in television sports when competition among channels for fragmenting audiences intensifies.

A very different criticism has sometimes been levelled at television commentary, with equal vigour and probably equal justification on both sides of the Atlantic. It is a dilemma whose resolution is likely to become ever more impossible as competitive television increases: the apparent inability of television commentators in all sports to bring a reasonably detached, and where necessary critical, perspective to their observations. What Klatell and Marcus describe as 'the woeful state of television sports journalism' in the United States is equally applicable to Britain. Some might argue that television commentary can scarcely be called a branch of journalism, and that the commentators' professional skill lies in conveying the atmosphere of an occasion and such information as is necessary to enhance viewers' enjoyment of the game. It is not their job to criticise, or to look for 'stories' outside the immediate scope of the game. But that is a narrow, bland and dispiriting view of television's responsibility and ability to inform huge numbers of sports followers on a range of issues concerning the funding, structure, organisation and politics of individual sports. At the most mundane level, this might involve a critical evaluation of team selections in the same way that print journalists will volunteer their (often colourful) opinion on the quality of selection. Such editorialising need not be quite as trenchant as the less restrained tabloid journalists, who will not shrink from questioning a manager's sanity. Without resorting to insults, however, it should be possible for television commentators to pass on some of their knowledge and expertise in the form of opinions in similar vein to those of their print colleagues.

At a much more serious level are the often contentious issues which characterise all sports, whether amateur or professional. It may be the announcement of a Rugby Union team to tour South Africa, or an unofficial England cricket team to do likewise. It may be the wrangling, conniving and manoeuvring that goes into preparing bids to host the Olympic Games or soccer's World Cup tournament. It may be the boardroom diplomacy which is increasingly coming to dominate League football in the light of vastly improved revenue opportunities. All these issues receive a proper airing in the sporting pages of most newspapers, but are generally ignored by television's practitioners. The result can be more than an unfortunate lacuna in the sports viewer's appreciation of wider issues surrounding a particular event; it can lead to a distorted portrayal of action on the screen.

A particularly vivid example was described by Frank Keating in the *Guardian*, introduced by the fairly uncompromising assertion that 'The numbing complacency of English soccer's bureaucratic freemasonry of nonentities continues to boggle the mind.' His quarrel was, first, with the FA Chief Executive's apparently unconcerned reaction to yet another bout of English soccer hooliganism in Stockholm following a World Cup qualifying match with Sweden. This had consisted essentially of large numbers of skinhead youths, tattooed and draped in Union Jack flags, terrifying the locals with a variety of fascist rituals – including Sieg Heil salutes. But it was not just football's officialdom which bore the brunt of Keating's anger. Part of the problem, he believed, was the complacency of English commentators in translating such overt acts of racism to the screen: 'It goes without saying that the BBC commentator at the match, John Motson, offers not even a passing reference to the banked Nazi salutes of the Brits; nor the slightest hint of explanation about the evil, droning hum of boos and jeers plainly heard each time one of England's two black players, John Barnes or Des Walker, comes anywhere near the ball.' Keating cites another example from an England–Holland encounter, when Ruud Gullit was 'humiliatingly and unhesitatingly taunted for a full ninety minutes, yet Motson laughed it off with "And Gullit getting good-natured barracking from the crowd".' And he describes how Barry Davies, during John Barnes' first derby match for Liverpool against Everton, glossed over Everton chants of 'Niggerpool, Niggerpool, Niggerpool'. No one is suggesting that it is a commentator's duty to draw attention to the problems of racism endemic in some British sports. There is, however, surely a duty to convey to the armchair viewer the full flavour of the stadium and events surrounding the match, even if some of those details are distinctly unsavoury. The problem, of course, is that such an approach carries with it a serious potential danger: it will on occasion show the sport in a rather unpleasant light.

It is at this point that the somewhat ambiguous position of the sports commentator becomes clearer. For their role as interpreter is seen as more closely resembling an ambassador and enthusiastic follower of the sport than an objective reporter. It is so defined not by the nature of their job, which should lend itself easily to offering background material and opinions, but by the nature of their employer. Television channels are not in the business of casting aspersions on events for which they have forked out large sums of money, or on bodies or individuals with whom the next round of delicate negotiations will be held. Television companies, and by extension their own screen representatives, will want to maintain good relations with the owners of a product much coveted by other channels. It is for precisely this reason that most American contracts provide for selection of commentators to be either shared by or entirely handed over to the rights holder. For the vast amounts of money they lay out, rights holders want to ensure that their property is not about to be devalued by a reporter with aspirations to investigative journalism. They want their sport glorified.

This, of course, is a consideration which sits rather comfortably with television's own concerns. It is quite conceivable, though a proposition never likely to be tested, that a genuinely detached commentator who was prepared to address difficult or controversial issues would have a depressing effect on ratings. Given that it is the marginal viewers who represent the difference between ratings success and failure, and given that these viewers are unlikely to be mesmerised by some internal sporting conflict or controversy, television channels will want to minimise this audience wastage by emphasising the positive, the alluring and the entertaining. This has been just as true in the public service-dominated competition of British broadcasting as it has been a part of America's private sector competitive system.

There is no suggestion of deliberate collaboration between television executives and television commentators to keep rights holders happy at all costs. In many cases, a sympathetic treatment is as much an automatic display of loyalty from ex-professionals or those steeped in the history and traditions of their particular sport. Since few of them are trained journalists, certain tenets of good journalistic practice are likely to fall victim to partisan enthusiasm. It is nevertheless an unfortunate characteristic of television sports on both sides of the Atlantic that, with a few exceptions, we have to rely on news, current affairs and the occasional dedicated sports journalism programme to bring us some of the reality behind the glossy image.

In addition to visual and aural factors – both concerned specifically with translation from stadium to screen during the course of an event – there is the contextual element of translation. Televised sporting events do not happen in a vacuum, with coverage beginning at kick-off and ending at the final whistle. They are trailed well in advance; they are

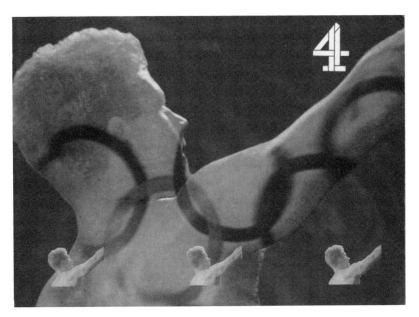

Packaging: Channel 4's promotional logo for the 1988 Olympics

introduced with sophisticated graphics, with evocative and sometimes powerful music, with carefully chosen and seductively filmed images. In other words, there is a complex and highly professional packaging operation designed to convey a more attractive and seductive context for the event.

Packaging can take several forms. Introductory music and graphics can be exploited to establish a certain mood, or anticipation of an exciting programme to come. For occasional spectacular events, like football's World Cup, the Olympics or the Commonwealth Games, significant efforts are made to establish a seductive atmosphere by tailoring presentational techniques to the particular event. The choice of Vangelis' title score for *Chariots of Fire* to accompany BBC coverage of the Los Angeles Olympics, for example, was a carefully planned decision to capitalise on the mood and story of a successful film. For weekly regulars, different sports programmes tend to establish familiar introductory music which provide continuity despite a change in the graphics or action sequences from year to year. Although concrete evidence is impossible, powerful and dramatic opening sequences will almost certainly attract marginal viewers to certain sports. The BBC's *Ski Sunday* is an example of the art at its most spectacular.

165

As well as presentational techniques, the programme's format will be important. It might include a panel of experts, whose own standing and level of professional success will play some part in attracting viewers. There may be action sequences from equivalent events in previous seasons or from the same competition in the current season. There may be footage featuring the more high-profile participants. There may be interviews, recorded in advance as scene-setting exercises to allow viewers some insight into the characters about to take the sporting stage. There will generally be some explanation about the relative importance of the event, its significance to participating teams or individuals, and some informed (and occasionally ignorant) speculation about the result. Long-running competitions, like snooker or the Olympics, will often introduce a humorous element, linking together footage of sporting (or production) blunders during the course of the competition.

Most intangible, but arguably most effective as a means of crowd-pulling, is the advance trailing and promotion of a televised sporting event. All channels, in their efforts to maximise audience size, will publicise forthcoming programmes. Sports programmes offer a particular challenge, since the most committed followers would be expected to

Publicity: boxer Frank Bruno before his WBA Heavyweight championship fight against Tim Witherspoon, with ITV boxing commentator Reg Gutteridge

166

tune in anyway. For promotional purposes, marginal viewers are therefore more than just an uncertain proportion of the total viewing audience: they become the targets of advance publicity designed to make the sporting programme as irresistible as possible. For this reason, there is a constant temptation to exaggerate certain elements of a contest which might serve to heighten tension and evoke a dramatic atmosphere.

Experimental evidence demonstrates how this might work to enhance audience appreciation of a sports programme. A study by the same American research team set out to assess the effects of highlighting relationships between opposing players or teams. Its aim was, first, to discover whether this contextual information influenced enjoyment of the contest; and second, whether any such influence was affected by a hostile as opposed to a friendly relationship between combatants. A hundred students watched an identical segment from a routine tennis match, dubbed with three separate commentaries: one third heard that the opponents were good friends; one third heard that they were bitter enemies; and in the third group, no mention of the relationship was made. Again, results were unequivocal. First, there was no difference in the appreciation scores of those who listened to the 'friendship' and 'neutral' commentaries. Second, those who heard the 'animosity' version scored higher on every measure of appreciation: they found the clip more interesting, exciting and enjoyable. Third, while viewers' own interest in sport did not impinge on scores, the commentary effect was more marked among irregular sports watchers – those marginal viewers whom channels are always keen to lure away from the competition. The authors acknowledge this study as evidence of the powerful instrument in the hands of sports commentators to manipulate spectators' attitudes to sporting events. In fact, the lesson goes beyond commentary. Animosity can be exploited as part of a channel's build-up and promotional efforts in order to contrive an atmosphere of suspense and drama, if necessary highlighting one or two individuals as the focus of attention.

There is, therefore, considerable scope in both the commentary and the contextual elements of sports television to employ certain techniques which owe less to the honest and accurate portrayal of sporting events and more to the tenets of mass audience programming. For those who would advocate entertainment as the ultimate goal of television, there is no argument about ethics or propriety or fairness: if the viewers prefer it, the channels should deliver. Those more concerned about preserving integrity within the translation of sports to the screen find themselves increasingly embattled – not necessarily because sports themselves are insensitive to the issue, but because certain television environments

167

dictate acceptable practice. It is entirely logical that commercially competitive television systems should be a little less rigorous about faithful representation, and a little more cavalier about dramatic embellishment.

Even a cursory examination of both American and Australian sports presentation illustrates the point. The thrust of American commentary and sports packaging is to enthral and captivate, to raise suspense and anticipation for the most uninspiring of contests. Joan Chandler, bemused by the practice of English cricket commentators who have 'no compulsion to fill in the action gaps', sees this as the legitimate desire of American producers to entertain and cajole their audience into watching. She interprets this as part of the natural process of creating a spectacle, which simply elaborates on the dramatic without destroying the essence. Benjamin Rader disagrees: the jazzed-up commentary, he says, ultimately reduces the big-league event to an everyday experience. The plethora of so-called 'big plays' is in fact routine, eventually serving only to reduce any sense of audience wonderment at real athletic achievement.

Certainly, some British commentary might benefit from greater concentration on information and explanation to assist the sporting ignorant. But Rader must be justified in his concern that the heavy emphasis on drama will eventually lower viewers' appreciation and enjoyment threshold. A goal or a penalty in soccer is a genuinely dramatic moment, around which whole matches revolve. If other elements of a match are constantly hyped because the genuine drama is too occasional to enrapture the marginal viewer, the proper focal point becomes gradually eroded and cheapened. It is the long-term consequences of this shift of emphasis which inflict greatest damage. With the advent of easy editing facilities, it becomes increasingly possible to recreate events in the interests of greater suspense and enjoyment. Klatell and Marcus offer the perfect example: a champion skier who draws the first run, shatters the world record and is patently unbeatable, thereby rendering the rest of the competition redundant in deciding first place. Committed ski buffs will continue to watch for the pleasure of seeing a difficult craft brilliantly executed; but in the absence of competition, the average viewer will be tempted to switch over. Faced with the prospect of declining audiences, it is a small step for an edited version simply to reverse the order and dub a new commentary (stressing, no doubt, how this champion skier has overcome terminal illness, a stormy divorce, and the recent death of both parents to make his heroic comeback at this competition). Would anyone notice? And would they care? After all, if ABC News can portray a staged re-enactment as real-life current affairs in the interests of audience retention, what price accuracy in portraying sporting events?

Australian television allows a glimpse of how a very British sport can find itself transformed by commercial television. When Packer's Channel Nine finally wrenched Test cricket away from the Australian Broadcasting Corporation, it invested considerable financial and technical resources into coverage. Some of the innovations – aerial shots of field placing, split-screen comparisons of respective bowling actions – were valuable contributions to a better view and a better understanding of the game. Others were little more than cheap production tricks which had little to do with explaining a complex game to the uninformed. At the most banal level came the introduction of a ridiculous cartoon duck, which tearfully accompanied a batsman dismissed for nought (in cricket terminology a 'duck') to the pavilion. It would stretch the bounds of criticism to suggest that this ill-conceived celluloid bird might interfere with appreciation of the game; but its contribution to revealing some of the game's inscrutability was precisely zero. Cartoon characters in live sports have only one objective – to keep those with minimum interest in the game (particularly children) tuned in. This is, no doubt, precisely why Sky imported the same triviality into their coverage of the 1990 West Indies–England Test series (along with the excitable commentary of Tony Greig). More serious is the well-established production technique known as 'honey shots'. These involve voyeuristic cameramen seeking out, then focusing on, attractive and preferably scantily clad young women in the stands. Such pictures are targeted deliberately at male viewers who may not be riveted by the game but whose expectations of seeing more pretty girls may dissuade them from switching over.

Finally, there is the aggressive nationalism which precedes and accompanies every Test series. No matter who the opposition or what the relationship between the teams, forthcoming matches are elevated through promotional trailers to battles of such apocalyptic proportions that unsuspecting viewers may feel the country's very survival depends on victory. It is a charade of tension-building which contributes nothing to an appreciation of the game. And it is not just the televised game's natural viewers who suffer through such contrived vulgarisation, but the game itself. The warfare terminology initiated by television is echoed by newspapers, carried into the grounds, and eventually creates an atmosphere of poisonous hostility which panders to populist jingoism and undermines the integrity of the sport.

At the root of these contrived images of nationalism and hostility is the same commercial drive which moulded ABC's approach to the Los Angeles Olympics. Other countries may have been dismayed and offended by the interminable parade of American athletes on screen

169

(whether successes or failures), but ABC needed to recoup its enormous outlay by ensuring maximum possible audiences. Just as most Australians are not dedicated cricket watchers, so most Americans are not dedicated to international athletics. Commercial television channels, competing against popular programming schedules on other channels, need to tantalise the waverers and cajole them into staying with a sport they are not naturally inclined to watch. Any device, any gimmick, any trick is justified if it ensnares a few more viewers and raises the rating score. The sports fan, of course, is stuck – the victim of a passion for a particular sport and exclusive television deals which allow no respite from cheap trivialisation.

In an ideal world, a competitive television environment would strike the perfect balance: gradually introducing non-enthusiasts to the intricacies and pleasures of new and diverse sports, using all the sophisticated wizardry of new technology while remaining faithful to the innate spirit of the game. All the evidence suggests that, while the visual spectacle is enhanced by innovative camerawork, both commentary and contextual artifice is increasingly exploited to entice the uncommitted. In the end, the overwhelming considerations are those which transcend any concern for honest reproduction. As competitive commercial television in Britain begins to raise the stakes for televised sport, it remains to be seen whether British sports are prepared to heed these lessons from abroad.

8

POTTING THE GOLD – THE SPONSORSHIP GAME

When England's cricketers first ventured to Australia, in the winter of 1861/2, they were not obliged to subsidise their own travelling and accommodation expenses: the tour was sponsored by a little known Australian company called Spiers and Pond. Despite the absence of television and radio, it is reported that this obscure catering company emerged £11,000 richer from their sporting investment. This story, taken from the Howell Report (described in more detail below), illustrates two significant facts about sponsorship. First, that it predated by nearly a hundred years the widespread introduction of television cameras at sporting events; and second, that since its inception sponsorship has been less a form of corporate altruism than a strictly commercial transaction with strategic marketing objectives. Those marketing objectives have changed little, although the means of assessing their success or failure have become considerably more sophisticated.

While sponsorship's commercial exploitation may not have changed, the exposure opportunities available to sponsors have certainly been transformed by the advent of television. Neither print nor radio affords the same scope for promoting corporate logos and brand names by skilful use of visually appealing images, and it was therefore always certain that cameras would bring with them a greater awareness of the commercial potential of sponsorship. There has developed an uneasy but indispensable relationship between the trilogy of sport, television and sponsorship which has produced some difficult, occasionally farcical, moments. On balance, an equilibrium has probably been maintained; but there are signs that in some events, and some sports, there are hostages to sporting fortune which have yet to be clearly understood.

In Britain, there have been two specific conditions which accelerated sponsorship's momentum as a serious means of channelling money into sport. First, as we have seen, sponsorship provides the only route to promoting commercial messages on two non-commercial channels which have historically dominated British television sports coverage. Despite careful construction of constraints and limitations, explained in more detail below, the BBC cannot (and almost certainly would not wish to) exclude some element of corporate promotion filtering through to viewers. Advertisers have long regarded the BBC's more upmarket audiences with undisguised envy, and have recently sought every opportunity to persuade the government of the commercial wisdom of forcing it to accept advertising. Thwarted finally (and against all expectations) by a government-appointed inquiry in 1986, companies will continue to exploit the only indirect means of transmitting commercial messages through the BBC.

The second spur to sponsorship was a prohibition some years ago, in line with most Western countries, on the television advertising of cigarettes and tobacco. Tobacco companies, excluded from direct access to the most powerful medium of persuasion, have spent substantial sums of money on sports sponsorship to ensure that their names, if not their messages, are constantly paraded before the public gaze. The association of tobacco companies with major sporting events requiring long hours of coverage – Embassy with snooker, John Player and Benson and Hedges with cricket, State Express with golf – has created almost impossible dilemmas for broadcasters aware of the dangers of tobacco advertising but mindful also of their responsibility to sports which rely on substantial income from these companies. To understand properly the tensions which simmer below, and occasionally burst through, the surface of this three-way relationship, we need to examine the three different perspectives: the sports bodies, the sponsors, and the broadcasters. While individual sporting events will find them harmoniously wedded in apparently common purpose, their objectives and aspirations will often have little in common. Sometimes, the result is an enjoyable and exciting sporting occasion. Sometimes, the consequences can be disastrous for television, for sponsors, or for the particular sport.

The competitor's tale
Precisely how much sport earns from sponsorship is almost impossible to calculate, since deals are essentially private transactions between individuals, teams or governing bodies and private companies. Most of the major agreements are publicised, and the amounts specified. Many smaller deals, especially at regional or local level, are too insignificant to

be reported or notified to the press. When the Howell Report assembled figures for Britain in 1983, it found discrepancies between two sets of figures produced in 1981 – one setting the total at £40 million, the other at £60 million if back-up costs were included. By 1985, the Institute of Sports Sponsorship was estimating expenditure at £140 million per annum. More recently, estimates for 1988 from Sportscan put the total value of sports sponsorship at nearly £200 million, provided by over 2,000 companies. It is generally believed that every sponsorship pound is supported by a pound of PR or advertising, thereby doubling the money made available for the promotion of sport and sporting events. Particularly when set against the money distributed by the Sports Council, sport's income from and dependence on sponsorship is substantial.

In 1981, the Central Council of Physical Recreation (CCPR) was sufficiently concerned about the complex relationship and increasing dependence to initiate an independent inquiry. Its Chairman was Denis Howell, Minister of Sport under the last Labour administration and a former Chairman of the CCPR. This committee published the results of its extensive inquiry, including seventy-three recommendations, at the end of 1983. One of its main concerns was the disposition of both sports governing bodies and competitors towards sponsorship and the increasing inconsistencies in how different sports approached this relationship.

At the forefront of these concerns was the issue of maintaining jurisdiction over the sport, and the point at which there might develop an unhealthy dependence on individual benefactors. 'The Committee finds that while some governing bodies do maintain total control of their sponsorships, others are content to accept financial assistance without supervising the effects of sponsorship upon their sports.' With masterly understatement, but with advice aimed squarely at the more inexperienced authorities who may have lacked understanding of commercial objectives, the report continued: 'We would hope that governing bodies could so arrange their financial affairs that the loss of any one source of income would not lead to the near collapse of the sport in its current form.' Sensible words, which many governing bodies have since acknowledged and acted upon. Unfortunately, as subsequent case studies demonstrated, wise accounting had less to do with the nature or number of sponsors than with the extent or existence of television coverage. Some sponsors, as we shall see, would certainly make a commercial decision to withdraw after a set period – and sometimes at disastrously short notice – regardless of decisions made by television producers. Others, however, would enter into deals on the understanding, either implicit or explicit,

173

that their beneficence would be paraded via recognisable corporate logos on television screens throughout the land. No cameras, no deal. And any number of reserve or potential deals would be unlikely to preserve an event if its survival was dependent entirely on sponsorship.

Amateur boxing's plight was featured in the report as an example of a sport suffering through insufficient attention from broadcasters. The secretary of the Amateur Boxing Association recalled wistfully the nineteen tournaments which used to be televised, reduced now to three programmes a year. Professional boxing still maintains a major presence, but declining television interest in the 45,000 registered amateurs has a depressing impact on income in a sport which, as the ABA secretary said, 'caters mainly for the lower income groups'. Such income could have socially beneficial consequences. 'We have a community role to play as we are a disciplined sport, and yet we provide an opportunity to let youngsters let off steam in a controlled way. We are a boom sport but are not able to attract "boom" money.' With greater television exposure, of course, it would be difficult to keep potential investors out of the ring.

A classic example of how television's desertion can leave sports bodies in dire straits through no fault of their own is canoeing. When the British Canoeing Union (BCU) hosted the 1981 World Championships, Sun Life of Canada agreed to put up £25,000 contingent on television coverage. The BCU could not negotiate a firm contract with the BBC, and Sun Life withdrew leaving 'severe financial embarrassment' in its wake. Only the generosity of other small sponsors, BCU members, and an increased Sports Council grant prevented a large deficit. Under these circumstances, the frustration of governing bodies with broadcasters is understandable even if not entirely justifiable.

Some sports, of course, are in a position to negotiate deals without guaranteed television coverage because of the profile of participants. The Howell Report's example of fencing's twenty-five-year-old deal with Martini and Rossi is entirely due to the more upmarket nature of the sport and its players. Not only is this sort of deal atypical, but it is inevitably worth less to the sponsor than a deal which potentially affords access to many millions of television viewers. While every governing body would accept the wise counsel offered by Howell, none would be prepared to refuse substantial sums of money even when dependent on circumstances and decisions entirely beyond their control. Once television commitments have been made, of course, the problem of finding and replacing sponsors virtually disappears. The Howell Report was full of praise for the sterling efforts of the Amateur Swimming Association in building a portfolio of sponsors at every level of the sport, but had to acknowledge that the ASA's contract with the BBC 'gives a special bargaining power in the field of sponsorship negotiations'.

Some of the individual competitors interviewed testified to the value of sponsorship money, both in amateur events as the competition became increasingly intense and for professionals who sought an income more in keeping with the requisite investment of time and effort. For anyone who still believes that pure amateurism remains an attainable ideal in the modern sporting world, the Howell Report is required reading. Even before citing the evidence of competitors, it states unequivocally: 'We were left in no doubt that the burden of surviving and succeeding in sport and also in life cannot be treated idealistically as in the past.' Then came the testimony, perhaps the most stirring from ex-Olympic competitor turned professional cyclist, Mick Bennett: 'In my first Olympics in 1972 I had to buy my own jersey and tyres. I lost my job in order to train to represent my country. I paid for my own bike, and only asked for 8p a mile car allowance yet I was refused.' Without any subsidy, his team had to live and train together on the continent. They subsequently won a Commonwealth gold, World Championship silver and two Olympic bronze medals. Top equestrian competitor Lucinda Green echoed the sentiment that total dedication was required by modern competitors, which in turn entailed sacrificing any normal means of earning a living: 'Sport today is all-consuming if you want to reach the top. There is no means of earning a living in a normal way and at the end of, say, ten or fifteen years, competitors can go out of sport without money or a job.'

Having cited evidence, the Howell Report essentially accepted the end of amateurism. 'The demands on competitors, on their pockets and on their time has increased to an extent where they are becoming full-time performers. The slide from pure amateurism to semi- or full professionalism ... may not be idealistically acceptable but its inevitability was a view often expressed to us.' Once this 'slide from amateurism' has been accepted as a *fait accompli*, competitors' concern that they should be free to exploit every means of self-marketing at their disposal becomes more understandable. Whether sponsorship logos on clothes should be permissible then becomes less of a sports policy issue and more of a broadcasting policy issue. Personal sponsorships are a lucrative source of additional income, whether the money goes into 'trust funds' for amateur athletes or direct to bank accounts for professional cricketers. Competitors want to be free but responsible. According to Steve Ovett, 'The principle of wearing logos is OK but it needs to be responsible. We do not want to be walking billboards.' But cricket's Bob Willis pointed out areas of potential conflict in characteristic style: 'We feel hard done by. I have

175

to whiten out the flashes on my boots, yet, at Wimbledon, people on court are done up like Christmas trees.'

Without clothes advertising, almost entirely a function of the wide-spread presence of television cameras, there would be less money. With less money, we are told, amateur athletes could not compete at the highest levels. And yet before that first Wimbledon telecast in 1937, amateur athletics seemed to have survived quite happily since the begin-ning of the century. It is a fascinating but unanswerable question: is it simply a gradual process of evolution that athletes are fitter and races run faster than fifty years ago? And that this evolution happens to coincide with the widespread availability of athletic and sporting spectacles via the broadcast media? Or have the vast sums of money unlocked by those same broadcast media, in particular the money available to individuals via personal endorsements, allowed athletes to devote time to training which their predecessors had to devote to earning a living? It is a sobering, and certainly not implausible, thought that television has been indirectly responsible for creating those very pinnacles of sporting achievement which it then conveys to its armchair spectators.

The sponsor's tale

In straightforward business terms, sponsorship of sport offers a uniquely cost-effective means of promoting both corporate and brand images – if televised. The Howell Report illustrates television's potential worth by reference to the two most televised sports: snooker and cricket.

Through its own research, the Howell Committee identified the scale of broadcast mentions of the sponsors during the 1983 Embassy World Professional Snooker Championships. Although verbal mentions are theoretically limited to two per programme, it identified considerably more during longer transmissions. Even within the statutory limits, however, a total of 78 programmes over seventeen days afforded a minimum of 156 verbal credits. In addition, *Radio Times* gave twenty-eight mentions to Embassy over the last ten days of the tournament 'with as many as three on a single page'. And there were regular written captions giving latest positions, which always featured the Embassy name. The Committee was told that, for their £135,000 sponsorship fee or £1,400 per hour of television, Embassy's airtime was cheap at the price. Given an uncompromisingly hostile environment for tobacco advertising, Embassy must have been delighted with their investment. Although they were sufficiently sensitive not to publicise any research, it can be assumed that awareness of the Embassy name will have risen during and immediately after the world championship fortnight.

Tangible evidence of the impact of widely televised sponsorship comes from Cornhill's experience with cricket. In 1977, when the insurance company first cemented its relationship with the Test and County Cricket Board, only 2% of the public could spontaneously mention Cornhill when asked to name insurance companies. During 1981, Cornhill assessed its television exposure and emerged with fairly positive evidence: 140 hours of coverage, during one of the most exciting Ashes series in cricket history, provided them with 7,459 banner sightings on screen; 234 verbal mentions on screen; 1,784 references on radio; 659 mentions in the national press, and 2,448 in the provincial press. Not to mention a staggering 21 million calls to British Telecom's score service in 1980. It is therefore understandable that by 1982 their 'spontaneous awareness' score among the general public should have leapt from 2% to 17%. Cornhill's return on their substantial investment was more than the 250 tickets they received per match to oil the wheels of customer liaison. According to Howell, the company itself estimated that 'an increased annual premium income of £10 million could be attributed to the sponsorship'. It is a vivid example of how a little known, and relatively small, financial institution can enhance both reputation and profits through association with both an appropriate sport and a high level of television coverage.

It is also a vivid reminder of why companies decide to undertake sports sponsorship, and their criteria for success or failure, continuation or termination. It is quite clear from conversations with corporate sponsors that decisions have, with very few exceptions, nothing to do with philanthropy and everything to do with hard-headed commercial interests. Some companies certainly display a sense of obligation and responsibility within a relationship once it is forged. But without exception, and hardly surprisingly, sponsors must put the interests of their company before the interests of particular sports when selecting their sponsorship portfolios. Those with a corporate message to convey must examine a wide range of criteria before committing themselves to substantial investment. For many years, selection of appropriate sports was neither considered nor scientific, often dependent on a personal contact at the chairman's level, an instinctive hunch, or a marketing director's individual passion. As marketing techniques have become more sophisticated, and measurement instruments have been refined, sponsorship decisions have been subjected to increasingly rigorous analysis to ensure they remain consistent with overall marketing strategy.

When escalating costs forced Prudential Assurance to withdraw from cricket some seven years ago, there remained what their sponsorship

Cornhill Insurance have sponsored Test cricket in England since 1977

director calls 'a culture of sponsoring things'. There was, however, no consolidated strategy on how the budget could be most efficiently spent. A coherent rationale emerged, based on the need for an activity of widespread interest and participation, fairly upmarket, and played to a relatively late age. Tennis was the obvious candidate, and Prudential proceeded to sink their money into LTA Championships, on all surfaces and at all levels. This process of matching corporate requirements to sponsorship initiatives has certainly not attained the level of a science. Some relationships are clearly inappropriate. Insurance companies might be unwise to have their names associated with dangerous activities like skydiving; brewers are strongly discouraged from sponsoring motor-car or motorcycle racing. But in choosing between the remaining possibilities, instinct plays an important part. As one sponsor put it: 'You get a feel for its profile and its audience and its ambience, and therefore you come to a range of feelings about whether sponsorship is going to be appropriate. . . . It's a very imprecise art.'

Thus when Courage decided to regenerate its name, there was no systematic enquiry which concluded that rugby was the perfect vehicle. More limited involvement in the North and a restructuring of English club rugby coincided with a new Courage initiative; the result was the Courage Club Championship involving nearly 1,200 clubs in the 110 leagues. A similar process cemented a relationship between Courage's new brand Miller Lite and the IAC athletics meeting at Crystal Palace (originally under the auspices of Coca-Cola). In both cases, arrangements that were ultimately of great mutual benefit evolved gradually rather than being scientifically designed to suit. These considerations are particularly important given that companies can receive twenty or thirty approaches a week, whether it be 14-year-olds determined to conquer Everest or PR companies under contract to individual clients. Only a tiny proportion will ever come to fruition.

Just as judgments about initiating sponsorship deals tend to be subjective, so assessment of their effectiveness and usefulness to the sponsor, and decisions about withdrawal, are equally prone to instinct. 'No one really knows how sponsorship works,' said one marketing man, and therefore measurement tools are at best approximations. Unlike an advertising campaign, whose specific message and impact is measurable and subject to pre- and post-testing, sponsorship's impact is less tangible and difficult to differentiate from back-up PR and advertising efforts. Consumer awareness is the traditional yardstick of success, a criterion which has served Cornhill well and is exploited by most effect-conscious strategists. But, as another sponsor commented, 'All these things are little imprecise measures that you've put together and then you add a fairly large dose of judgment; I don't believe anybody does it any better than that.'

Lack of objective evaluation measures therefore makes the decision to withdraw sponsorship that much less predictable. It may be that consumer awareness has reached a plateau, and continued investment is therefore deemed surplus to requirements. As the Howell Report commented of an unnamed sponsor whose initial investment was £400,000 but which was then asked to increase its commitment: 'If [the company] enjoyed awareness levels in the 90% area, as it did, and the cost of sponsorship moved towards seven figures, then it was contemplating spending significant money for a peripheral gain.' Similarly, brands or

179

corporate names may start to become so indistinguishable from the event that any impact is lost. Gillette's £6,500 deal with the MCC in 1962 pioneered sponsored one-day cricket, which continued from 1963 to 1981. By that time, Gillette had decided it could not justify a higher bid than the £130,000 then on offer. According to Howell, 'Gillette fully appreciated that the very success of the competition which it had initiated meant that its value to sport was now probably more than its own sponsorship could sustain.' But it was equally likely that Gillette had extracted every ounce of benefit from the deal, and that further association would bring very little commercial benefit. For precisely that reason, Courage decided to withdraw its Hofmeister sponsorship of snooker: 'People were no longer thinking what the brand name was in connection with the event; it was tripping off the tongue too lightly.'

It would be unfair to portray corporate sponsors as marketing opportunists seeking to exploit sport only as long as sport provides a decent commercial return. Altruism, certainly, is rarely a motivating force and sometimes sponsors can show themselves in a rather harsh light: 'I have to make a very commercial judgment about what's available and what good it will do us, and when it ceases to be of value I equally have to make a hard-nosed decision and say, "I'm sorry, we're not going to renew our contract." ' The same speaker was both concerned about the future of sports which became over-dependent on particular benefactors, and aware of reciprocal responsibilities. The moving force may be essentially commercial, 'but once the deal is done I think a sensible sponsor feels that he wants to play a part in helping that sport in some ways that are not going to give him direct commercial return.' This might include donations to the Referee Society or assistance for a Disabled Trust or just attending meetings and social functions, all of which will simply establish a presence and help to keep in touch with the concerns of administrators.

At a more abstract level, there were some reservations expressed about current political doctrine and the potential impact of an economic downturn. Given a government which expects and encourages corporations to donate, responsibility is seen as being devolved from the public sector to the private sector. One sponsor questioned whether decisions made on the basis of corporate benefit, where business was essentially dictating which were the healthy sports and which were underfunded, were in the best interests of British sport. 'Business is getting the vote' not just in deciding which sports can flourish but in choosing between sport and, say, charities for AIDS sufferers or the homeless.

More than one sponsor was disturbed by the prospect of a less rosy economy. One made it clear that sponsorship would be the first budget under the axe should company profits start to fall dramatically. Government might push commerce to pick up the tab, but companies are capricious in times of economic hardship. 'I haven't seen too many sports getting into serious trouble,' said another sponsor, 'but I think that's a function of being in relatively prosperous times. In other circumstances it might be very different.' These are ominous words which, nevertheless, are unlikely to be taken to heart until circumstances dictate a more realistic assessment. The essence of sponsorship is that, when times are good, there is an inevitable ratchet effect which regularly raises the ante. Professionals become accustomed to higher incomes, governing bodies become accustomed to being able to stage regular and prestigious events, competitors at all levels assume their championships are inviolable. One company's strategic rethink can be problematic, but at least allows an opportunity to seek benefactors elsewhere; if cash becomes universally tighter, overall opportunities dwindle and some sports will suffer. Almost certainly, it will be those which command the least valuable television airtime.

For underlying most of the major sponsors' strategic thinking was the importance of television cameras at their events. Some minor event sponsorship was justified by the targeted profile of participants. But sponsors are in no doubt that major deals are dominated by television considerations: 'If it's not on television there's no point to it,' was a characteristic comment. This sponsor, in return for a quarter of a million pounds, had a minimum number of peak-time television hours written into the contract, with a promise of rebates if this was not delivered. Even a minimum audience size was specified. When Canon announced its historic £1 million a year sponsorship of the Football League in May 1983, in the midst of unresolved negotiations between broadcasters and the Football League, it was explicit about the conditions: 'We would have to look at the situation again if there were no television.' Ironically, the sticking point for those negotiations was the contentious issue of shirt advertising, contrary to both IBA and BBC codes of practice but desperately sought by football clubs. Arsenal's astonishing half-million pound deal with the Japanese electronics corporation JVC was, no doubt, equally contingent on successful television negotiations. It was neither the first nor the last time that broadcasters were to find themselves at the centre of a storm, amid accusations of inconsistency and rank hypocrisy.

The broadcaster's tale

As the critical point of this eternal triangle, broadcasters are frequently beleaguered: by sports complaining about lack of airtime, by sponsors complaining about lack of consistency, by internal codes of practice designed to ensure that television does not become a corporate plaything, and by the audience who would ideally like their sport without advertisements or sponsorship banners, and for free. It is a high-wire balancing act from which, inevitably, there are falls.

Broadcasters are well aware of their responsibilities both to sports and to the audience. If they became bloody-minded about levels of exposure to commercial messages, sponsors would start to withdraw, sports would suffer, and ultimately audiences would not have television access to events which they enjoy. Jonathon Martin acknowledges that a realistic attitude to sponsorship from the BBC is important because 'some great events just would not happen any more without sponsors'. Most obviously, there is in television audience terms the consistently most popular sporting event of the year, the Grand National – which would not have survived after the Topham family had Seagram not intervened. BBC television's interest in hockey generated sponsorship interest which in turn helped to fund pre-Olympic matches around the world. By contrast, broadcasters are also aware of the exploitative or 'piggy-back' role of some sponsors. This can occur with events which are not in need of financial assistance to ensure their very survival. They are either popular showpieces which a new sponsor wishes to exploit, or created specifically as commercial vehicles in a bid for more television time. Snooker's massive popularity over the last few years has spawned a plethora of sponsored tournaments which, apart from providing a great deal of cheap television time, does no harm to the annual incomes of those on the professional snooker circuit. In such cases, there is neither a contest of great national importance crying out for a corporate saviour nor a grass roots sports industry able to benefit from an injection of corporate cash.

Television's accommodation of sponsorship needs is not of course entirely dictated by selfless recognition of sport's requirements. Not only would certain audience-pulling events not happen without investment by sponsors seeking television exposure, but their presentation and organisation is likely to benefit from increased resources. The result is a more attractive event and therefore a better television programme. Even more significantly, facilitating income to the sport through television exposure serves to reduce the cash demands that sports will make in return for television rights. Throughout the 1970s, the Football League were content with a joint agreement between the BBC and ITV, because they had only just begun to realise the huge financial potential of sponsorship. The more airtime they could fill, the more sponsorship money they could unlock; better still if football appeared on both networks. ITV's unsuccessful dawn coup for exclusive rights in 1979 served only to inflate rights costs to both channels, but by 1983 more was required. At the end of negotiations in March of that year, Football League club chairmen rejected a £2.6 million per annum deal because the TV companies would not give way on shirt advertising which was bound to provide a substantial additional source of revenue.

At a further meeting in April, both BBC and ITV remained adamant that their rules would not allow for shirt advertising. The Howell Report quotes an LWT spokesman, in what sounds like a rather plaintive plea: 'I am sure, in the end, clubs will feel site advertising revenue is just as important to them as revenue for shirt advertising.' Unfortunately, site advertising had in most cases been thoroughly milked, and anyway could not provide the same lucrative source of funds. The chairman of Tottenham was blunt about the counterbalancing of relaxed sponsorship rules and rights fees: 'I am sure the major clubs would not be looking for an increase in the cash from television if shirt advertising could be agreed. This will provide hundreds of thousands of pounds of extra revenue for clubs.' On 15 July, television surrendered. Shirt advertising would be permitted as long as total coverage did not exceed sixteen square inches and the sponsor's name was no higher than two inches. In return, the networks could screen ten League games, and the League Cup Final, live. And the cost? The same £2.6 million which club chairmen had originally refused.

Once shirt advertising was conceded, there was little left for television to offer in the way of sponsorship. League clubs had taken every advantage of the opportunities available, netting annual sponsorship cash of nearly £20 million. As John Bromley put it: 'They sold the shirt advertising; they sold the ground advertising; they had sponsored the ball; they were getting to the point where there was no more sponsoring possible.' Saturation point meant either accepting little prospect of a real increase in income or looking for other sources of revenue. Right on cue, British Satellite Broadcasting entered the frame to force ITV up to unprecedented heights, and almost overnight the focus of Football League revenue switched from sponsorship to television rights. The American model had come to Britain.

While soccer enhances its cash value through the transition from sponsorship to rights fees, most sports are still sponsorship-driven and therefore television-dependent. For that reason, restrictions which broadcasters apply in their coverage, and the consistency with which these restrictions are implemented, are constantly under fire both by sponsors themselves and by the governing bodies whose sports they serve. The Howell Report was emphatic: 'It cannot be doubted that there is a wide diversity of practice amounting to "double standards" . . . no steps appear to have been taken to rectify an anomalous situation which continues to rankle with sports administrators and is a mystery to the general public.' Ostensibly, the rules are relatively simple: the sponsor's name accepted in the event title; a maximum of two banners within sight of main camera positions; two verbal mentions within the programme; a single mention per programme in the *Radio Times* or *TV Times*; and one written credit on captions during programmes. As with every attempt to apply a single rule across all sports, these guidelines defy consistent application simply because sports are not consistent activities. The Howell Report itself demonstrates the intrinsic difficulties of comparing two banners during a snooker tournament, when one camera is permanently trained on a small playing area, with the Boat Race or a golf tournament where a single banner would have only fleeting exposure. In the second case, most major sponsors would find the promotional return for their investment unacceptable.

Ultimately, all but the most uncompromising are agreed that sponsors should not dictate the rules and that broadcasters should be allowed discretion within their guidelines. For the BBC, Jonathon Martin accepts television's responsibility 'to be consistent and fair across the board'. There is a general guiding principle that 'sponsorship should be in the background, literally, and the sport should be in the foreground'. This notion of the broadcaster retaining control is reinforced by the experience of other countries – like Italy and Spain – where ground advertising threatens to dominate the television image. Martin compares the relative tastefulness of the familiar two tiers of advertising around football or cricket grounds with Italy where 'you'll find three/four/five tiers, you'll find some of the advertisements revolve, some of them flash, some of them are luminous'. A Spanish basketball match featured a flashing advertisement over the basket every time a ball went through it, 'the ultimate in a kind of pin-table sport on television'.

Sponsors, by their nature, will always want to extend the boundaries of acceptable exposure to maximise their return. Sports bodies and negotiators will want to expand the corporate coffers and keep their benefactors happy. It is scarcely surprising that there is a simmering battle with broadcasters attempting to prevent, or at least delay, degeneration into

European-style excesses. They are well aware that today's excesses become tomorrow's standard practice and that every concession is a prelude to further pressure to relax restrictions. When the anti-smoking lobby demonstrates angrily against the 'excessive' exposure of tobacco products during snooker, and television producers attempt through some acrobatic camerawork to make the Embassy banner as inconspicuous as possible, there is still every sign that television remains master of its domain and can restrain the commercial drive. But as television becomes more competitive, as sponsors continue to push for airtime concessions, as the revenue needs of sports continue to escalate, and as the political pressure for 'deregulation' of broadcasting increases, producers will find it increasingly hard to adhere to standards which are by their very nature inconsistent. Sponsors will secure more victories, whatever the sensibilities of television viewers. And that illuminated basketball sign may not be so far away.

Where next?
American experience gives little clue about whether and how fast sponsored events might come to dominate the television sport agenda. As we have seen, titanic struggles for television rights between networks have ensured that sports and stadia are bought 'clean' to avoid contamination of the network's much prized advertising airtime. Compared to Europe, therefore, where strong non-commercial channels have encouraged sports to find more indirect means of generating revenue, there has been no developed tradition of event or team sponsorship. For British viewers accustomed to America's apparent lust for commercialism, it is strange to watch American footballers in uniforms which promote nothing more than their own name and number.

Over the last few years, however, the balance has been shifting dramatically. American sports ratings have been alarmingly in decline to the point where networks have been regretting one or two massive settlements and threatening dramatic cuts in future. Just as British soccer negotiators started to look to higher television fees when sponsorship funds had been exhausted, so their American equivalents are seeking a reverse process: encouraging interest from sponsors to compensate for a threatened shortfall from television. It is a more difficult task, since networks take into account the 'free' publicity they are offering when negotiating rights fees. In addition, there is a price for any accreditation provided by the network. CBS has demanded that, if a company is part of the event title and expects on-screen credits to that effect, it must buy a minimum of 25% of the available airtime.

A perfect example of this evolving relationship is the case of the El Paso Sun Bowl. Klatell and Marcus relate how this historic tournament, the oldest independent college bowl in the United States, provided the focal point for a festival involving thousands of southerners. CBS was the long-standing network rights holder, but had seen ratings decline in the three years from 1983 to 1985, decided to drop it and thereby condemned it to penniless extinction. Its imminent demise was, apparently, a 'matter of civic bereavement' which was averted only by the valiant intervention of the John Hancock Insurance Company. Hailed as the corporate saviour, the company's purchase of the rights fee ensured both the event's survival and continued television exposure by CBS, whose rights payment had now been underwritten by Hancock. In return, the company was allowed to paint its own logo on the artificial surface, over a 20-yard centre area which would have featured in most of the televised game. Even then, CBS was not prepared to acknowledge the 'John Hancock Sun Bowl' until it undertook to purchase at least 25% of available airtime.

Boxing, too, is subject to the same trend. When Marvin Hagler fought Sugar Ray Leonard for the world middleweight title in 1987, Budweiser paid $750,000 for its logo on the ring mat and ring posts. This is one area in which British television has yet to emulate American sponsorship trends. When Alan Minter fought Tony Sibson for the European championship in autumn 1981, his boxing shorts sported the name 'Daf Trucks' down both sides and across the middle. It was such a blatant contravention of BBC rules (agreed in consultation with the British Boxing Board of Control) that television coverage was halted. It is not simply a matter of principle in such cases. As American experience demonstrates, television expects some financial compensation for making itself commercially available; if competitors attempt to secure clandestine sponsorship deals, the channel is unable to calculate the most appropriate rights fee and leaves itself vulnerable to exploitation with no return for itself.

All the signs are that the two countries, from very different starting points, are gradually converging in their practice. As American networks seek to expand the potential revenue base and share costs with sponsors, so British sports, having successfully established lucrative sponsorship deals, are seeking to exploit emerging competition among television channels. In the midst of this evolutionary (and to some extent revolutionary) process is the growth of one sponsorship area of increasing concern to both sports administrators and television executives: the rise of international sports marketing organisations seeking to represent all interests in the equation and therefore subject to potentially damaging conflicts of interest.

It is entirely logical that sponsors who have invested a great deal of money in a particular sport or event will want to maximise their impact and presence. Apart from ensuring that television coverage is exploited to its optimum, there are press journalists to chivvy when the sponsor's name is regrettably omitted from tournament titles in the following day's newspaper reports; there are hospitality facilities to arrange, along with ample supplies of good food and drink; there are guest lists to compile; there are advance press and PR arrangements; there are peripheral promotional gimmicks like balloons, T-shirts, pens, plastic replica trophies and autographed hats. There are, in fact, a huge number of promotional details for sporting events which are beyond the effective capacity of most companies because they do not constitute a mainstream PR effort. For which reason, it is entirely sensible to contract such activities to specialist agencies with substantial experience in the field who, for a modest fee, will undertake all the necessary administrative and promotional work.

Similarly, it is entirely logical that governing bodies of individual sports, especially those with little experience of negotiating sponsorship deals, should seek the expert advice and help of an agency in securing – for a modest fee – the most profitable and most appropriate sponsor. And it is equally logical that individual competitors, be they athletes, golf players, snooker or tennis professionals, will not necessarily have the time or business acumen to maximise their earning potential. Many will therefore devolve responsibility to a full-time agent who can generally be relied upon to guarantee their clients' appearance at prestigious and high-earning events – for a modest fee.

There is growing concern that recipients of these modest fees (which aggregate to a distinctly less modest total) tend to be identical organis-ations who will happily represent sponsor, governing body, individual competitor and even television channels simultaneously; and that the conflicts of interest involved are potentially horrendous. Can the same organisation work in the best interests of a sports body client when it is simultaneously seeking to maximise the revenue of individuals within that sport and to promote the interests of sponsors in that sport? In a chapter headed 'Ethical Considerations' the Howell Report expressed its concern about the growing trend in such international marketing groups. The growth of an increasingly complex web of relationships was un-wittingly highlighted when the report quoted the blunt marketing philosophy of Horst Dassler, late president of Adidas: 'We exist to sell boots and shirts and wherever the action is, we need to be there.' At roughly the same time, Horst Dassler had combined with the Japanese advertising agency Dentsu to create International Sports and Leisure Marketing (ISL). And it was ISL in whom the International Olympic Committee invested the marketing rights for both Summer and Winter Games in 1988.

Equally well known is the International Management Group (IMG), founded by Mark McCormack, and its subsidiary Trans World International (TWI). A Japanese whisky company, Sun Tory, wanted to circumvent domestic television restrictions on whisky commercials; golf was an ideal vehicle, given its wide exposure on Japanese television. IMG arranged the tournament and the television deal, as well as representing the sponsors. As a bonus, McCormack himself provided some of the television commentary. The discomfort felt by some senior administrative figures at what was perceived as excessive involvement was described by Philippe Chatrier, President of the International Tennis Federation, in his evidence to Howell: 'What happens is that sport allows him to find their money via sponsorship – this is the soft option – and then finds he is gradually taking control. The principal weakness of sports bodies is their lack of organisation and their failure to adapt to the modern world in terms of running their sports.'

Although a comment on IMG, and in this case McCormack in particular, it is more generally applicable to all such groups. It is complicated even further by the introduction of satellite sports channels with substantial airtime availability, and therefore equally enthusiastic about the prospect of international organisations with the contacts and expertise to put together attractive tournaments. British Satellite Broadcasting blazed a trail by awarding TBI a lucrative contract (worth £155 million over five years) to supply ten hours of programming a day to its sports channel. Sky appointed TWI to provide coverage of the 1990 Test series from the West Indies; which meant, of course, that TWI also provided highlights packages for the BBC of the same series. It is difficult to see how such arrangements, which might benefit television, sponsors and individual highly paid athletes, can ultimately benefit sport. But with the influx of yet more airtime waiting for yet more television-specific events to be created, it is just as difficult to see the environment changing. It has certainly not improved since Howell issued its explicit statement of concern some five years ago: 'It seems to us most undesirable that an organisation should be able to represent a governing body, sponsors, a significant number of top players, negotiate television, cable and satellite contracts and sell merchandising rights. The situation is pregnant with conflict of interests and cannot carry public confidence.'

All the evidence suggests a continuing and increasingly fraught gestation period. Certainly, sponsorship deals have been a constant and beneficial source of revenue for many sports which in turn have repaid their benefactors as a vehicle for brand or corporate promotion. Television has been the major conduit for such promotional campaigns, although the role of print media (particularly national newspapers) should not be underestimated. To date, television has been responsible for establishing and – with differing levels of consistency – abiding by guidelines. Both independent and BBC television have managed to remain masters of their sports schedules, trying to ensure that audiences remain the main focus of attention rather than sponsors.

With corporations becoming increasingly hard-nosed and rigorous about the commercial return from sponsorship, and with sports searching increasingly for new avenues of revenue to supplement Sports Council grants and to enhance the earning power of professional or semi-professional competitors, pressures on television will continue to grow. As regulation of commercial television in particular is relaxed, limits on verbal mentions, caption credits and written credits in publication lists will seem increasingly incongruous. At the same time, no doubt, the pressure on governing bodies will grow to allow players to take advantage of a relaxed television regime. Individual endorsements by athletes may have seemed inconceivable not long ago, but are now an accepted part of every athletics meeting. Corporate logos on white cricket shirts may seem equally inconceivable now, but ten years hence it is more than possible – the need to augment income from other sources makes it distinctly probable. And if terrestrial television channels are short-sighted enough to emulate the joint BBC/ITV resistance movement of the early 1980s, governing bodies and professional players will not be forced to sit on their hands waiting for these Luddite television executives to repent. They can, if they are prepared to sacrifice a proportion of their potential audience, take their business elsewhere.

9

A SPORTING CHANCE FOR SATELLITE?

On 5 February 1989, Rupert Murdoch's four direct-to-home satellite channels began transmission, sending television pictures into any home in the UK with either a satellite dish or cable connection. On the first day of transmission, it was estimated that the total audience for these channels was not much in excess of 10,000 viewers. From the beginning, it was desperately important to attract viewers to these additional channels by attempting to provide unique material unavailable on other channels. And it was a mere twenty-one days after launch that Sky transmitted live and exclusively a sporting event of considerable national interest which had been prised away from ITV. At 3 o'clock in the morning of 26 February, the only British viewers able to watch Frank Bruno being pulverised by Mike Tyson were those few thousand with access to Sky television.

More than one observer remarked wryly that the long-running battle for exclusive rights between Sky and ITV was a good deal more interesting, and more fairly matched, than the fight itself. It certainly had its quirky elements. ITV believed they had sealed a $2 million deal with Tyson to cover four fights of which the Bruno fight was to be the fourth and – by some margin – the most important. Among other evidence of a binding contract, ITV cited paper napkins from Le Rififi Club in London's West End, on which figures had been agreed between John Bromley and Don King, the American boxing promoter, following a boxing dinner at the Cumberland Hotel. Bruno's agent, however, negotiated separate contracts with Sky, for live coverage, and with the BBC, for highlights. ITV were comprehensively beaten. After a week's court hearing, the judge decreed that not only did ITV's contract have no force in law, but that King did not even have authority to act on Tyson's behalf. Costs amounted to £400,000, believed to be double what the BBC had paid for the rights to highlights. And as a final insult, the 14.3 million viewers which the BBC attracted at 3 o'clock the following afternoon was one of the largest sporting audiences of the decade.

Once again, it was boxing which from the beginning was prepared to exploit new television opportunities to increase earning potential. Perhaps it is because a professional boxing contest has only two individuals to agree to terms and because, as Nick Higham wrote in the *Listener*, 'It's a world in which deals really are done in smoke-filled rooms by men with dinner jackets and large cigars.' Perhaps it is because a square ring inside a stadium does not require any huge investment of competence or resources to provide adequate coverage, and is therefore ripe for the untested technical standards of new cable and satellite companies. Or perhaps it is simply that boxing's larger-than-life characters and promoters are just a little more willing to step into television's unknown. Whatever the reasons, the cycle had come full circle. Just as Jack Solomons had tried to exploit the BBC's interest by raising the stakes in the late 1940s, so Bruno's television agent Geoffrey Petts continued the tradition into the satellite era.

Debates about the potentially dramatic and revolutionary effects of this satellite era have proved every bit as fierce as boxing contests. In one corner stand the bullish optimists, consisting mostly of the new players themselves and other entrepreneurs concocting strategic plans for entering what they hope will become a highly lucrative market. In the opposite corner are more detached commentators, some financial institutions, and several major advertisers who want to see real signs of progress before sinking money into new enterprises. Before we examine the potential impact of new media on sports television, three vital elements of the new technology equation need to be thoroughly explored. Who exactly are the new providers of sport on television (the players)? What are their strategies likely to be, and how will these be influenced by a new regulatory framework (rules and tactics)? And what are the audience prospects for new channels (the prize)?

The players
While Sky's four channels provided the first satellite-delivered programmes to be available to *all* British viewers, there had for some time been a small minority of households who could receive additional channels via cable. In the early 1980s, following the government-appointed Hunt Committee's report, cable was heralded as television's next revolution. Amid speculation about the end of Britain's BBC/IBA duopoly and the dawning of a new age of choice and opportunity, the Cable Authority was formed to distribute cable franchises and oversee development of the

cable industry. Unlike its European neighbours, the British government was not prepared to commit any public money; if cable was indeed to revolutionise television, it would be an entertainment-led revolution with capital injected solely by the private sector. The private sector did not jump at the chance. By the end of 1989 less than two million UK homes were passed by cable, much of it provided by upgrading systems which had already existed. But those who subscribed did have access to more than the four broadcast terrestrial channels. As well as movie channels, a children's channel, a pop video channel, Sky Europe and Superchannel, their monthly fee bought them a 24-hour sports channel – Screensport.

Screensport is part of a television enterprise set up, somewhat implausibly, by retailers W. H. Smith in 1983 along with a children's channel and a magazine-type channel called 'Lifestyle'. In February 1989, W. H. Smith Television were sufficiently confident of satellite television's future to spend £42 million on broadcasting direct from the medium-powered Astra satellite (encouraged, no doubt, by Sky's decision to take the same route). Screensport therefore has a fully dedicated transponder on Astra which transmits 24-hour sports programming to anyone with an Astra receiving dish. Its content, however, has been limited to events and tournaments which other mainstream channels tend to pass over: rallycross and motorcycle racing, for example, and heavy emphasis on American sports like college basketball, American Football, and professional ice hockey. Screensport is hampered in its access to high-quality European sport by an agreement between European broadcasters and its closest satellite rival, Eurosport.

Eurosport also has a dedicated Astra transponder, and is therefore available to the same audience as Screensport. Although it was originally advertised as one of the four Sky channels, its ownership is in fact a more complex arrangement between Sky and the European Broadcasting Union (EBU). The EBU consists of thirty-eight essentially public service broadcasters from thirty-two countries, with a reciprocal agreement on live events: when one broadcaster televises an event in its own country, coverage is offered at no charge to other EBU members. Almost all major European sporting events are therefore tied up by the EBU, who have excluded new commercial channels from their exchange system. Eurosport is a joint venture between some of the major EBU members (including the BBC) and News International, owners of Sky television. While many have expressed surprise that powerful terrestrial broadcasters should be prepared to make programmes available to a new commercial satellite enterprise, the terms of the deal made it an irresistible bargain

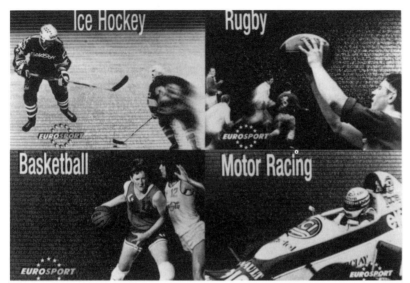
The satellite promise of Eurosport

for the EBU. Sky Television offered to underwrite all the costs and potential losses of running the channel while agreeing to share all profits. At no cost and no risk, it was a financial bonus for the EBU which they could not turn down. The result is a 24-hour satellite sports channel with some of the best European sports programming on offer.

This arrangement, however, has not satisfied the European Commission. Screensport, itself denied access to those same EBU events now available on their arch rival's satellite channel, lodged a formal complaint against the deal in Brussels. The Commission in turn served a formal notice of objection, alleging that both the EBU consortium agreement and the joint venture with Sky were 'likely to restrict and distort competition in the Common Market'. Such anti-competitive practice would infringe Article 85 of the Treaty of Rome. Although the case still awaits a final decision from the European Court, it is unlikely that the Eurosport deal can survive in its present form. Almost certainly, the European material which is currently only available on one Astra transponder will soon be available on two.

Finally, an entirely different satellite operation started in April 1990. Once direct broadcasting from satellite (DBS) became a technical possibility, frequencies for such operations were allocated by international agreement to each country which could then operate such channels according to any specifications or regulatory controls which they saw fit. In the UK, the government decided that the British operation should be commercial (thereby offering new opportunities to advertisers), should be funded entirely from the private sector, and should be overseen (like ITV) by the IBA. The IBA in turn invited tenders for a British DBS service, eventually won by British Satellite Broadcasting (BSB). Unlike Screensport, Eurosport and other channels which simply rent transponders from the privately owned Astra satellite, BSB has had to finance its own high-powered satellite.

BSB's history has been troubled. Its launch plans received a rude shock when Rupert Murdoch announced his intention to launch four Sky channels from Astra aimed at the UK. Not only was satellite competition a surprise, but the Sky operation was based on a traditional transmission system (PAL) which was entirely incompatible with BSB's new high-tech standard of D-MAC and therefore required an entirely different (if somewhat clumsier) satellite receiving dish. Finding itself in an unexpected satellite war, BSB pursued an aggressive marketing campaign based on its smaller, square dish ('squarial') which it hoped would persuade consumers to wait for the less unsightly version before launching themselves into satellite television. Unfortunately, preparation of the requisite microchips was less advanced than they had hoped: a launch planned for September 1989, already conceding seven months to Sky, was delayed amid speculation that it might struggle to raise the requisite extra capital. Finally launched with funding apparently secure at least for another four years, BSB is now transmitting its five channels with one distinct advantage for viewers prepared to invest in the most advanced television sets: a high-definition capability which can significantly enhance picture quality. One of those five channels is dedicated to continuous sports programming.

Rules and tactics
Unlike their terrestrial rivals, satellite channels have two objectives to ensure survival and success. While terrestrial channels need concentrate only on attracting a reasonable audience share from 21 million households, satellite channels must first persuade viewers to buy reception dishes and then compete for their share of available viewers. To assist in the first of these objectives ('dish driving' as the marketing jargon has it), what better means of persuasion could there be than exclusive live coverage of a major sporting spectacle?

While most sports, as we have seen, appeal to only a minority of the population, there are a few sporting high points which will command huge audiences. Many who find horses exceptionally dull will sacrifice twenty minutes to watch the Grand National; few would describe themselves as ardent rowing fanatics, but are still seduced by the annual Oxford *v* Cambridge Thames ritual. And audience sizes for these events illustrate why they represent highly desirable prospects for competitive satellite channels: 15 million at the height of the Grand National; 8 million for the Boat Race; over 10 million for the FA Cup Final; over 11 million and 9 million respectively for Wimbledon Men's and Women's Championship Finals. And all of these on a Saturday (or Sunday) afternoon when audiences can rarely scale the peak-time heights of evening schedules.

Any of these events would represent a considerable coup for a satellite channel, especially when involved in a desperate battle to convince reluctant consumers of the advantages of one type of satellite-receiving equipment over another. For channels which are prepared for substantial losses in the early years of operation, a very considerable outlay would be justified if the consequence was a significant boost to sales of satellite dishes. To date, of course, exclusive purchase of these events has been prohibited by the 'Listed Events' clauses of successive Broadcasting Acts which have placed events of national importance out of bounds. Government proposals in the new Broadcasting Bill will finally end the 35-year-old restriction on exclusive access to events of national importance and provide satellite channels with their 'loss-leader' opportunity.

For a government ideologically committed to the free market, such a move is scarcely surprising. Sports governing bodies have argued consistently that Listed Events constrained their ability to negotiate and prevented them from obtaining a proper market price for their most valuable commodity. When the Home Office canvassed opinion to its proposals for abolishing this long-standing provision, sporting bodies and commercial television companies spoke in almost total unanimity in favour of abolition. Only the BBC attempted to argue the case for guaranteed universality, but it was a lonely voice in the free market wilderness, itself accused of blatant self-interest. Even Peter Dimmock, architect of the original proposal in the 1950s in order to protect the BBC's public service sporting tradition, professes himself astonished that sporting bodies have tolerated its existence for so long.

The potential repercussions of repealing this provision are discussed below. Meanwhile proper examination of government proposals demonstrates some ambivalence. For while the Bill proposes to remove all barriers to exclusive access, it is not willing to permit purchase of major events for televising on a pay-per-view basis. It is a strangely contradictory policy, which attempts to prevent the disenfranchisement of low-income viewers but still allows exclusive access to satellite channels requiring considerable investment in receiving equipment. Unless major changes are made during the Bill's parliamentary passage, that is how it will stand. For new channels utterly dependent on convincing very large numbers of apprehensive purchasers of the virtues of satellite dishes it could quite literally provide the means of survival. It certainly constitutes a landmark in the history of television sport in Britain.

In regulatory terms, then, almost anything goes for television sport in the satellite era. Apart from frenetic bidding for exclusive rights to major showpieces, what tactics will competing channels employ to attract a reasonable and ultimately profitable slice of the viewing audience? To some extent Screensport have been hampered both by their limited access to top sports and by a smaller operating budget than both BSB and Eurosport. Their delayed start notwithstanding, BSB have already made their mark on the sports negotiating scene. Their entry into the League soccer negotiations, although ultimately thwarted, was symptomatic of BSB's determination to secure events of proven audience appeal. Bob Hunter, Managing Director of the sports channel, is convinced that a dedicated sports service with a 'big event' as the centrepiece will attract a significant number of people deprived of live or major sporting action on evening terrestrial channels. Around this centrepiece will be scheduled a series of sports-related programmes featuring news, personalities, chat-shows, quizzes etc. Hunter cites a number of sports which command significant followings but are almost never available at peak viewing hours: Rugby League, tennis, volleyball. A good sports service will not only lend unaccustomed time and resources to these sports but will develop a characteristic coverage involving different approaches: plenty of analysis, different style and quality of commentary, innovative use of cameras.

Most important of all, however, is the quality of the sport. Viewers watch sport, says Hunter, 'to see people who play better than anyone else', and it is incumbent on a dedicated sports service to provide the best. The best, of course, is not necessarily to be found in the UK – while BSB may be a British service, sport is international and quality sport transcends national cultural and language barriers. A classic example is French Rugby Union, whose club style is almost indistinguishable from the international variety. Rugby at that level of excitement would, like American Football, represent ideal television sport: 'very concentrated action for very short bursts and then nothing happening', allowing time for replays and analysis.

This principle can be extended around the world and, potentially, to any sport. The superior individual skills of South American soccer are rarely seen on British screens, nor the classic teamwork of some European soccer teams at their best. Similarly with ice hockey, once a popular British sport but with a much smaller following today. Expose television audiences to the best of American, Canadian, even Russian ice hockey, and television might even induce a revival akin to the American Football craze initiated by Channel 4's coverage. It is, potentially, a stirring vision which at least for the foreseeable future establishes BSB as complementary to rather than competing with the BBC. When ITV secured its deal for League soccer, BSB was happy to forge an alliance with the BBC in a parallel deal with the Football Association for Cup matches. It suited both sides: enough live action to be shared on two channels, with the BBC content to continue its evening highlights programmes. BSB's battle is with its satellite competitors.

In that respect Adrian Metcalfe, having recently left Channel 4 for Eurosport, agrees with Hunter. He perceives sport on terrestrial channels as becoming increasingly marginalised since the days when it was live and comparatively cheap, a situation transformed in a very short time by the arrival of video and fierce competition for rights. In an interview with the *Independent*, Metcalfe stated his conviction that dedicated sports channels would return viewers to those good old days: 'In a sense we're going back 20 years or so to when *Grandstand* was at its height and *World of Sport* was starting. Television had time for sport then.' Now, however, ratings concerns and increased production costs have conspired to eliminate sport from evening schedules. For those reasons, the time is right for a dedicated sports channel: 'We're putting sport back in that peak-time slot, and we won't be worrying about it over-running because, like the old days, we won't be pushing out anything but sport.'

Although representing competing interests, both Hunter and Metcalfe share an approach to new sports channels which is founded squarely on two assumptions about audience behaviour. First, that as more channels come on stream and the traditional process of family viewing gradually breaks down, viewers will wish to take every advantage of the new opportunities at their disposal and learn to dip in and out of television channels as they do with records or books. Secondly, that the single European market of 1992 will extend to the sports viewing tastes of individual European nations. The second assumption must for the moment rest on optimistic speculation about the enthusiasm of a British audience for South American soccer or French rugby. On the first assumption, however, initial soundings – if premature – are not promising for satellite.

197

The prize

In most areas of economic activity, theory suggests that demand and supply will eventually achieve some kind of equilibrium. Television's technical revolution has certainly provided a remarkable abundance of supply which has, almost overnight, more than doubled the volume of available airtime in the UK and throughout Europe. This particular economic equation, however, has been driven almost entirely by technological availability rather than consumer demand. Although numerous surveys have for many years attested to the dissatisfaction of at least a third of UK viewers with their television service, this is scarcely a devastating indictment for a leisure activity which takes up almost a quarter of the waking day. It has never suggested the sort of simmering disillusionment likely to drive significant numbers of disaffected viewers into the arms of new channels.

And so it has proved. Even before medium- or high-powered satellites began transmitting signals for direct reception by individual households, cable afforded thousands of homes the opportunity to sample new and different channels. Figures for the take-up of cable options demonstrate a very muted consumer reaction, despite the ability of cable systems to target potential purchasers with direct door-to-door selling. By the end of 1989, figures from the Cable Authority showed an overall take-up rate of around 18% of households to whom cable is available (compared to a comparable take-up rate of 75% in America). Evidence also shows that even when households have decided to subscribe to cable, around two-thirds of their viewing continues to be of existing terrestrial channels. The remaining one third, distributed over several channels, does not represent a very lucrative prospect to new market entrants.

If reactions to cable have been muted, consumer response to satellite television might fairly be described as catatonic. Even allowing for entrepreneurial overstatement, first projections from Sky television that 3 million dishes would be sold within a year have long been consigned to the realms of fantasy. Even with the help of national advertising campaigns, substantial editorial coverage in News International's five British newspapers, and assorted free offers through the same route, dish sales or rentals barely reached half a million by the end of 1989. At a time of relative economic prosperity, it has been an uninspiring start to a process widely expected to revolutionise British viewing habits.

It is far too early to anticipate the impact of additional channels on viewer behaviour in the longer term. Some have suggested that comparison with the video phenomenon, also slow to take off in its early years but with penetration now standing at two-thirds, indicates a gradual evolutionary process which ultimately succeeds. Video, however, provides a greater flexibility, allowing both time-shifting of off-air material and playing pre-recorded material like films. There is no real equivalent to satellite television which can provide effective comparisons: an explosion of new and unfamiliar material, requiring additional payments from viewers accustomed to receiving 'free' television. Comparisons with the considerably more mature cable market of America are unhelpful, since the more populous and wealthier American local markets can command immense economic power; they are consequently able to sustain a much higher level of economic activity – including several cable television franchises.

Even in America, however, where conditions for successful cable channels are a great deal more favourable, subscribers to cable spend most of their viewing time watching network (terrestrial) television. Worried as they are about the steady inroads being made into their own viewing figures, America's networks still command two-thirds of viewing time in cabled households. Both American and British experience to date suggests how viewing patterns might unfold over the next ten or fifteen years. While increasing numbers might be convinced of the pleasures of the additional choices provided by satellite television, almost all viewers will continue to derive most of their television from traditional terrestrial channels. Prospects for satellite in the UK will not be enhanced by the arrival in 1993 of a fifth terrestrial channel, covering around two-thirds of the country, available in the traditional manner without installation of expensive equipment. All the evidence suggests that for the foreseeable future the new generation of television channels will be fighting for a small slice of peripheral viewing from a minority of connected viewers.

Under these circumstances it is difficult to reconcile the futuristic visions of those in satellite sports television with the reality of audience behaviour. While traditional family viewing patterns may have been disrupted by the widespread purchase of second, third and fourth television sets, existing technology still makes it difficult and more expensive to connect every set to cable or satellite. If access to new channels is confined to the main living room set, peak-time sports watching may find itself the subject of vigorous family negotiation. Sporting tastes, as we have seen, cannot be reduced to a single homogeneous genre, and arguments may revolve round the selection of a particular sport rather than sport in general. It is almost certain that, whatever the theory about new patterns of television viewing, the reality in most households will be a great deal less flexibility than new programmers might wish for.

The next decade and beyond

It is perhaps an illuminating statement about satellite television generally that its effect on televised sport will for the next few years be almost wholly independent of audience behaviour. New channels are resigned to several years of financial losses while they continue to pour money into sustaining 24-hour programming. At least in the short term, competition for television rights to popular events and tournaments should represent a considerable financial boost both for sports professionals and sporting bodies. The future of television sport will be determined as much by the attitudes of sports representatives to this potential windfall as by the marketing and scheduling strategies of new and existing channels locked in intense competition.

Who will benefit? Most likely recipients of these cash windfalls will be those involved in the major crowd-pulling events, and the most popular or traditional sports. Major events should reap substantial financial benefits after abolition of Listed Events, since both terrestrial and satellite commercial channels will want to enter the bidding. For ITV, as we have seen, it has been the presence of a non-commercial and well-established BBC which has consistently inhibited their ability to command large audiences for major sporting events. With a cash-limited BBC unlikely to keep pace with inflationary bidding, the field will be clear for ITV to exploit its resources and secure exclusive rights for the first time. Simultaneously, the dish-driving ambitions of satellite channels will ensure their own continued financial interest. What ultimately happens to sport's annual showpieces will depend on reactions to competing interests from those bodies which control the rights. There will be at least three considerations which, depending on the event and the governing body involved, will have differential influences on where these events are shown: reactions of sponsors; a sense of responsibility to the sport's supporters throughout the country; and feelings about technical competence.

Sponsors are accustomed to substantial and universal audiences for major events, and will not be impressed by the restricted nature of satellite audiences. In this respect, BBC coverage is particularly valuable as the only indirect commercial access to BBC audiences; whatever means one uses to compare 30 seconds exposure of a corporate logo with a 30-second advertisement, it is impossible to place a value on commercial exposure through the BBC which cannot be achieved through spot advertising. It is scarcely credible that Cornhill would have been prepared to persevere with its long-standing and generous patronage of Test cricket had long hours of BBC coverage not been guaranteed. They would certainly not have achieved a 15% rise in corporate awareness through exposure on a minority satellite channel. Unless satellite bids are sufficient to compensate for money which would certainly be withdrawn by disgruntled sponsors, sports bodies will not want to alienate their primary source of income. For the time being at least, those which recognise the commercial needs of sponsors will want to continue with the safer bet of terrestrial television.

Such reservations will only apply to those events which tend to be sponsorship-dependent. One listed event in particular may be more vulnerable to vast satellite bids because of its dependence on television rights rather than sponsorship: the Wimbledon Championships. As a tournament which derives well over half its total income from the worldwide sale of television rights, and which deliberately avoids any more than the most discreet on-court sponsorship, the All England Club may find it hard to resist. German television viewers experienced a taste of Wimbledon's desire to maximise television revenue for the 1989 tournament when the EBU were outbid by the German conglomerate Bertelsmann, owners of the satellite channel RTL Plus. In a year when both the world's premier tennis singles titles were won by Germans, barely a half of German homes were capable of watching it. From the All England Club's point of view, of course, it was a perfectly justifiable decision. They have a responsibility to maximise revenue in order to pass the benefits on to British tennis via the Lawn Tennis Association.

There is, however, another element of responsibility to the national game which may transcend financial considerations for those who have control over major national events. Whatever financial inducements are offered for Wimbledon or Test cricket or the FA Cup Final, there will be some substantial heart-searching before such high-profile events are removed from universal access. Televised events, as we have seen, serve to stimulate interest in both participation and live spectating. Any sport which chooses deliberately to remove its annual showpiece from terrestrial television risks damaging its own prospects of greater interest and involvement. Apart from which, there will be serious public relations consequences, as governing bodies are portrayed as grasping gold-diggers with little regard for those who are unable or unwilling to purchase satellite receivers. Sports which choose to make the transition from free television to paying television cannot expect to be universally popular with their followers.

Apart from reservations about sponsors and fans, sports bodies are also likely to be influenced by the untested technical expertise of satellite channels. Some Outside Broadcasts can be nightmares, even with advanced technology and years of experience; new channels will be stretched, and sports bodies will want to be convinced that their investment in mobile units and their competence in handling difficult live transmissions is comparable to those with decades of experience. Encouraged by Channel 4's commitment to new sports coverage, specialist independent producers have started to emerge with new and refreshing ideas on coverage. But some time is bound to lapse before rights holders will want to renounce an established relationship with a trusted terrestrial broadcaster in favour of an untried satellite channel with a substantially smaller potential audience.

Sport's major events, then, are likely to stay on terrestrial television in the short term. The balance, however, will have shifted substantially in favour of ITV, who can satisfy rights holders on all reservations bar one: the demands that a commercial broadcaster might wish to make in return for their substantial investment. Assuming governing bodies are confident of their ability to resist excessive commercial demands, events which have for fifty years been the pride of BBC television can soon be expected to make the transition. Top of the list, resisting for the moment any temptation to remove itself from universal access, is likely to be Wimbledon – the one event which must represent the archetypal television sport for commercial television, combining an appeal to upmarket and traditionally light television viewers of both sexes with pauses in play ideally suited to commercial breaks. Given the immense financial value of Wimbledon airtime, it is likely to be worth a very large bid indeed from ITV.

In the longer term, assuming that at least one satellite sporting channel establishes itself as a profitable concern, it is highly probable that some of sport's major spectacles will find their way on to satellite – almost certainly in a complementary package with terrestrial television like the BBC/BSB deal on Cup soccer, or the Sky/BBC deal on the 1990 Test cricket series in the West Indies. If not the top listed events, then certainly a number of high-profile events with strong popular followings: Rugby's Five-Nations championship, golf's British Open or Ryder Cup, horseracing classics other than the Grand National or Derby would all be prime candidates. Others may negotiate deals which allow exclusive live coverage to satellite, with a concession on highlights to one of the terrestrial channels in order to placate the wrath of the dispossessed. The biggest losers in the longer term, apart from the BBC, could be large sections of the television audience. There will be viewers who cannot afford satellite equipment; viewers who cannot receive a signal for geographical reasons (interference from weather, living outside the satellite footprint, surrounded by high buildings); and viewers who are simply not prepared to make the investment for the sake of a single event. It is the ultimate irony of the modern communications era that significant numbers of viewers may eventually be deprived of a sporting showpiece which has been freely available for over half a century.

What of the next tier down, those sporting contests which do not represent the climax of a sporting season but command a substantial popular following? BSB have already demonstrated the attraction of League soccer to satellite channels, and ITV's viewing figures have proved BSB's point. It is very difficult, however, to conceive of other domestic tournaments which would attract the same level of audience interest. Many cricket lovers might appreciate the opportunity to watch county cricket live on television, but their daytime numbers will not provoke a buying spree among satellite heads of sport. For most other popular sports, whether horse-racing, tennis, golf or snooker, there is enough programming available on terrestrial television to satisfy the appetites of all but the most ardent supporters. In most cases, it is specific events rather than the sport itself which command the viewing figures necessary to establish them as a useful satellite commodity.

Nor are new channels likely to regard minority sports as great audience pullers. Although some sports like ice-skating or showjumping will command high viewing figures at times of particular national interest, they are not automatic draws. Sports which have languished either on the fringes of *Grandstand* or in annual Channel 4 slots – basketball, volley-ball, table tennis etc. – will be grateful for the opportunity of more airtime but, as we have seen, do not regard it as any substitute for exposure to a universal audience. From the channel's perspective, these sports might persuade a few fans to invest in dishes but cannot provide the surge of interest which a major event would produce. From the sport's viewpoint, relinquishing rights to a minority channel may bring in extra cash but will not serve the wider objective of encouraging greater participation in, and more widespread knowledge of, the game.

There are two further reasons why British sport may be cautious about the satellite revolution. First, new channels looking for the cream of sporting action will be turning increasingly to Europe, thereby fulfilling two criteria: access to high-quality sport for comparatively low cost, since coverage will already have been arranged by the domestic broad-caster; and scheduling of popular sports which viewers will not be able to see on terrestrial television. For viewers, there will be the twin benefits of more frequent opportunities to see their favourite sports played well, and increasing familiarity with the clubs, tactics and personalities of Britain's economic partners. That may not comfort British governing bodies, but it might help foster an increasing sense of European harmony in a country not renowned for its hospitable attitude to Europe.

A second reason for caution is more cost-related. With substantially more airtime to fill, channels will be susceptible to approaches from sponsors or advertisers keen to promote their products via sporting events. Before Superchannel, the ill-fated attempt to launch a Pan-European satellite enterprise, was taken over by Italian investors it featured a substantial amount of peak-time sport, some of which was provided by advertisers and therefore obtained at no cost. One motor race was organised, sponsored and filmed entirely by Renault and consisted of unabashed Renault advertising: cars, billboards, participants' uniforms and spot advertising all promoted Renault. Superchannel had no part in the creative process, but were given the programme for no fee. It is a form of barter (perhaps we should call them 'sponsports') gaining increasing mileage on American networks to whom agents or promoters will sell an event for a nominal $1 fee. In return, the promoter has rights to all the advertising space in that programme. It is not an alluring prospect. While it represents cheap television which may keep a satellite channel in business, both production values and content are ceded to the advertiser. Sport under these circumstances is no more than an incidental marketing tool.

Welcome as it is, therefore, more airtime for sport will present as many dilemmas as solutions. At the centre of the dilemma will be the professional and governing bodies who seek to protect the interests both of professionals and of the grassroots participants and spectators. For many of these organisations, competitive satellite and terrestrial television will unlock substantially higher cash rewards in rights fees. But reciprocal demands will be made and concessions will be required. Governing bodies will need to delineate precisely their boundaries of acceptable compromise. A series of difficult decisions over the next five or ten years about the destination of major national events, about the creation of new television-inspired events, and about rights for live action versus recorded highlights will have implications not just for the future of new satellite channels but for the integrity and dignity of sports themselves. As the non-commercial dominance of the BBC is gradually eclipsed – by demands made on its own increasingly overstretched airtime as much as by the inroads of new channels into commercially attractive events – television decisions will be increasingly dictated by commercial television audiences rather than sporting criteria.

There will be more emphasis on the demographic profile of audiences, less concern for bringing on new and less popular sports; relaxation of television restrictions on sponsorship (which in the case of Eurosport is anyway unenforceable); and, most potentially damaging of all, a drive to create drama and suspense through the introduction of contrived sporting contests. American boxing illustrates how pressure from new channels can dilute and ultimately undermine events of national importance. Interviewed on *This Week* as part of a documentary enquiry into boxing, Seth Abraham, a senior Vice President of America's Home Box Office Sport, volunteered: 'We're looking for programming that is going to attract new subscribers. Championship boxing brings in new subscribers.' In the same programme the editor of *Ring*, America's premier boxing magazine, gave a trenchant verdict on what new channels like HBO had done to boxing: 'In the old days, there were eight divisions with one champion in each weight class. Now there are sixteen divisions and four different organisations. They sprang up because television wanted championship fights. Television has created a monster.'

What monsters British cable and satellite channels can invent will depend both on the common sense of sporting administrators and the tastes of British audiences. Experience so far suggests that neither American nor British audiences are impervious to the contrived nature of events if they are promoted with sufficient brouhaha. We may not yet be in the realms of wrist-wrestling and rattlesnake hunting. But in addition to some top European sport and greater access to more mainstream British sports, we can surely expect more of the audience-building Budd *v* Decker concocted recipes.

New channels will certainly bring substantial benefits to British sports fans, as the decision by Sky to cover England's 1990 cricket tour of the West Indies demonstrated. Apart from providing full coverage for dish-owners, Sky's investment enabled the BBC to show late-night highlights of a contest which went untelevised in 1986 (and which started, no doubt to Sky's delight, with one of the biggest upsets in cricket history). But in other areas, this might be scant compensation for the transformation in coverage, content and accessibility of televised sport. At least one respected sports writer foresees a bleak future. Looking forward to the 1990s at the end of 1989, the *Guardian*'s Matthew Engel wrote: 'In Britain, we can probably kiss goodbye to the pattern of televised sport we have grown to know and mostly love. Watching the best-presented sport in the world on national television has been a reason for living here. The advent of satellite TV is likely to change all that, as sports choose to sell their major events to smaller audiences for more money.'

It has indeed been a rich and varied diet available to viewers since that first Wimbledon transmission more than fifty years ago. But in many respects, the second fifty years of television sport may prove to be significantly less beneficial, both to the audience and to sport itself, than the half century which has just ended.

BIBLIOGRAPHY

Patrick Barwise and Andrew Ehrenberg, *Television and its Audience*. London, Sage Publications, 1988.

BBC, *Annual Report and Accounts 1987/8* and *1988/9*. London, BBC, 1988 and 1989.

Bill Bonney, *Packer and Televised Cricket*, Faculty of Humanities and Social Sciences media paper no. 2. Sydney, New South Wales Institute of Technology, 1980.

Asa Briggs, *History of Broadcasting in the United Kingdom*, Volume IV, London, Oxford University Press, 1979.

Jennings Bryant, D. Brown, Paul Comisky, Dolf Zillman, 'Sports and Spectators: Commentary and Appreciation' in *Journal of Communication*, vol. 32, no. 4, Winter 1982.

Edward Buscombe (ed.), *Football on Television*. BFI Television Monograph. London, British Film Institute, 1975.

Centre for Leisure Research, *A Digest of Sports Statistics for the UK*. (2nd edition) London, Sports Council, 1986.

Centre for Television Research, *Programme Range and Quality – an International Comparison*. Leeds University, 1986.

Centre for Television Research, *Television in the United States: Funding Sources and Programming Consequences* by Professor Jay G. Blumler. Leeds University, 1986.

Joan M. Chandler, *Television and National Sport: the United States and Britain*. Chicago, University of Illinois Press, 1988.

Paul Comisky, Jennings Bryant, Dolf Zillman, 'Commentary as a substitute for action' in *Journal of Communication*, vol. 27, no. 3, Summer 1977.

Peter Dimmock (ed.), *Sports in View*. London, Faber and Faber, 1964.

Matthew Engel and Ian Morrison, *The Sportspages Almanac 1990*. London, Simon and Schuster, 1989.

John Goldlust, *Playing for Keeps: sport, the media and society*. Melbourne, Longman Cheshire, 1987.

Barry Gunter and Michael Svennevig, *Behind and in Front of the Screen: television's involvement with family life*. London, John Libbey, 1988.

Allen Guttman, *Sports Spectators*. New York, Columbia University Press, 1986.

Denis Howell et al., *Committee of Enquiry into Sports Sponsorship* ('The Howell Report'). London, Central Council of Physical Recreation, 1983.

Independent Broadcasting Authority, *Annual Report 1987/8* and *1988/9*. London, IBA, 1988 and 1989.

Jeremy Isaacs, *Storm Over 4*. London, Weidenfeld and Nicolson, 1989.

Emlyn Jones, *Sport in Space: the effects of cable and satellite television*. London, Sports Council, 1985.

David A. Klatell and Norman Marcus, *Sports for Sale: television, money and the fans*. New York, Oxford University Press, 1988.

Miller Lite *Report on American Attitudes toward Sports*. Milwaukee, Miller Brewing Company, 1983.

Office of Population Censuses and Surveys, *General Household Survey 1986*. London, Her Majesty's Stationery Office, 1989.

Jeremy Potter, *Independent Television in Britain, Volume 3: Politics and Control, 1968–80*. London, Macmillan, 1988.

Ron Powers, *Supertube: the rise of television sports*. New York, Coward-McCann Inc., 1984.

Benjamin G. Rader, *In Its Own Image: how television has transformed sports*. New York, The Free Press (Macmillan), 1984.

Bernard Sendall, *Independent Television in Britain, Volume 1: Origin and Foundation, 1946–62*. London, Macmillan, 1982.

Bernard Sendall, *Independent Television in Britain, Volume 2: Expansion and Change 1958–68*. London, Macmillan, 1983.

Garry Whannel, *Sport on 4*. London, Channel 4, 1988.

INDEX

212